LIVE & WORK in...
FRANCE

LIVE & WORK in...

·REVISED AND UPDATED·
THIRD EDITION·
3RD

FRANCE

Comprehensive,
up-to-date,
practical
information about
everyday life

ALAN HART

howtobooks

Published by How To Books Ltd,
Spring Hill House, Spring Hill Road,
Begbroke, Oxford OX5 1RX. United Kingdom.
Tel: (01865) 375794. Fax: (01865) 379162.
info@howtobooks.co.uk
www.howtobooks.co.uk

How To Books greatly reduce the carbon footprint of their books by sourcing their typesetting and printing in the UK.

First edition 1998
Reprinted 1999
Reprinted 2000
Second edition 2003
Reprinted 2003
Reprinted 2004 (twice)
Third edition 2008

British Library Cataloguing in Publication Data
A catalogue record for this book is available from the British Library

ISBN 978 1 84528 219 6

Cover design by Baseline Arts Ltd, Oxford
Produced for How To Books by Deer Park Productions, Tavistock, Devon
Typeset by PDQ Typesetting, Newcastle-under-Lyme, Staffs.
Printed and bound by Bell & Bain, Glasgow

NOTE: The material contained in this book is set out in good faith for general guidance and no liability can be accepted for loss or expense incurred as a result of relying in particular circumstances on statements made in the book. The laws and regulations are complex and liable to change, and readers should check the current position with the relevant authorities before making personal arrangements.

Contents

Preface

Ten years on from the first edition of *Living and Working in France* (the original title of this book), much has changed in a country which was traditionally perceived as something of a closed world. France has become more open and interactive with the wider world, even if she still fights tooth and nail to maintain her identity. Much of the change in attitude has probably stemmed from two phenomena.

The first is the enormous emigration of French young people towards the United States and the United Kingdom. These migrations represent the biggest French exodus since the 17th century. The influence that the returning migrants have is being felt in France. Whilst France continues to defend her culture, institutions and traditions, the strong emphasis on lifestyle rather than competition leads to a real desire to adapt the best of both French and foreign models in the world's favourite holiday destination.

The second phenomenon is the impact of the Internet. In spite of all the drudgery of French paperwork, the French government departments and state-owned industries have made huge advances in developing multi-lingual websites. These sites have broken down much of the austere mystique which surrounded life in France, so that as you slide out of one system and into another, you do not feel like an eternal interloper.

Over the years, I have had the pleasure of meeting quite a number of readers at book signings in France and the UK. The questions they ask have provided me with ideas on how to develop this new edition to best meet the increasing need for a guide which can assist in demystifying moving to France.

The first question is – how do I learn the language? There is no simple answer. Despite bilingual websites, and French linguistic competency, a grasp of French remains essential to a successful move. Throughout this book I have tried to introduce you to the basic ideas and assumptions of French life, so that you can understand your new colleagues and friends quickly, and really start to build the relationships you will need to feel at home in France. Using the highlighted words and phrases will enable you to start building up your vocabulary and your cultural knowledge.

The second question is – why concentrate so much on bureaucracy? The answer is because if you get it right the first time round, you can really get down to enjoying *la vie française* in all its fascinating complexity. On a more practical side, you will also need to have your paperwork in order to open your bank account and guarantee your cheques; to register your children for school; to be able to work; and to provide you with social security cover and also access the generous French benefits you will be paying for out of your salary.

Bureaucracy in France is part of the way of life, providing the framework on which you paint in your own local colour, whether that it is rooftops of Paris, or the mountains of the Pyrenees. If it all seems a tremendous waste of time to you, remember what the definitive Frenchman, Napoléon, (a Corsican!) is supposed to have said: 'Du sublime au ridicule, il n'y a qu'un pas'. It is but a step from the sublime to the ridiculous. Deal successfully with the ridiculous first and then you can enjoy the sublime in peace.

This book is dedicated to all those who have helped me to make my home in France. My thanks go once again to Nikki Read and the How To Books team, who continue to support me and my best wishes go out to all the readers of this book for a *bonne continuation*.

Alan Hart

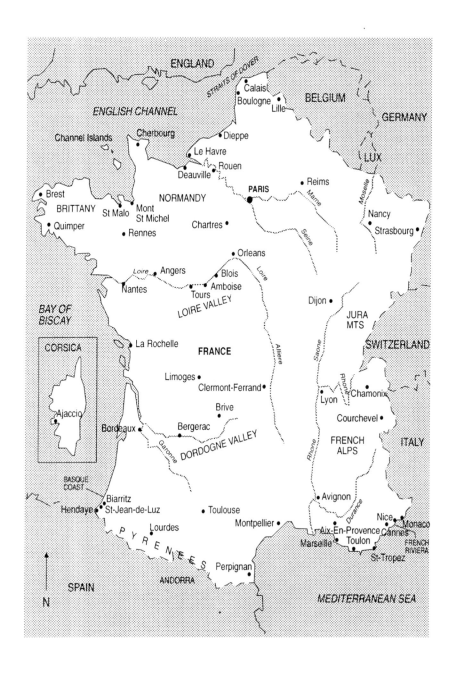

Fig. 1. Map of France.

Introducing France

OVERVIEW: THE GEOGRAPHY OF FRANCE

France, which covers 549,000 square kilometres, is the largest
country in western Europe. It is a land of climatic and
geographical contrasts, and enclosed by the mountainous ski-
slopes of the Alps and the Pyrenees lie the verdant pastures of the
Ile de France and Limousin; the vineyards most notably of the
Loire valley and the area around Bordeaux; the remote hills and
rugged plateaux of the Auvergne; the industrialised landscapes of
the north; and the sophisticated, cosmopolitan resorts of the
Mediterranean south.

The five principal rivers are the Seine (which flows through Paris),
the Loire and the Rhône (along which grow many fine vines), the
Garonne in the west, and the Rhine in the east which forms a
natural border with France's old enemy and new trade and
political partner Germany. In addition, a lattice of canals,
completes a superb transport network which accounts for 40% of
all the waterways of Europe.

North and north-western France (Brittany, Normandy, Picardy,
the Ile de France) generally enjoy a 'British' climate of milder
winters and pleasant summers. Eastern and central France
(Alsace, the Vosges, the Rhône valley, Burgundy, the Auvergne)
generally have colder winters with heavier snow, and more clearly
defined seasons. In the south and south-west (Provence, the Midi,

Aquitaine, the Basque country) winters are occasionally cold but summers are almost invariably – sometimes tropically – hot, from Nice in the east to Biarritz in the west.

THE PEOPLE OF FRANCE

Town and country

The total population of mainland France and Corsica in 2008 was 64.4 million people. The vast majority of the population is concentrated in the industrialised regions of northern and eastern France and the Rhône valley, and approximately 80% of the French population now lives in urban zones.

Despite the continuing predominance of Paris, according to the 1999 census figures the real population drift has not been to the capital but to a certain number of other cities and regions. The high-speed TGV rail links to Paris have also created an estimated 10,000 commuters every day to the capital, who thus benefit from both city salaries and country life. Nantes, Toulouse, Montpellier and Lyon have all grown by more than three times the national average, and Lille, Rennes and Strasbourg have also seen important increases in population. Of the great cities, only Marseille has remained stagnant in terms of population growth.

Recent studies by the government agency INSEE and the 1999 census figures, have confirmed this drift back to the countryside. The Ile de France with 70,000 departures a year, and northern France have generally seen the most important migrations with a drift south by the ageing population, even though the French are only third in the European order of domestic regional mobility, (*Libération*, 14 February 2002). The beneficiaries of these new migrations are the west and south-west which have seen the greatest number of new arrivals.

With 47.3% of the current population aged between 40–59 years old, this trend could well continue in the near future with both the arrival of a 'Papy-Boom' generated by the retirement of the 'Baby Boom' generation, who will be added to the 12 million retired people in France in 1999. Other reasons for the shift in population include both improved communication with the south, and a general desire for the more relaxed lifestyle of *la douce France* symbolised in both French and foreign popular imaginations by small friendly country towns and villages.

Nonetheless, long-term public concern over the continuing 'desertification' of certain areas of rural France (such as the Auvergne) continues, as do regular government subsidies to the traditional industries of farming and fishing which are still treated with great reverence. France remains the world's leading exporter of agricultural products, and no French politician dares to ignore the rural vote and lobby, not least because the *Chasse, Pêche, Nature et Tradition* (Hunting, Fishing, Nature and Tradition) party won 4% in the 2002 Presidential elections.

But France's real wealth now lies in the newer high-technology industries. These are to be found in and around Paris, which dominates France economically, and around the other major cities of Lyon, Marseille, Lille, Bordeaux and Toulouse.

ORIGINS

As is witnessed by the diversity of languages, cultures and names, the French have experienced several waves of immigration over the centuries. Roman Gaul was conquered eventually by Clovis who was baptised as the first Christian king of 'France' in 481 AD by St Rémy at Rheims. In 1996 the 1500th anniversary of this baptism, claimed by some as a means of celebrating France's Catholic heritage and reviled by others in the name of the secular state born of the Revolution, provoked a fierce debate during the Papal visit.

Several centuries later Charlemagne's Holy Roman empire based on France splintered under his divided offspring, and left the kings of France in reality only as kings of the Ile de France until the end of the 15th century. The independent kingdoms and duchies of Brittany, Burgundy, the Languedoc and Provence, and the disputed territories of the Loire valley and the South-West which provoked the Hundred Years War with England, all developed their own cultural identities and in some cases their own languages. These are still important today, most notably in Brittany, the Basque and Catalan regions bordering Spain, the island of Corsica, Provence, and in the oft-disputed Germanic region Alsace-Lorraine which even has some laws unique to the region.

Immigrations

Strong regional accents are to be found throughout France, some of which can be difficult even for native French speakers to understand! In the south the influence of Italian and Spanish immigrants is strong. This Mediterranean influence has been added to over the years by Portuguese immigrants, mainly to be found in the industrial centres. Between the two World Wars, nearly three million immigrants came to France, mainly of Slavic origins – White Russians fleeing the Revolution, and Poles in particular.

More recently immigrants have arrived from France's former colonies in Africa, most notably the *maghreb* countries of Algeria, Morocco and Tunisia. Together with the former French colonials (or *pieds noirs* – literally 'black feet'), this has been a very significant immigration, and France now has over four million Muslim residents principally of African origin. In addition, as with previous immigrations, there have been distinct effects with the development of a dialect and culture, mainly in city suburbs, combining north African and French influences.

Finally, there is also a large and thriving British community not only in Paris, but also in Provence and the Dordogne, and scattered throughout the country. It is almost impossible to quantify the real number of British residents in France at any give time because of the non-requirement for visas. The official 1999 census figure was 75,000 British residents, up from 52,000 in 1990 (*Libération* 10 November 2000). Clearly the *Entente* is still more than *Cordiale* a century after the signature of the Franco-British treaty in 1904!

UNDERSTANDING THE FRENCH

The essential problem with understanding the French is that they are 'neither fish nor fowl', neither Latin nor Anglo-Saxon, but a mix of the two cultures. From the former they take their romanticism, a large part of their looks, their religion, and their love of intrigue and tendency to corruption and lawlessness. From the Anglo-Saxons they have acquired the other half of their looks, much of their culture, and commercial brilliance hampered by their innate need to argue about everything.

The French themselves agree on their own bizarre character. At the beginning of the Presidential election campaign in France in

2002 *L'Express* (3 January 2002) wrote: '*There is a French magic, a particular temperament which mixes the indomitable defensiveness of an Asterix, the personification of our "exception", and the mad energy of a Popeye... who always fights to maintain an eminent place in the world, and to seduce.*'

Any resemblance to the antics of Asterix the Gaul and his companions is more than passing and fictional; the French love the cartoon character who best reflects their past but also their current character.

'Asterix contra mundi'

The fact that Asterix has an enduring appeal to the French may perhaps explain the popularity of the anti-globalisation (*mondialisation*) campaigner José Bové, who bears more than a mild physical similarity to the fictional character. Bové's popularity explains much about the French character which otherwise remains incomprehensible to foreigners and especially to Anglo-Saxons. The problem that France has with Europe, and indeed with the rest of the world, has a number of origins.

Firstly it is due to the fact that the French believe passionately in *l'exception française*, the French exception in politics and culture. They truly believe that they have lessons to teach the rest of the world, without necessarily having anything to learn.

The French often demonstrate a sense of superiority which can grate on foreign nerves. This all explains why, for instance, the French have more court rulings outstanding against them for infringements of European law than any other EU state. France sees the European Union not as a coalition of states reaching consensus on various issues, but as the Francisisation of Europe.

However, this belief in exceptions is frequently the cause of problems for those on the outside looking in, expecting France to take the 'logical' path when in fact she reverts to Gallic independence in order to keep the peace amongst her strident in-fighting factions. As the right-wing *Figaro* (29 June 2002) grumbled recently, '*as a result of her "exceptions", nobody understands France: her 35 hours, her incessant strikes, her simultaneous records of growth and unemployment, the inability of successive governments to impose indispensable reforms ... and her overall richness which jumps out and hits you between the eyes.*'

Secondly it stems from a sense of 'victimisation', and of constant attack from the English-speaking nations and their common language. The French rightly complain that English is too dominant as a language in the world; but have yet to produce a convincing argument why their language should replace English dominance. Bové's attacks on multinationals have struck a chord with his fellow citizens precisely because he stands for the individualism they cherish in the face of multi-national companies. Following the EU ruling in July 2002 that all food product labels in Europe should be in English, *Le Figaro* (10 August 2002) declared, '*we would say that* [France's] *table and her language are in the sights of Brussels!*' There is nothing more likely to irritate a Frenchman than attacks on his language or his *cuisine*.

The third reason for the seeming arrogance of the French is their fear of foreigners. Part of this fear derives simply from the perfectionist French fear of making a fool of themselves in front of foreigners. But according to a survey in October 2000, 60% of the French population thought that there were too many foreigners in France, and 43% consider themselves to be 'a little' racist. Of the 26% who considered themselves not to be racist, the majority considered that immigrants are a source of cultural enrichment.

Read in isolation these comments might seem alarming; but read in the context of the other comments above, they go a long way to identifying the complexity of the French character. After all, one half of the population dreams of moving to Paris, and after a few years in the city, they dream of moving out and buying a home in the places they originally wanted to escape from, as the 1999 census figures prove. How can you reason with a mentality like that? The answer is that you cannot. You simply have to take it all in your stride, make allowances, and try to be sensitive. In so doing you will disarm the French who do take time to get to know and accept newcomers, French or foreign alike. You will overcome their reticence, their *froideur*, their seeming arrogance, but first of all you have to learn the rules of the game and then play to win.

The 'average' French person
An 'average' person is no easier to find in France than anywhere else in the world. Generally the French are conservative, with a strong almost nostalgic belief in the 'traditional' values of family, home, and a protective and generous welfare state. The French are generally a very private people who do not wish to reveal more about themselves than is necessary. Personal questions about family, lifestyle or business are often avoided or rebuffed. Private

lives are considered to be just that, and lifestyles and relationships are not considered topics of public discussion as in Britain or the USA.

They are a highly individualistic people, who shy away from organised activities and concern themselves with their own personal situations. (The French describe this as, '*Chacun pour soi*', or the more popular version, '*Chacun défend son bifteck*' – roughly translated as 'everybody looks out for himself'.) Negative aspects of the French character which often strike foreigners are intolerance, particularly of non-French methods and modes of thinking; patriotism which at times appears to verge on xenophobia; and condescension towards foreigners. Criticism and complaining are national pastimes, and the French are past-masters of wisdom by hindsight. However, the many positive traits to the French character should also be remembered. The great French senses of passion for the causes they defend, and of style for which they are renowned, are matched also by a clear appreciation of intelligence and talent in all its forms. Philosophy is a compulsory school subject, and the country of Pascal, Descartes and Voltaire is still deeply influenced by their thoughts and those of their successors.

The unexpected flair which suddenly appears seemingly from nowhere, either in business, sport or the arts, resulting in the '*French magic*' described by *L'Express*, is what makes the French such a fascinating and endearing people. Even if at times their individualism is their greatest fault, it is also one of their greatest strengths of character in providing true local colour in the face of an increasingly standardised European Union. In conclusion, whilst the French can appear to be haughty, they are in fact very welcoming to foreigners who try to communicate with them in their own language, and attempt to understand their culture.

SOCIAL VALUES

Marriage is still the bedrock of French society, although *union libres* (common-law marriages) are widespread. Family life is supported and encouraged by generous benefits (*allocation familiale*), school equipment benefits, tax breaks and reduced transport costs for large families. The 1990s saw a rise in childless or single-parent families, and also in the number single-occupant households. However there was a significant change in attitudes in 2000, with marriages up by over 50,000 in comparison with 1995. Births in 2000 increased by 4%, and the number was matched again in 2001, a 'baby-boom' phenomenon which has not occurred for 20 years. However, by 2050 it is estimated that a third of the population will be aged over 60, so the new-borns will have to work harder and longer later on to support the generally ageing population.

The reduction of the working week to 35 hours was 'sold' to the French people as having a number of important benefits, such as job creation, but also allowing families to spend more time together as the recuperation days (*récuparations du temp de travail*, or *RTTs* as they are commonly known) have had significant impacts in some but not all classes of society. Wealthier households are now taking more regular breaks, and the prolonged summer vacations are not always standard practice any more.

In the face of fierce opposition, the Socialist government succeeded in introducing the *PACS* (*Pacte de Solidarité Civile*) in

1999, granted limited rights to cohabitating couples of both the same and the opposite sex. Hailed as a great advance for gay rights in the conservative Catholic French culture, the *PACS* has proved unexpectedly popular amongst young heterosexual couples across France and not simply in the gay-friendly major cities. In September 1998, 49% of French people approved the idea of the PACS; by September 2000, approval had risen to 70% (*Libération* 28 September 2000). Figures recently released have shown that in fact the majority of PACS are between 30-something heterosexual couples. It should be noted that alternative lifestyles other than traditional marriage and family life are sometimes less well-received outside Paris.

French society has withstood a remarkable number of changes in the last four years, not all of which have been good. Despite the partial loss of national identity by entering into a single currency, there was a good-humoured camaraderie as everybody came to grips with the Euro in the early hours of 2002. However six years on, one thing everybody seems convinced of is that the cost of living has risen since the introduction of the Euro.

The food crises of the late 1990s turned French stomachs in 2000, when cases of ESB were detected in French herds despite a 'Fortress France' approach by the government. Next on the culinary agenda came Organically Modified Crops (*OGMs* in French), the target of José Bové and his campaigners. The potential impacts on the agricultural industry of both problems, together with continued restrictions on hunting, left the *la France profonde* ('middle' France) agitated and in favour of radical action.

For the majority older generation in France, the end of military service perhaps represented the 'thin end of the wedge' in terms of a certain evolution in society which they clearly do not approve. The French are rightly known as a very formal people, who place great emphasis on good manners and respect. One of the recurrent wails of recent years in France which came to the fore in the elections in 2002 was the decline of respect in society. Both old and young accuse each other of showing disrespect towards each group. For newcomers, there are certain basic rules which must be learnt quickly in order to integrate French society.

Formality and courtesy

From the earliest age the French are taught to address adults as *Monsieur*, *Madame* or *Mademoiselle*. The latter form of address should be reserved for young ladies. Be careful that you do not unintentionally cause offence by misusing the term Mademoiselle. Even when you know full well that a lady is a spinster, she ought to be addressed as Madame. To address her as Mademoiselle is to imply that she is an 'old maid'! Neighbours may well remain Monsieur or Madame forever. Unless you have been specifically introduced to a French person by their first name, avoid using that name until invited to do so. What is considered friendliness elsewhere will be considered over-familiarity in France, and will be dealt with accordingly!

Another cardinal rule of courtesy in France is the use of *tu* and *vous*. French people will let you know when they are ready to be *tu-toied'*. Otherwise, stick to using the more formal *vous* form of address as *tu* implies an intimacy which is mainly inappropriate. Foreigners are often forgiven this fault on the grounds of ignorance. Demonstrating your knowledge of this rule will considerably enhance your standing with French people.

A basic gesture you will see all day and everywhere is the shaking of hands when people meet, and again when they say goodbye. Ladies may offer their cheeks to close friends for the *bises* (more properly the *bisous*). How many kisses (or pecks on the cheek) are exchanged depends once again on intimacy, and even geographical location – Parisians often give one on each cheek, whilst provincials may give several on each cheek. Once again, stick to the formal handshake until you are invited to use this form of greeting.

Many of these rules are universal, although amongst younger people in their 20s and under, the rules are much less hard and fast. The *bises* are exchanged more freely, and *tu* is an acceptable form of address. But where their social etiquette is concerned, let the French guide you until you are confident that you know the rules of the game. Showing you know how to behave 'properly' will paradoxically often lead more quickly to a relaxed atmosphere and relationship.

Women in society
According to the 1999 census figures, 82% of women in the 30–44 age range were either working or looking for work. Birth rates for 2000 and 2001 showed an increased number of young mothers (under 25) and older mothers (over 35) even though the average age was still 29, reflecting the average age of marriage in the two years. However, the figures are said to suggest a more general desire on the part of French women to pursue careers rather than raise families. Anglo-Saxon women may well find France a great deal more sexist than either the United Kingdom or the USA. Whilst women have made significant advances in business and have always been prominent in the arts, Anglo-Saxon women still

sense a great deal of chauvinism in the attitudes shown to them. President Nicolas Sarkozy has named several high-ranking women ministers, but his *UMP* party still prefers to pay a fine rather than observe a French law requiring male–female parity amongst its candidates.

Religion

Just as in England where most people are nominally Church of England, in France most people are nominally Roman Catholic. In spite of the Revolution in 1789, and the separation of Church and State in 1905, the Catholic inheritance is still strong. Whilst Mass attendance remains on average low, and one priest more often than not serves several villages, there was a revival of interest in Catholicism amongst young people following the World Youth Day celebrations in Paris at the end of the 1990s. Protestants make up 1.7% of the population, included in which are the Anglicans in France with over 30 chaplaincies across the country. With approximately 600,000 members, the French Jewish community is the most important community in western Europe, and they have produced many distinguished writers and politicians. There are also now reckoned to be about 600,000 Buddhists in France.

Recent estimates place the number of Muslims in France at just over four million, mainly immigrants of north African origin with between a third and a half holding French nationality. Islam is now the second major religion in France. The strains that are placed upon French Muslims with divided loyalties between Islamic law and western culture have led to a number of clashes both within the French Muslim community (especially over the conduct and dress of French Muslim women), and in society as a whole with Algerian Islamic extremism gaining significant footholds amongst the alienated younger communities of the poorer city suburbs.

THE LEGAL SYSTEM

Britain is a common law country in which the system of justice depends heavily on custom and precedent. However France is a civil law country where the legal system is based entirely on a body of written law. A system of administrative justice was laid down by Napoleon I in the *Code Napoléon*, which was later also adopted by other countries. Today there are 55 *codes* (compilations of laws, decrees, and circulars) governing all branches of French law. Amongst these are the *Code Civil,* the *Code Pénal*, and the *Code Fiscal.*

In France there are actually two judicial systems: administrative and judiciary. The administrative system is responsible for settling lawsuits between the Government and the individual. This provides French citizens with exceptional legal protection. Suits are brought to the *Tribunaux de Première Instance* and appeals may be made to the *Conseil d'Etat* (Council of State). This is one of the most prestigious bodies in France. One of its roles is to advise the Government on the conformity of proposed legislation with the body of existing law.

Running parallel to the administrative system is the judiciary which is responsible for civil and criminal cases. The criminal courts include the *Tribunaux correctionels* (courts of correction), the *Tribunaux de police* (police courts), and the *Cours d'assises* (assize courts), which try felonies. Appeals are referred to one of the *Cours d'appel* (courts of appeal).

All court decisions are subject to possible reversal by the Supreme Court of Appeals (the *Cour de Cassation*). All judges in France are career professionals who must pass a very competitive examination. In criminal courts the judge has a more active role in the case than in Great Britain and conducts most of the questioning of the witness. A French jury is actually a mixed tribunal where six lay judges sit with three professional judges. A two-thirds majority of this 'jury' may convict. The jury of peers (as used in Great Britain) was abolished in 1941 in France.

More than ever before, the French judicial system has been at the heart of national life in recent years. The Socialist government ended the traditional political control of judges which was generally used to thwart political corruption investigations, and the result has been an astounding number of investigations, but few actual trials, of the main right-wing political elite, with the closest attention centring on former President Chirac himself who faces a number of unanswered major charges of bribery and grand fraud from his time as Mayor of Paris.

The right-wing Raffarin government introduced a string of tough new measures to strengthen the various police forces, and cut back on public disorder offences ranging from organised mafia-style violent crime, to juvenile delinquency, to prostitution and even illegal rave parties. The crackdown on crime was led by Nicolas Sarkozy who at the time was the Interior Minister.

THE POLITICAL SYSTEM

The French system of government is a combination of presidential and parliamentary systems.

The President of the Republic

The President is elected by direct universal suffrage for a term of five years (known as a *quinquenat*). Elections normally take place in two rounds, which lead to political realignments between each ballot (*scrutin*) as the leading right-wing and left-wing candidates draw together their forces.

He appoints the Prime Minister, presides over the Cabinet, and concludes treaties. When the president is not of the same political party as the prime minister and parliamentary majority, it is known as a *cohabitation*. Major policy decisions on defence and foreign policy remain the reserve of the President, who is Head of State and Commander-in-Chief of the Armed Forces.

He may submit questions to the French Parliament by a national referendum, and he may dissolve the *Assemblée Nationale*, the lower house of the French Parliament.

The Prime Minister

The head of the government is the Prime Minister, who heads the cabinet. He submits government bills to parliament and is responsible for their implementation once they have been voted into law. He or she is selected by the President and is normally the head of the majority in the *Assemblée Générale*. However, this does not have to be the case.

He or she draws up membership of the cabinet, which can and does include people from outside the political world brought in to bring special expertise to a particular area. Current examples of this are Christine Lagarde, the Finance and Economy Minister (formerly head partner of a major Anglo-Saxon law firm);

Rachida Dati, the Justice Minister (formerly a court prosecutor); Martin Hirsch (former President of the Emmaus charity for the homeless and destitute); and Junior Housing Minister Fadela Amara (founder of a militant women's rights association in the tougher suburbs).

The separation of powers within the French constitution allows these ministers to be drafted in, regardless of whether they succeed in being elected to Parliament. They all sit in the *Assemblée Générale*. The role of the Prime Minister and his cabinet under the separation of powers is to prepare legislation for debate and approval – or rejection – by the two houses of the French Parliament.

The French Parliament
The French Parliament is bi-cameral, that is, it has two chambers as in most democracies.

♦ The 'Lower House', the *Assemblée Nationale* (National Assembly) is the more important of the two houses. It may initiate laws, overrule the *Sénat*, and by a 'motion of censure' force a government to resign. The 491 *Deputés* (members) of the *Assemblée* are elected for a five-year term by a two-round majority vote.

To be elected on the first ballot, a candidate must obtain an absolute majority (rare in France) of the valid votes cast, i.e. more than 50% of the votes. If no candidates meet this requirement, a second ballot takes place on the following Sunday for candidates who have received at least 12.5% of the votes in the first round. The realignments and redistribution of votes between the two ballots are crucial to a candidate's success or failure. The *Président* of the *Assemblée Nationale* (currently Bernard Accoyer) is the third most important person in the order of precedence in the Republic.

◆ The *Sénat* (Senate) is the second elected body, made up of 283 Senators, indirectly elected for nine years by an electoral college. Distinguished former *Deputés* and ministers often move up to the *Sénat* in order to continue in political life but in a reduced capacity.

Local government

France is divided into 96 *departements* (each known by its name and number) managed by a *Préfect* appointed by the central government, and 36,000 *communes* led by *maires* (mayors) who are agents of both the central government and of the municipalities. These two tiers form the backbone of an administrative system established by Napoleon I to rule the country under the watchful eye of central government.

However, since 1972 continued efforts have been made to decentralise that system in favour of elected local authorities. In that year, 22 regions were created by grouping together several *departements*. This was intended to bring local government more under the control of local people. Further reforms ten years later, in 1982, further decentralised decision-making powers to regional councils, general councils in the *départements*, and municipal councils in the *communes*. Recent governments have continued to decentralise power to the regional assemblies whilst at the same time retaining the cohesive nature of the French republic and refusing to initiate a process of devolution in the face of strident minority claims for independence, most notably in Corsica, the Basque country and Brittany.

One French political particularity is multiple office holding (the *cumul des mandates*) despite repeated efforts at reform. Many national politicians stand for mayor in their constituencies, and even in major cities, allowing them to concentrate power in their own hand, and making sure that if they lose a national job they still have a local fiefdom.

POLITICAL PARTIES

The *UMP*

By the time of the presidential elections in 2002, the bickering right-wing parties had almost all drawn together to back Jacques Chirac and oppose the Socialist Lionel Jospin in the *Union pour un movement populaire (UMP)*. Chirac's original political party, the Gaullist *Rallye pour la République (RPR)* was dissolved in 2002 to form the basis of the new *UMP*. The current Interior Minister, Michéle Alliot-Marie, was the last leader of the *RPR*. Alliot-Marie's ambitious media-friendly predecessor as Interior Minister, Nicolas Sarkozy, transformed the *UMP* into his own electoral machine, and it swept him to power in 2007.

The *UMP* led by Prime Minister François Fillon, and former Prime Minister Jean-Pierre Raffarin amongst others, is pushing through an ambitious campaign of tax cuts and economic and hard-line immigration reforms. Sarkozy makes no secret of his admiration for the American and British political models, in a country where many still regard these ideas as bewildering at best. Sarkozy has also announced a major reform of the all-powerful civil service (*la fonction publique*), which accounts for about 25% of the workforce, with less *fonctionnaires* and a reduction to the costly retirement schemes they benefit from. The last person to try that was Prime Minister Alain Juppé in 1995. Significantly in 2007, Juppé failed to make it back to Parliament and the Government. Major social upheaval could follow these attempts, even if public opinion is now more in favour of addressing these pressing issues.

Sarkozy has caused uproar also in the political world by bringing in Socialist and former Centre Party ministers (*les ministres de l'ouverture*), in a so far successful effort to divide and rule. Despite his protestations, there is little doubt that Sarkozy would prefer an American presidential system, and François Fillon is often tipped to be the last-ever Prime Minister of France.

Le Nouveau Centre and the Mouvement Democrate (MODEM)

In the 1970s, former President Valéry Giscard d'Estaing founded the centre-right party *Union pour une Démocratie Française (UDF)*. By the end of the 1990s, the party had adopted an 'independent ally' position beside the *RPR* and *UMP* parties. Nonetheless the leader François Bayrou increasingly distanced himself from Nicolas Sarkozy, and ran a highly successful presidential campaign against Sarkozy in 2007, claiming 18% of the vote and third place.

Bayrou refused to support Sarkozy, but almost 20 *UDF* members of parliament threw in their votes with the *UMP* candidate. This group has now formed the *Nouveau Centre*, whose main preoccupation appears to be trying to finish off François Bayrou's political career. The leader of the *Nouveau Centre* is the current Defence Minister, Hérvé Morin.

Bayrou meanwhile, has formed a new party, the *Mouvement Démocrate* (or *MODEM*), building on his electoral success. Although he is reduced to four members of parliament, his Christian Democrat brand of politics is particularly appreciated in Paris and other major cities, and the Catholic west. This will probably ensure his political future as he wanders in the wilderness in the coming years.

The Socialist Party (*PS*)

In 2007, the Socialist Party suffered its second consecutive Presidential and General Election defeat. The presidential nominee was Ségolène Royal, the now ex-partner of the General Secretary François Hollande. However, her rivals and internal enemies failed to accept the choice and her campaign stalled. A curious style of old-fashion family values, 'secret' Blairism, and a belief in her own destiny as France's answer to Spain's Prime Minister Zapatero, left Socialist voters bewildered and others unconvinced, even if her 'participative public debates' for establishing priorities and election promises proved a popular gimmick. With her semi-mystic utterances, her habit of wearing white, and her political failure, French satirists have nicknamed her 'The Immaculate Deception'.

The party is currently recomposing itself, yet again, but this will be a long-drawn out process which means that they are unlikely to hold national power for some time to come.

The principal components in the current Socialist Party are:

1. The **Left wing** – The 'old guard' led by Henri Emmanuelli and Jean-Luc Melenchon takes a hard-left stance in the militant defence of workers' rights. They also led a successful campaign to reject the proposed European Constitution.

2. The **Jospin clan** – The current leadership of the party rests with the General Secretary François Hollande. A mild-mannered man, capable but not sufficiently popular to really rally the troops, Hollande is now the subject of all the attacks for ten years of electoral failure. The rising star of the moment is the Mayor of Paris, Bertrand Delanoë, the openly gay mayor who has had an enormous success in the capital, and is now also considered a future presidential candidate for the Left. He is a long-term friend of former Prime Minister Lionel Jospin. The former Prime Minister famously 'left politics' after his presidential defeat in 2002, but he keeps coming back with increased frequency.

3. The **Liberal Wing** – The Liberals were led by Dominique Strauss-Kahn, who was Jospin's Finance Minister and for a while by former Prime Minister Laurent Fabius. Both contested the Socialist presidential candidacy against Ségolène Royal. Fabius changed direction, adopting a more hard-left anti-European line (which failed to give him credibility or support). Strauss-Kahn is now president of the International Monetary Fund, nominated by President Sarkozy who neatly dispensed with one of his principal rivals. Strauss-Kahn was accused of collusion with Sarkozy for accepting, but is still taking a close interest in French politics.

The *PS* is now faced with the difficult task of both safeguarding its new supporters in the upwardly-mobile 'BoBo' classes especially in Paris and Lyons where they made huge inroads in 2001, and winning back the working classes which they lost in the 2002 elections. The commitment to a united Left, working with the Communist and Green parties, appears to remain both a priority and a necessity. However the French Left suffers from incessant bickering and rivalry, and the further Left you go on the political spectrum, the harder it is to find any form of consensus, despite a successful anti-European coalition during the Constitution referendum.

The Communist and Green parties

One of the other great shocks of political life, although it was not unexpected, was the virtual disappearance in 2002 of the French Communist Party (*PCF*) now led by Marie-Georges Buffet. With help of the *PS*, a few Communist *Deputés* were re-elected, and in 2008 they are now fighting for their financial and political survival The *PCF* still maintains an orthodox Leninist line of defence of workers' rights, without appearing credible or interesting to the workers.

The Green Party (*Les Verts*) are led by the *Deputé* Noël Mammere and the *Senateur* Dominique Voynet. The Greens are traditionally known for their in-fighting, but have had some major successes. In the Jospin government the environment ministry was held by two successive Green Party leaders, and in Paris the Green Party have taken full control of the transport portfolio, with a spectacular impact. Several Green leaders have recently defected to François Bayrou's *MODEM* party.

The extremist parties

The 1990s saw the rise of the extreme-right political parties in France. The elections in 2002 demonstrated the extent to which the extremist parties in France have become the real power-brokers in French politics. Although they failed at this game on a national level, at a local level they still wield considerable power.

◆ The '**Nationalists**' (*souverainistes*) – Philippe de Villiers' *Mouvement pour la France* represented about 5% of the electorate in 1995, and his strong Catholic moral stance and a firmly anti-European line still finds much favour in his own homeland in rural western France. Jospin's former Interior Minister, the renegade Left-wing politician Jean-Pierre Chevenement tried and failed to become president in 2002 with his populist cross-party *Pôle Républicaine*. His political ideas left the voters confused, and Chevenement failed even to be re-elected to parliament. A Gaullist *député*, Nicolas Dupont-Aignan, also tried and failed to revive the *souverainist* vote in 2007. These groups are small, electorally insignificant, but vociferous.

◆ The **extreme-Right** – Ever since its creation in 1981, there has been a sinister rise in support of the *Front National* (*FN*) led by Jean-Marie Le Pen. In 1995 Le Pen gained 15% of votes cast in the Presidential elections, and in 2002 he went through to the second round with 18%. Le Pen's demagogic style mixes tough anti-immigration talk, blaming immigrants for France's unemployment and advocating repatriation, with a sweeping invective against President Chirac and the former *RPR* for their support for European Union. Le Pen's rallying cry is 'the French first'. Many protest voters are drawn to the *FN*. In

Spring 1998 the *FN* once again took nearly 16% of the votes in the regional elections, leaving them as power-brokers in many regions, leading to mayhem on the Right. Le Pen's 2007 presidential campaign floundered because on the one hand his daughter and heir, Marine Le Pen, tried to tone down her father's more extreme outbursts; and on the other hand Sarkozy leapt into the breach and used tough-line rhetoric to successfully attract *FN* voters.

◆ The **extreme Left** – For years, nobody took the Trotskyist Arlette Laguillier of 'Workers' Struggle' party, *Lutte Ouvrière (LO)* seriously. Suddenly in 2002, she took almost 7% of the votes in the first round of the Presidential elections, contributing to the defeat of Jospin and calling for a new revolution rather than a vote for Chirac against Le Pen. Her main rival is a young part-time politician named Olivier Besancenot of the extreme Revolutionary Communist League (*LCR*), who took 4% of the votes in the presidential elections in 2002 and 2007. Besancenot, young, good-looking and silver-tongued, is seen as the rising star of the French Extreme Left, and poses a real problem for the French Socialists.

RULERS AND REPUBLICS SINCE 1789

Since their first revolution in 1789, the French have been ruled by a number of kings, consuls, emperors and presidents in succession. The First Republican rulers (1792–5) were replaced by the Directory (*Directoire*), which in turn gave way rapidly to the forceful character of the First Consul, military genius and from 1804–14 the first Emperor of the French, Napoleon. Napoleon was not simply a great general, but also a great law-giver, and the codification of French law is still largely based upon his *Code*

Napoléon laid down in this period. After his final defeat in 1815 at the battle of Waterloo, Napoleon was replaced by the restored Bourbon monarchy under Louis XVIII (1815–24) and his reactionary brother Charles X (1824–30), the younger brothers of the beheaded Louis XVI. July 1830 saw another revolution in France, less bloody than its predecessor. The life of Charles X was spared, but his throne was lost to his more egalitarian cousin Louis-Philippe, (whose father Philippe, Duc d'Orléans, known as Philippe Egalité, voted to execute his cousin Louis XVI!).

Louis-Philippe adopted a more restrained and deliberately *bourgeois* style of monarchy, which lasted until 1848 when revolutions swept across Europe toppling monarchs in their wake. Hence France went through her third revolution in less than 50 years.

A Second Republic was established, under the nephew of the first emperor. Unsurprisingly, this second Bonaparte could not resist following family tradition, and had himself declared Emperor of the French as Napoleon III in 1851. Unlike his uncle, Napoleon III was a great Anglophile, and it was indeed to England that he fled when he was overthrown by the Commune in 1870 after the Franco-Prussian War. During his reign, many of the foundations were laid of Franco-British *rapprochement* which came to fruition in the *Entente Cordiale* in 1904. The Third Republic which was eventually established in 1875 lasted until 1940, when France capitulated to the invading Nazi forces and was divided into the occupied territories of the north, and the southern régime of Marshal Pétain based at Vichy which eventually came under Nazi control. Following the liberation of France and the end of the Second World War, a Fourth Republic was established from 1946–58.

The new Fifth Republic, adopted by referendum in 1958, was inspired by the ideas of General Charles de Gaulle, the French wartime resistance leader, who went on to become President (1958–69) and whose spirit still dominates French right-wing politics. Increased presidential power and a reduced capacity for the *Assemblée Nationale* (Parliament) to bring down the government were built in to the new constitution to try to eradicate the political instability of the Third and Fourth Republics.

De Gaulle was succeeded as President by Georges Pompidou, who opened to the way to British entry to the Common Market before his death in 1974. He was succeeded by Valérie Giscard d'Estaing as President who beat François Mitterand to the presidency in 1974. In 1981, however, Mitterand's historic 14-year reign began as the first Socialist President of the Fifth Republic. His style of leadership inspired a confidence which allowed him to survive many crises, and which earned him the affectionate nicknames of both '*Ton-ton*' (uncle), and quite simply '*Dieu*' (God).

Jacques Chirac's election as President of France in 1995 was a close-won victory which reflected the divided state of France. The reins of government were already divided in a *Cohabitation* between the Socialist President François Mitterand and his right-wing Prime Minister Edouard Balladur. The Presidential election gave Chirac a slim majority, but the tables were turned in 1997 with the election of his Socialist presidential challenger, Lionel Jospin, as the new Prime Minister.

The Chirac presidencies, 1995–2007

Chirac's first Prime Minister, Alain Juppé (1995–97), began the path to British-style economic liberalism, and state-owned industries were prepared for privatisation in order to raise funds for both France's enormous social security debt, and the financial criteria for the Euro. Cuts in public spending and record unemployment (12.5%) led to an almost general, bitter strike by public-sector workers in the winter of 1995.

In the spring of 1997, President Jacques Chirac took a political gamble which did not pay off, when he chose to dissolve a year earlier than was necessary the existing *Assemblée Nationale*, where the ruling right-wing coalition which he headed had a majority. Deep unpopularity at the austerity measures and plans for the liberalisation of the French economy led to a massive swing to the Left, and Lionel Jospin headed a Left-wing coalition government from 1997–2002, with the Socialists dependent on the Communist and Green parties for support in the *Assemblée Nationale*. Thus France re-entered once again the state of Right-Left *cohabitation*.

Both unemployment and crime were high, and youth unemployment was designated as one of the major priorities by both the President and the Prime Minister. Jospin initiated a mass employment programme, partly based on youth employment with state-backed jobs for young people to ease them into the job market. The other pillar of his plan was the 35-hour week programme. This provoked opposition from employers, workers who were angered at the loss of earnings from overtime, and the vast number of traditionally left-voting civil servants who were excluded from an unworkable reform. The job creations were not as numerous as expected, but unemployment came down to just over 9% in 2002.

In 2002, the Presidential election was planned for May, to be followed by a general election for the *Assemblée Générale* in June. Chirac and Jospin were amongst the last of a record number of candidates to declare their candidacies for the presidency, to the general irritation of the public and press. On 21 April 2002, the French electorate, accustomed to using the first round of the Presidential elections to send a message to the real candidates by voting for minority candidates who perhaps more nearly represented their views, put the writing on the wall for the entire smug French political class. In a shock result, Jospin was thrown out in favour of the extreme-right wing candidate, Jean-Marie Le Pen, and Chirac won less than 20% of the first vote. Following mass street demonstrations, a Left-Right Republican coalition in the second round delivered a rousing defeat for Le Pen. But this only served to demonstrate the persistence and depth of the *'fracture sociale'* which Chirac had claimed he would heal in 1995.

In 2002 the growing sense of insecurity which became the *leitmotiv* of the elections was really symptomatic of more fundamental problems in French society which need to be addressed. One explanation of the extremist vote has been that the *France d'en bas* (France of below) has taught a lesson to the *France d'en haut* (France 'up there' – i.e. removed from everyday life). The lower middle classes, sick of heavy taxation and a self-perceived drop in their standard of living, provided the backbone of *FN* support in 2002, whilst the tired and angry workers turned their back on their traditional *PS* and *PCF* leaders.

The appointment of Jean-Pierre Raffarin as Prime Minister in 2002 was a move to undercut the electoral power base of the *FN*. Raffarin, a regional politician, was largely unknown in Paris except for a brief period as Junior Minister for Small and Middle-Sized Business (*Petits et Moyens Entreprises* or *PMEs*), and whose most famous ministerial battle had been to defend the French *baguette* against European directives.

The rise of the extreme Left which cost Jospin the presidency (taking 11% of the vote in 2002) is symbolic of another crisis. Even though unemployment fell sharply, it remains concentrated in certain sectors of the population. Workers, disillusioned with the failure of the Jospin government to stop factory closures in areas already hard-hit by unemployment, or to significantly improve the finances of the *ouvriers* (workers), voted for the extreme parties with their simplistic solutions – revolution or repatriation. The *FN* vote in areas of high unemployment was also very high, as much as 30% in some areas of the North and East.

Forty years on from the first waves of mass immigration from former French colonies, the failure to achieve social advancement and acceptance for the immigrant communities is one of France's most painful sores. In March 2000, the level of unemployment amongst high-level graduates was 5% for French-born graduates, and 20% for *Maghrehbin* graduates. This has provoked large-scale deception for many immigrants seeking integration through education.

The end of the Chirac years was marked very heavily by foreign policy issues. Chirac suddenly acquired a renewed legitimacy in

French eyes when he led the international campaign against the war in Iraq. For once he appeared to have adopted the stature of his political hero, General de Gaulle, in defying the USA. However this success was followed by yet another failed political gamble, the European Constitution referendum in 2005. The spectacular failure of this referendum led to the fall of Jean-Pierre Raffarin, and Chirac appointed his personal favourite Dominique de Villepin as Prime Minister for the stagnant twilight years of his final presidency.

'President Bling-Bling' and the 'Sarkoshow'

In 2007, Nicolas Sarkozy finally realised the dream that he had talked about all his life, when he was elected President. Although he presents himself as representing a break with the political past, he is nonetheless a former *protégé* of President Chirac. Sarkozy earned his political spurs serving the former *RPR* party from a very early age, having made a strategic marriage in order to become Mayor of France's richest commune, Neuilly, at the age of 28.

Appointed as Budget Minister in the Balladur Government, Sarkozy betrayed his former political master Chirac in 1995 and backed Balladur as the presidential candidate. Sarkozy was by now divorced, and wooing Chirac's daughter, but the relationship ended when Sarkozy suddenly married his second wife Cecilia, the wife of a major TV presenter. Sarkozy had actually presided at Cecilia's first civil wedding. When Chirac was re-elected as President, Sarkozy began a period in the political wilderness, having earned Chirac's undying enmity.

In 2002, Jean-Pierre Raffarin called Sarkozy back to Government to deal with the poisoned chalice of crime, as France's Interior Minister. Sarkozy's tough line 'zero tolerance' rhetoric, and the start of his media omnipresence, made him a very popular minister at least with some sections of the population. His verbal excesses, however, have earned him a foul reputation in the inner-city suburbs where he is *persona non grata*. From 2006, Sarkozy devoted himself, in public and in private, to securing the *UMP* party nomination as presidential candidate. When he was elected President in May 2007, he had at last reached the top of the greasy pole of politics.

Sarkozy's first move was to apply the principle he had denounced in his rival François Bayrou's programme. Sarkozy appointed several leading Socialists as members of his government. Officially this is to harness all the reforming energies of the political elite in regenerating the country. In reality, it is also to ensure that no effective opposition can be formed to counter his reform programme or his personal power. French rulers since de Gaulle have often been accused of behaving more like princes than presidents. His critics accuse him of being a 'hyper-president', effectively destroying the role of the Prime Minister and the Government by hogging the limelight and the major policy decisions. These two characteristics of Sarkozy's style – dividing the opposition and ruling by himself – create a distinct reminder of Louis XIV, 'the Sun King', who employed the same methods. In addition, the President's media omnipresence (often referred to as the 'Sarkoshow'), his marital and extra-marital sagas, and his 'showbiz' celebrity lifestyle, have earned Sarkozy the nickname of 'President Bling-Bling'.

Sarkozy is determined to make his mark on the international scene, with a style mixing the economic policy of Tony Blair, the foreign policy of George W. Bush, and the personal lifestyle of Silvio Berlusconi. All of this is certainly in marked contrast to the traditional French idea of what a President and his entourage should represent – sober and refined elegance standing for everlasting ideals. Although he is pushing through a battery of fiscal and employment reforms, the results concerning the top popular political question, public spending power, have so far been meagre. Sarkozy's popularity had dropped from 38% in May 2008. Much of this was because of his failure to increase spending power, but also because of the incessant exposure of his luxurious and apparently hedonistic private life.

The real key to the situation will be Sarkozy's ability to curb his own excesses, verbal or otherwise. Sarkozy is right to say that the French have always had a strange relationship with wealth, despising it in public and coveting it in private. Times and attitudes have changed, but there is still deep-seated resentment at the wide-spread poverty which many French people face, and which is at the core of the spending power debate. Recent major insider dealing scandals at EADS and the *Société Générale* have also fuelled the traditional French attitude. The danger is that in his overt pursuit of all that glitters, Sarkozy could waste his political capital in the pursuit of fool's gold, and lose the opportunity for achieving real structural change which, despite everything, is what the French now want.

2

Making a Successful Move to France

To make a success of your move to France, you need to plan as much as possible. Remembering to bring the right papers with you, and then to take them to the right appointment in France in your earliest days can and will save you many headaches later on. A successful move can be divided into three parts: before and during your arrival, which are considered in this chapter, and immediately after your arrival, which is considered in Chapter 5.

Four important points to remember are:

1. Moving home is reckoned to be one of the most stressful experiences known to humans, along with death and divorce. You will have a hiccup or two somewhere along the line even if you plan well. Try to retain what the French most admire in foreigners – their sense of humour!

2. To the French, bureaucracy is not a means to an end but a way of life. A French civil servant really could not care less how many times you have turned up at their counter. They literally have all day to sit there and find reasons to make you come back and keep them busy tomorrow. Correct preparation will allow you to get off the administrative roundabout as quickly as possible, but it cannot be avoided.

3. Losing your temper is on the whole very counter-productive with the French administration. You might as well tell the wind not to blow in your face. Stay calm, try to smile even if you are

developing a deep personal loathing for the person across the counter, and avoid screaming fits.

4. Take a good supply of reading material and always arrive early at French administrative centres.

PREPARING BEFORE YOUR DEPARTURE

Passports

Under the internal arrangements (the Schengen Agreement) citizens of the European Union (EU) can enter France with just a national identity card. However, **British citizens need a valid British passport in order to enter France** (or indeed any other country covered by the Schengen Agreement), as the United Kingdom does not adhere to the Agreement.

Commonwealth citizens with residency rights in the UK are not recognised as British citizens under EU regulations. You will therefore be subject to entry requirements related to your country of origin. **Channel Islanders and Manx citizens** are not included in the EU provisions, unless they or a parent or grandparent were born in the UK, or they have been resident in the UK for five years.

Visas and residence permits

EU citizens do not require visas in order to enter France. Regulations for visas for non-EU citizens vary, and you will need to check current regulations with the French Embassy or Consulate nearest to you. For non-EU citizens, a number of different visas are available:

◆ *Visa de transit* – allows three days travel across France by
  train.

◆ *Visa de circulation* – often given to business people. This allows
  several stays of up to 90 days, with a maximum of 180 days in
  any one year. This visa is normally valid for three years.

◆ *Visa de court-séjour* – a short-stay visa valid for up to 90 days,
  permitting re-entry to France during that period.

◆ *Visa de long-séjour* – a long-stay visa for those studying,
  working or living in France for more than 90 days. You must
  already have this visa if you decide to stay for a longer period
  than originally intended. Otherwise, you will be obliged to
  return to your home country in order to apply for this visa.

Minimum requirements for Americans seeking visas to live and
work in France include a valid passport; several passport-size
black and white photographs; proof of your financial means and
ability to support yourself during your stay in France and also
support any dependents you may have; and your work contract
with French Labour Ministry approval. Full details are given later
in the chapters on finding employment in France. American
tourists can enter and stay in France for up to 90 days without a
visa.

**All foreigners intending to reside in France for more than three
months, except for citizens of the original EU member countries,
must obtain a residence permit (*carte de séjour*). Temporary
residence permits for non-EU citizens are normally valid for up
to one year.**

Driving papers

You are obliged to carry your papers with you whenever you are driving a vehicle in France. Failure to produce them can lead to a fine. You can bring a car into France for up to six months in any one year without having to complete customs formalities. See Chapter 12 for further details on licences, car importation and car registration.

Professional papers

Take with you all relevant professional certificates, diplomas, and so on, which may be required if you are setting up your own business. You will also need to enquire at your nearest French Consulate about the *carte de commerçant* required in some cases by those seeking to create their own business.

Personal papers

You should bring with you copies of income tax documents for the last four years, and any documents relating to investments and stocks and bonds. Receipts for your moving expenses, if they are not reimbursed by your employer, may be needed for tax purposes.

Documents checklist

Check that you have all of the following papers ready as you prepare for your departure.

☐ Valid passport.
☐ Valid visa for non-EU citizens.
☐ Full certified copies of your birth certificate, that of your spouse, and those of your children.
☐ Full certified copy of your marriage certificate.
☐ Valid driving licence.

☐ Car registration and insurance papers.

☐ *Carte de commerçant* if this is required and professional certificates.

☐ Au pairs need their *Déclaration d'Engagement* from their employer. Non-EU citizens will also be asked for a medical certificate.

☐ Students should bring with them evidence of admission to a study course.

☐ Bank statements, tax declarations and other financial documents. Proof of your financial resources may be demanded before you are granted a residence permit, depending on your nationality and occupation.

☐ Vaccination certificates for your pets.

DECIDING WHERE TO LIVE

Deciding where to live in France will involve balancing professional, family and perhaps educational obligations, and personal preferences. Deciding what sort of accommodation to live in, whether to buy or rent, and in which area of the city, are personal choices which will be shaped by your circumstances and future plans. Think carefully about the following points when you decide where to live:

- ◆ **Size** – Do you prefer to have a larger home in a less popular but cheaper area, or a smaller home in a more central and/or expensive area?

- ◆ **Facilities** – Which facilities do you want to be nearest? Shops, schools, entertainment, your workplace?

- ◆ **Transport** – What public transport facilities are there nearby? Do you need parking space?

◆ **Safety** – How safe is the area? Is it really as safe, or as dangerous as you have been told?

If you have the opportunity it is a good idea to briefly visit the *quartier* (district) where you are considering living. Bear in mind the points above, be observant when you visit the *quartier*, and decide on your priorities before taking a decision.

Local considerations

Each town, *commune* or *arrondissement* (in Paris, Lyon and Marseille) has its own mayor and local council, and state-run services from education to taxation are operated on the basis of sub-divisions of the *arrondissements*. This can have varying degrees of importance at different stages of your life. For instance:

◆ Your chances of finding a place in a municipal *crèche* for your child will be affected. The number of places available varies greatly in different areas.

◆ Your children will be assigned to state schools according to the *arrondissement* you live in, and the sub-divisions become crucial when it comes to entering your child into one of the élite *lycées*.

◆ Your local housing tax (*taxe d'habitation*) will vary according to not only the size of your apartment or house, but also to its last official listed valuation by the local authorities, which will take into account average market prices per square metre at the time of the valuation. The presence of large businesses or factories can have a very beneficial effect for local residents in terms of their *taxe d'habitation*.

◆ Local authorities rival each other on the quality of services they offer to their residents. Mainly, this is part of the party political game, but the results of a sustained programme over a number of years to restore a certain *quartier* or maintain a general standard of living across the neighbourhood can make a considerable difference.

◆ In March 2008 new municipal councils were elected. A change in the political wind may well set in motion a levelling of the differences between *arrondissements* and the towns.

Environmental considerations

When you do narrow your choices down, it is worth taking a trip to the local *mairie* to find out what is planned in the area in the near future. If there are plans to move the school a kilometre away, or to cut a new *métro* line under your street, or to build a block of new flats on the site opposite, you may want to reconsider.

You should also be wary in rural areas of the danger of flooding, which has been a particular problem in both northern and southern France. Village centres are not immune from major problems. When you view a property, ask if the building is in a flood-risk zone (*zone inondable*). Many buildings were constructed in such zones even up until very recent times. The age of a building is no guarantee against the risk of flooding in some areas.

Final considerations

As you begin your home search, there are three basic rules to remember:

1. Furnished rented accommodation is generally more expensive than unfurnished accommodation.

2. The suburbs are generally less expensive than the city centre, although everything depends on location.

3. Weigh up a larger home in a more distant location against increased travelling time and monthly cost, as well as perhaps inferior amenities – although that calculation can work in both directions.

DECIDING WHAT TO TAKE WITH YOU

French kitchens are normally smaller than English kitchens, and you would probably be safer buying large kitchen machines and appliances within France. British electrical appliances do work in France. However, you must remember to either change the three-pin plug to a two-pin plug, or buy adapters. English televisions and video recorders will not work in France, and these will need to be purchased or rented locally.

Self-assembly furniture stores do exist in France, and buying furniture does not need to cost a fortune. You will need to decide if it is cheaper to buy furniture in France or to ship your own furniture to France. Furniture storage is generally very costly in France and the UK. French beds come in three standard sizes – single, small double, and large double. Whilst your sheets and bedding will almost certainly fit these sizes, you should bear in mind that the standard French pillow is square.

Find out about the climate of the town or region to which you are moving, as regional variations in climate are very noticeable. You will need a fair share of winter and summer clothing if you are moving to France for a prolonged period. Clothes can be bought reasonably cheaply in France in high-street stores such as Monoprix or Prisunic, or from catalogues (some of which have stores) such as La Redoute if both your budget and your storage facilities are limited. The table below (Figure 2) gives conversion sizes for English and French clothes measurements.

	Men's suits							Men's shirts							Men's shoes					
UK	36	38	40	42	44	46	48	14	14.5	15	15.5	16	16.5	17	7	7.5	8.5	9.5	10.5	11
France	46	48	50	52	54	56	58	36	37	38	39/40	41	42	43	41	42	43	44	45	46

	Dress sizes						Women's shoes					
UK	8	10	12	14	16	18	4.5	5	5.5	6	6.5	7
France	36	38	40	42	44	46	38	38	39	39	40	41

Fig. 2. Clothes size conversions.

Import rules and regulations

The excellent website provided by the French Customs Service (**www.douane.gouv.fr**) gives clear precise explanations, including how to import pets, plants and medicines. They also lay out the French duty-free policies. Click on the British flag for the English-language pages and take a good look at the various sections for help and advice.

Detailed rules about the importation of household goods should be discussed with the customs section of the French consulate. On the website, you will find French Customs contact details in London and Washington. If you use a professional moving firm, they should also be able to inform you about necessary customs formalities.

♦ For EU citizens, goods on which you have already paid VAT in another EU member country are exempt from VAT payments when imported into France. This should be specified on the 'CMR' form provided by a professional removal firm. If you have receipts which show that VAT has already been paid, it is wise to have these available for inspection if required. You should also prepare an itemised inventory of your effects, both for customs inspection, and in case of an insurance claim.

♦ Non-EU citizens are also exempt from VAT payments on their belongings, *providing that* they have been in their possession more than six months, *and* that VAT has been paid in another EU country. You will be required by the French customs officials to produce receipts to this effect. Items purchased less than six months before your arrival, or outside of the EU area, will be subject to VAT payment. You have one year from the date of your arrival in France to import your possessions before they become subject to VAT payment. You must obtain a stamped *Certificat de Changement de Domicile* from your 'home' French Consulate, and your detailed inventory must also be stamped by the same consular authorities. Restrictions on what is considered duty-free should be checked with the French consular services to find out which of your personal effects and possessions may be subject to tax upon importation.

♦ Details on the importation of vehicles are given in Chapter 11.

♦ There are restrictions on which plants can be imported into France (particular varieties of 'herbs' and 'pot plants' are not appreciated...), a limited number of plants can be included amongst your personal effects. Check out the Customs website section in English on plants and vegetables for precise details.

Works of art and collectors' items may require special import licences, as do firearms and ammunition. For these items, you must contact the French Consulate for further details, or consult the French-only pages of the Customs website. For all of these items, you must contact the French Consulate for further information. You can also contact the French customs office at the Centre Renseignement des Douanes, 238 quai de Bercy, 75572 Paris, Cedex 12, tél. 01 40 01 02 06.

Bringing your pets

Pets imported from another European Union (EU) country must be accompanied by their EU Pet Passport, including all the relevant personal and medical details.

All animals entering an EU country must be identified by a micro-chip or tattoo mentioned on the passport and an anti-rabies vaccination certificate. In addition, a rabies control must be carried out at least three months before entry into France. Bring the results of this test with you as well.

Certain breeds of dangerous dogs are now forbidden in France, and others must be kept muzzled. For precise details regarding pet importations, contact your local French Consulate. You can also find advice in English on the website of the French Consulate in London **www.consulfrance-londres.org**.

PREPARING FINANCIALLY

It can cost a lot of money to set up your new home in France. If you rent an apartment or house, you will have to pay two months' rent in advance as a deposit (and up to three months' for commercial premises), and also the rent for the first month – i.e. three months' rent in advance.

If you use an agency to find your new home, there will also be their fee to pay, normally equivalent to one month's rent. You will then have the cost of electricity and gas connections, and the rental of a telephone line to pay as well.

It can be difficult to secure a rental contract from French landlords, especially if you are a foreigner. Even young French couples are asked for written guarantees, either from their parents or their employers, as a precaution against unpaid rents and bills. Make sure that you bring a significant sum of money with you to cover both these initial expenses, and day-to-day living expenses. Driving licences and residence permits also have to be paid for.

PREPARING CULTURALLY

Many people come to France specifically to improve their French, or quite simply to learn the language for the first time. You will find that a grasp of the most basic phrases and words will help you enormously when you arrive. Do not count on 'everybody speaking English' to you; many can, but not everybody will. You will certainly need to understand what is being said to you when you apply for your residence permit, for example. You will also integrate more rapidly and increase your own personal standing if the French see that you are trying your best to communicate with them in their own language.

You should also try to find out something about the country to which you are moving. There are plenty of excellent introductions to French history and culture available in bookshops. The varied and generally very good French press is also widely available. Reading articles on current life in France will not only help you understand your new environment, but will also improve your language skills.

REGISTERING AT YOUR EMBASSY

British citizens are not required to register at the Embassy or the nearest Consulate-General.

American citizens are not obliged to register at their Paris Embassy, but are strongly advised to do so. This will not only help establish your rights as a US citizen in France, but will also make it easier to deal later with the re-issue of passports, or emergency situations which may occur which involve contacting your family in the USA, and also ease the registration of any children born in France with US citizenship.

OBTAINING YOUR RESIDENCE PERMIT

If you intend to stay in France more than three months, you must apply for a residence permit (*carte de séjour*). Failure to apply for your permit within three months of arrival is a serious offence and could lead to a heavy fine.

Citizens of a member country of the one of the original EU countries are no longer required to apply for a residence permit. You must have a full British passport for this exemption. EU citizenship rights are not granted to Australians with British residency rights, and there are certain restrictions on inhabitants of the Channel Islands and the Isle of Man.

Citizens of one of the new member countries which joined the EU in 2004 are still required to apply for a *carte de séjour* if they wish to have an 'economic activity', i.e. you wish to work or open your own business, the law goes on to state that you do still require a *carte de séjour*. Students from these countries registered at French universities or colleges are not required to seek a residence permit.

ı-**EU countries** need a long-term visa (*visa de long*
arrival in France. Residence permits will not be
issueu .... t the appropriate visas. Americans and Canadians do
not need entry visas for France, but Australians do. **In Paris** you
will need to ask your Consulate which police centre (*centre
d'acceuil des étrangers*) you need to apply to. The centre will
depend on where you live. **Outside Paris** you should initially apply
to the local town hall (*mairie*) who may refer you to a *préfecture*
(police headquarters) for that *département*. Americans who are
moving to work in Paris should refer to Chapter 6 on Finding
Employment for a more detailed explanation of the process they
need to follow.

The bureaucracy you encounter to obtain your *carte* can be agony.
It is advisable to take several copies of all your documents with
you, a good book, and to allow plenty of time. You will receive a
temporary *carte* (*récépissé de demande de carte de séjour*) initially,
proving you have applied, which is valid for three months. This
will eventually be replaced by your permanent *carte*.

Documents needed to obtain a *carte de séjour*
The following is a list of documents which are usually required no
matter what your nationality or status. **Regulations often change,
so check the precise requirements with your local *préfecture* or
mairie.**

☐ Your full birth certificate (a 'certified' copy).

☐ Your passport.

☐ Four passport-sized black-and-white photographs.

☐ Either the rental contract on your apartment; or a bill from France Telecom or *Electricté de France* (*EDF*) in your name showing your address; or a *certificat d'hébergement* from the person who is lodging you dated during the last three months, plus a copy of their *carte d'identité* or *carte de séjour* (if they are also non-French).

☐ If you are in paid employment, either: two copies of your *lettre d'embauche* (job offer) on headed paper from your employer, or your original contract, plus a copy of three most recent pay slips if you have already begun work.

☐ For various categories of independent workers, you will be required to provide proof that you have taken the correct administrative steps to establish your business legally in France. Take advice upon this point.

☐ If you are retired you must be able to prove your financial ability to support yourself and your dependents. You must also prove that you have sufficient health cover.

Cartes de séjour are normally limited to the length of your 'guaranteed' stay (i.e. the length of your employment contract) in France. Within Paris, refer to your own Embassy for details of your local permit centre. Outside Paris, you should ask at your local *mairie* (town hall), where you may be referred to a main *commissariat* (police station).

Student *cartes de séjours* are normally limited to one year, and are renewable. Further details are given for applications for student *cartes de séjours* in Chapter 11 on education.

MANAGING YOUR MONEY

Currency exchange offices are located at airports, railway stations and most banks. If you have the time and the choice, compare exchange rates to find the most favourable rate, and also check to see how much commission you will be charged. In central Paris, you will find many currency exchanges centred around the rue Scribe and the Place de l'Opéra, near the bus stops for Roissy airport.

Introducing the Euro (€)

On 1 January 1999, France joined the single European currency, the Euro.

Notes (or bills): 5, 10, 20, 50, 100, 200, and 500 Euros. Any remaining French francs and notes can be exchanged for Euros at the Banque de France until 1 January 2012.

Coins: 1 and 2 Euros, and 1, 2, 5, 10, 20 and 50 Cents (equivalent to centimes, representing one hundredths of Euros). French cents are marked 'RF' to show they were issued in France.

The Euro is valid in all countries which participate in the European Monetary Union scheme, including Germany, the Benelux countries, Italy, Portugal and Spain. The scheme allows for other countries to join the system when they meet certain economic criteria.

FINDING OUT MORE

French embassies and consulates

◆ *French Embassy in the UK:* **www.ambafrance-uk.org**, and

www.consulfrance-londres.org for detailed information in English to help you prepare your move to France. The French Embassy, 58 Knightsbridge, London SW7. Tel: 020 7073 1000. The French Consulate-General (visas and immigration service) 6A, Cromwell Place, POBox 57, London SW7 2EW. Tel: 020 7073 1250. The French Consulate-General, 11 Randolph Crescent, Edinburgh EH3 7TT. Tel: 0131 225 7954. **www.consulfrance-edimbourg.org**.

◆ *French Embassy in the USA:* **www.ambafrance-us.org**. The French Embassy, 4101 Reservoir Road NW, Washington 2007 DC. Tel: 202 944 6000. The French Consulate, 934 Fifth Avenue, New York NY 10021. Tel: 212 606 3600. **www.consulfrance-newyork.org**. There are also consulates in Atlanta, Boston, Chicago, Houston, Los Angeles, Miami, New Orleans, and San Francisco. Full details in English on visa applications and procedures is available on **www.consulfrance-washington.org**.

Foreign embassies and consulates in France

◆ **The American Embassy: www.paris.usembassy.gov**. Office of American Services & Consular Section, 4 avenue Gabriel, 75008 Paris. Tél. 01 43 12 22 22.

◆ **The British Embassy: www.britishembassy.gov.uk/france**. The Paris Consulate is at 18bis rue d'Anjou, 75008 Paris, M° Concorde, Tél. 01 44 51 31 00.

◆ **The Canadian Embassy**: **www.amb-canada.fr**. The Embassy is at 35 avenue Montaigne, 75008 Paris, M° Alma-Marceau, Tél. 01 44 43 29 00.

♦ **The Irish Embassy**: www.embassyofirelandparis.com. 12, avenue Foch, 75116 Paris. Tél. 01 44 17 67 00.

Other organisations

♦ **www.service-public.fr** – the French government web portal, which will orientate you to all government websites. Some of these are in English. Click on the British flag to obtain a quick list.

♦ **www.prefecture-de-paris.interieur.gouv.fr** – official French website (with a section in English for students), outlining procedures for obtaining your **carte de séjour**.

♦ **Institut Français in London**: www.institut-francais.org.uk. 17 Queensberry Place, London SW7 2DT. Tel: 020 7073 1350, Monday–Friday 8.30am–10pm, Saturday 10am–10pm; Language Centre, 14 Cromwell Place, London SW7 2JR. Tel: 020 7581 2701. Children's Library, 32 Harrington Road, London SW7 2DT. Tube: South Kensington. Buses: 14, 414, 45a, 49, 70, 74, 345, 360, C1. For anybody seriously considering moving to France, or finding out about the French culture, language or lifestyle, a visit to the French Institute is a 'must' if at all possible.

♦ **The French Travel Centre**: 178 Piccadilly, London W1V OAL. Tel: 09068 244 123. Fax 020 7493 6594, **www.franceguide.com**. Open Monday to Friday 10h00–18h00, Saturday 10h00-17h00 also French Railways Ltd, The Rail Europe Travel Centre, 179 Piccadilly, tube: Green Park or Piccadilly Circus. French government tourist centre.

♦ **Alliance Française Glasgow**: www.afglasgow.org.uk. 3 Park Circus, Glasgow, G3 6AX. Tel: 0141 331 4080; and Alliance

Française Manchester **www.alliancefrancaisemanchester.org**, Church Gate House, 4th Floor, 56 Oxford Street, Manchester M1 6EU. Tel: 0161 236 7117, are part of the world-wide network of French Government language schools.

3

Renting Property in France

A survey in Paris in November 2000 showed that property, including both private residential accommodation and public buildings, is still largely in private hands. Some 49.8% of Paris buildings belong to *copropriétés* (collective ownerships), and 20.2% belongs to individuals. This does not mean that all of these are potential landlords, as many are also owner-occupiers. About 17% of the Paris property market belongs to companies, including holding companies of banks and insurance companies.

Your experience of negotiating your way into a lease will depend largely upon whom you are dealing with – a company or an individual. There is increasing alarm at the level of information being demanded of applicant tenants (see below). Even working for a big-name foreign corporation may not necessarily spare you from demands for an almost humiliating range of documents. This seems to be truer of rental agencies acting on behalf of landlords or companies than of the landlords themselves. The only advice that can be given in these scenarios is that you have to grit your teeth if you really want to break into the property market to rent an apartment in Paris.

There are two points you should consider when renting property in France. Furnished accommodation is generally more expensive than unfurnished accommodation; and suburbs are generally less expensive than city centres, although this will depend upon location.

FINDING THE ADVERTS

Obviously you can use real estate agencies (*agents immobilier*) when you first arrive, but there will be a charge to pay for their services. Many of the agencies now have websites which may speed up your initial search, e.g. **www.century21.fr**, **www.seloger.com**, or **www.immostreet.com**.

As a foreigner in France, you may well find it easier to deal directly with landlords, rather than use agencies. To find accommodation in your region yourself, local journals, newspapers and noticeboards are all indispensable for the new arrival. The best national press (with regional editions) are:

◆ *Le Figaro* **and** *Libération* **(newspapers)** – daily. Mainly agencies, some independent landlords. You will find more same-day appointments (e.g. be there at 12h00 today and tomorrow). The problem is, of course, that the first person who comes with the right profile for the landlord is normally the lucky new tenant.

◆ *Particulier à Particulier* **(www.pap.fr)** – comes out every Thursday, available at all major newsagents and kiosks. The major way to find an apartment, although some are from agencies with the vast majority of ads from independent landlords. Be prepared for an early start every Thursday – you need to get the *PAP* around 07h30, mark up the ads which interest you, and call as soon as possible. Some are let before the paper even comes out, and landlords receive hundreds of calls from these advertisements. Long-running advertisements should make you wonder what exactly is being offered and what are the snags.

English-language community noticeboards (e.g. churches) may also be a useful source of adverts. Keep a pen and paper handy and call as soon as you can. In advertisements on both noticeboards and in these magazines aimed at English-speakers, watch out for inflated prices for unsuspecting foreigners.

UNDERSTANDING THE ADVERTS

Once you have started to locate the housing advertisements, either independently or via agencies, you will need to understand the terms and short-hand used in property adverts so that you can concentrate on looking for the style of home which suits you and your budget. The examples given below will help you understand the jargon, and save you much valuable time.

*14e Studio **meublé**, salle d'eau. Prés Montparnasse. €385* / mois + charges. Tél. après 20h00.

Furnished studio in the 14th *arrondissement* of Paris. Includes a 'bathroom' (probably) consisting of shower, wash-basin and WC. Near to Montparnasse station. €385 per month plus building charges. Telephone the following number after 8pm.

Comment: This is probably a very small studio flat of about 18–20m^2. Much important information is missing. When you telephone to enquire about such studios ask: the size of the flat; on which floor it is situated; if there is a lift; what are the kitchen facilities; what furnishings are provided; how much are the building charges (i.e. how much is the total rent). If there is no mention that it is furnished (*meublé*), then you must assume that there is no furniture at all. This may also be one or possibly two *chambres de bonne* (maid's rooms) knocked into one flat. These are small rooms in the attics of large residential buildings. Single *chambres de bonne* are often let to students, but you sometimes have to share a WC and shower with other residents on the corridor.

3ᵉ Beaubourg. Immeuble ancien renové. Digicode, interphone. Studio 35m²; neuf, aménagement standing. Séjour avec 2 fenêtres, poutres apparentes, cuisine équipée, salle de bains, wc, rangements. Libre 31/12:625 Euros / mois charges comprises.

(Unfurnished) studio 35 m² in the third arrondissement of Paris, in the Beaubourg *quartier*, in an old building which has been restored with both door code system and entry phone. Newly redecorated to a good level. (Principal) living room with two windows, exposed beams, equipped kitchen, bathroom, WC, and built-in cupboards. Available from 31 December. €625 per month including building charges.

Comment: This is a much clearer advertisement. You still need to check about which floor the studio is on as it could well be sixth floor without a lift. Space is at a premium in French flats, and so it is important to know that there are built-in cupboards. Other terms for these are *placards* and *penderies* (normally referring to small built-in wardrobes). Check what is included in the kitchen area.

15ᵉ Convention. Immeuble pierre de taille, 2 pièces, 41m², clair, exposé sud. Fenêtre dans chaque pièce. Calme. Au 4e sans ascenseur. Digicode. Entrée, salle de bains (baignoire), wc, branchement lave-linge, séjour, coin-cuisine, chambre.

(Unfurnished) two-room flat in the 15th *arrondissement* of Paris near Convention métro. Two rooms totalling 41 m². South facing with a window in each room. Quiet, situated on the fourth floor without a lift. Door code. Entrance hall/passage, bathroom (with bath), WC, outlet for a washing machine, sitting room with 'kitchen corner', and bedroom.

Comment: This is a classic one bedroom flat. *Digicode* refers to the means of access to the building from the street. There may also be an entry-phone system as in the example above. The 'kitchen corner' is a classic feature of smaller flats. You will also see references to a *cuisine americaine*. This is a kitchen with a bar to separate it from the main room. *Pierre de taille* indicates that this is a good-quality stone building, probably well-maintained.

CLAMART (92) Maison 4 pièces, 80m², sur terrain 272m². Cuisine aménagée, salle de douche, wc séparées. Près commerces, écoles et transports. Dans quartier résidentiel calme. Chauffage gaz.

Four-roomed house in Clamart in Département 92, 80m² of a total property site of 272m². Fitted kitchen, shower room, separate WC. Near to shops, schools and transport. In a quiet residential area. Gas heating.

Comment: The number of rooms (two or more) does not normally include the entrance hall, WC, or bathroom. In this case, there will be a sitting room, at least two bedrooms, and either a significant kitchen, a dining room, or a third bedroom. The total property site probably includes a garden and parking space. It is a small house, but the advertiser is obviously seeking to attract a young couple with a small family. Note the facilities on offer.

Heating (*chauffage*) is either *individuel*, i.e. you control and pay for this yourself, or *collective*, in which it case it is included in the building charges. However, in the latter case it is switched on and off on a specific date which may not always suit you. Air-conditioned residential property is almost unheard of.

Houses may have attics, but few, if any, flats will. However, certain flats will include the use of an individual cellar (*cave*). You should check the security and state of the cellar before deciding whether to use it to store your belongings. Large flats may have a *chambre de bonne* attached several floors above, although many *chambres* are now rented out separately.

Some flats may also have a parking space attached to them. This will instantly increase the price of the flat, certainly in cities and large towns. Check whether the *parking* is in an attached car park, or a garage complex under the building. *Parkings* (also known as a *box*) can also be separately rented if needed.

VIEWING PROPERTY

Select the properties that interest you and telephone quickly to arrange to view them. If you are careful, you should be able to view several in one day, and so compare the properties more easily. In some cases the advertisements will simply announce a date, time and address to which you should come in order to visit. Expect to queue, and get there early.

Remember that when you go to view a property, you yourself are being viewed by the landlord as a prospective tenant. Competition is sharp for good homes, so you must be prepared.

◆ **Appear friendly and professional**. Smile and dress smartly. Nobody wants a difficult tenant, and a landlord will want to feel sure that you can pay the rent.

◆ **Take proof of your spending power**. Money talks loudly. Take along as many recent wage slips as you can, and also bank statements. They will almost certainly be asked for by the landlord. If you refuse to show them, it is very unlikely you will be accepted as a tenant. If you have just arrived, take along your engagement letter (*lettre d'embauche*) if you already have employment, stating your salary.

◆ **Have your cheque book ready** to make a down payment on a rental if you and the landlord agree terms. However, **BE CAREFUL** to ask for a receipt from the landlord, and preferably your signed rental contract.

Questions the landlord will ask you

Expect to be asked at least one of the following questions by a prospective landlord:

◆ If you are employed, '**Do you have a permanent contract?**'. If you have just arrived, take along past pay slips, and an *attestation d'emploi* from your employer, stating that you have an indefinite contract, and your annual or monthly salary before tax.

◆ If you are a student, '**Do you have a *carte d'étudiant?***' Renting to students is advantageous in one sense as there are tax benefits for landlords.

◆ '**Are you sure that you can afford the rent?**' Officially your monthly salary after tax and social security deductions must be three times the total rent on your home. In practice, this is rarely the case. However, it can be a sticking point, and with good reason. **Do not over-stretch yourself financially.**

◆ **'What guarantees can you offer for the payment of the rent?'**
Very frequently landlords will ask for *références serieuses* and
garanties parentales. This is a written undertaking either by
your parents, or your firm in some cases, that if you default on
the rent, they will settle any outstanding debts. It is not an
undertaking to be made lightly, as the standard notice period
for a rental arrangement is three months.

Rent guarantees

Students will almost certainly be asked for references and
guarantors, but so too will young people who are in full-time
employment (single or married). According to one newspaper
article (*Libération*, 13 September 2000), rental agencies are now
insisting on social security details, access to the previous three
months' bank statements, and even court rulings regarding
divorce settlements and loan repayment plans, in order to assess
your financial capabilities to pay the rent. Foreigners have
traditionally been singled out in the recent past for this kind of
treatment on the grounds you may flee owing months of rent.
Gentle negotiation and reassurance with an individual landlord
can often resolve the problem, however.

TAKING OUT A LEASE

Once you have found a property and been accepted for the
tenancy, you will have to sign the lease (*contrat de location* or
more properly the *bail*, pronounced 'bye'). This should usually be
a standard grey and green form, including mention of the laws
governing rental agreements. They can be obtained from Tissot,
19 rue Lagrange, 75005 Paris. The front and back will be filled in
and signed by your landlord and yourself, and the inside pages
will include the general terms of the agreement. Two identical

copies of the contract are signed and completed, one for you and one for the landlord.

The contract should include: the name of the landlord; your name; the full address of your flat including the staircase, etc; a description of the property; the length of the contract; the rent you are to pay, including building charges; when you are to pay it; and the amount of the *caution* you have paid for the property.

Beware of 'home-made' contracts which could lead to difficult situations should a problem arise. They will certainly not offer you the same legal protection and security of residence as the formal contracts. Some landlords may have had a separate contract prepared by a lawyer for larger properties. Read contracts carefully before signing them and if necessary seek professional advice. **Do not panic and never 'lease' a property without a contract (i.e. cash-in-hand).**

To conclude the contract, take along your *carte de séjour* and passport, or just your passport if you do not require a *carte de séjour*, and your deposit (*caution*) for the flat. In 2008 the Government reduced the deposit to one month's rent. This sum must be defined and mentioned in the contract. The first month's rent is also always paid in advance, so make sure you have sufficient funds to cover the first month's rent and the deposit.

ETAT DES LIEUX

The contract is not completed until one final process has taken place, known as the *état des lieux*. This should happen **before** you move in, and is undertaken with the landlord (or their representative), to establish the exact state of the property (e.g. cracks in the wall, broken windows, etc.).

Both of you keep a signed copy. Keep this safely in case your landlord later tries to make you pay for repairs which are not your fault. For furnished lets, you should also have an itemised inventory of the furnishings provided.

The *état des lieux* is the moment to try to negotiate minor changes in the presentation of the apartment before you move in. No landlord is going to agree to redecorate completely or re-equip an entire kitchen. Some will, however, agree that you need a cooker and that the damp patch in the bathroom must be dealt with before you can safely be said to be 'enjoying' the property. You are not obliged to forever hold your peace once you move in, but you can hopefully save yourself a lot of hassle by correct anticipation.

ADDITIONAL COSTS WHEN RENTING PROPERTY

In addition to the *caution* and first month's rent, you may also find yourself presented with a bill for the *frais* or *honoraires* as they are sometimes called. These will be the costs involved in preparing a contract, and undertaking the *état des lieux*. Landlords are within their rights to use a bailiff (*huissier*) to undertake the *état des lieux*. All of these charges will be at the tenant's expense.

The other additional cost you may face will be the estate agent's fee if you have used their services. This is also normally equivalent to one month's rent. Remember to check this before you take advantage of their services and include it in your budget.

Rent increases normally take place once a year on the anniversary date of the signature of the rental agreement. They are limited by law to an average figure indexed to national building trade costs. Generally, the maximum increases are about 4% per year, if they are applied by landlords. The decision to apply an increase or not is at the discretion of a landlord.

A new rent increase index is due to be introduced in 2008, which will be linked to inflation rather than to the construction industry.

YOUR RESPONSIBILITIES AS TENANT

The general conditions of the standard contract list 16 responsibilities, the first of which is to pay the rent on time! The other most important responsibilities are:

1. To use the premises in a calm and reasonable manner for the purposes for which they were intended. Also not to convert them to another purpose, e.g. offices.

2. To take out a standard insurance policy against fire, water damage, etc.

3. To obey the regulations governing the day-to-day running of the building and concerning the *parties communes* (lifts, corridors, etc.). These rules are agreed by the all the owners (*copropriété*).

4. Not to sub-let your property without prior written approval from your landlord.

5. Day-to-day minor repairs. Be careful to note that certain preventative maintenance tasks – e.g. an annual check-up for the boiler – are normally also the tenant's responsibility. This can prove to be important should you need to change the boiler (one of the landlord's responsibilities) later on.

6. If you rent a furnished property (*meublé*) then you are obliged to ensure that the furnishings stay in the apartment when you are living there, or that they are correctly and safely stored for return to the apartment when you leave. If you do decide to discreetly move one or two items of dubious taste out of your view and into your cellar, make sure the cellar is clean and safe and the items are well protected against pests such as wood lice or rodents. Otherwise, talk nicely to your landlord...

THE LANDLORD'S RESPONSIBILITIES

1. To ensure that the property is clean, that all repairs have taken place, and that all appliances included under the contract are in working order when the tenant enters the property. The landlord is responsible for ensuring that the wiring is in order and that all plumbing is in full working order.

2. To ensure that the tenant can 'peacefully enjoy' the use of the property. Should you find yourself with noisy neighbours or a problem elsewhere in the building, this will be important.

3. To undertake major repairs which are not the responsibility of the tenant.

4. Not to oppose improvements to the property which will not change the basic use and structure of the property. This means a tenant can redecorate an apartment, even against the wishes of the landlord. However, it is best to obtain agreement from the landlord otherwise you are obliged to restore the original decorations when you leave the apartment. Tenants are responsible for giving back exactly what they receive.

SHARING PROPERTY

Flat-sharing on the Anglo-Saxon model (i.e. a large apartment or house shared by a number of roughly financially-equivalent people looking to benefit from combined spending power and personal companionship) is becoming increasingly popular in France, especially in the 'twenty-something' fledgling executive group.

In the case of a formal property share – for example, two or more friends or an unmarried couple – it is best to arrange a separate formal lease between the landlord and each tenant in their own name dividing the rent between the tenants. Should one party then leave, the others will not be responsible for the rent of the person who has left. For unmarried couples who have signed a PACS contract (which requires cohabitation as a prerequisite), in the case of an untimely event the surviving partner is protected from eviction.

It is also a good idea to put the electricity bill in the name of one tenant, and the telephone bill in the name of another. This provides each person with another proof of residence (*justificatif de domicile*) and helps to ensure each person's rights should a problem arise. In the case of an informal flat share (i.e. sub-letting a room in a flat or house without a written contract, which is strictly illegal), you may be asked to pay a smaller deposit (e.g. one month instead of two). But you should still **be sure to ask for a receipt from the person to whom you pay the deposit**. Your rights in this situation are much less well-defined, so do be careful.

The French often say they do not like sharing with other French people as they are not good co-tenants! If you share a flat with a

French person because you want to improve your French, remember they may also wish to improve their English. Think carefully before entering into a flat-share and try to protect yourself as much as possible.

FINDING OUT MORE

In addition to the websites mentioned at the beginning of this chapter, you should also check out the following sites:

- *L'Agence National de l'Information sur le Logement* (*ANIL*) **www.anil.org** – the National Housing Board. **This is an essential website for anybody buying or renting property in France**. An important part of the site is multi-lingual – just click on the button to switch into English. Other parts of the site, including the 'spotlights on...' are only in French.

- Some of the suggested websites in this chapter also have advice columns (in French), such as the site for *Particulier à Particulier,* **www.pap.fr**. These are good sources of extra, detailed information, such as the formula used for rent increases (which allows you to check your landlord's requirements).

- **France-USA Contacts, www.fusac.fr**, 26 rue Bénard, 75014 Paris, tél. 01 56 53 54 54, fax 01 56 53 54 55; US office: France Contacts, PO Box 115, Cooper Station, New York. NY10276. Tel: 212 777 5553. Fax: 212 777 5554. Free and extremely useful magazine available in English-speaking churches, bars, and shops in Paris.

- *The Paris Voice*, **www.parisvoice.com**. Another very useful free English-language magazine, available in roughly the same places as FUSAC.

4

Buying and Renovating Property in France

Since the mid-1990s, French property prices have been spiralling higher and higher. The ripening of the new 'Bobo' generation and the fruits of a healthier French economy have allowed the French to indulge in what they love talking about: buying and renovating property. New laws encouraging the French to buy and lease property, either old or new, and tax incentives to help the French construction industry and new homeowners, have also contributed to the property boom.

In March 2001, the French magazine *Challenges* said that the French prefer to '*not only buy an environment to live in, but also a life-style*'. With the marked population drift to the south and the larger regional cities, it is becoming increasingly difficult to find bargains in popular areas such as the Languedoc-Roussillon around Montpellier, where the population is expected to increase by 21% by 2030. But in more rural areas, for example between Toulouse and the Dordogne, less expensive properties can still be found in the more remote communes.

One of the principal factors in regional property markets is the mass influx of foreign, and particularly British, buyers. A survey by Abbey National in 2000 found that 500,000 people from the UK owned property in France. In 2002, an English-speaking French bank had over 10,000 clients in the Calvados regions of

Normandy. More recently, tempers flared in Brittany when the *Grands Bretons* where perceived to be driving local Bretons out of their own property market by pushing up the prices. If you are now preparing to join the continental drift in search of a French lifestyle, then you must think and act carefully to turn your dream into a reality rather than a drama.

If you are considering buying property in France, you should note that the Government is considering a number of introducing a number of environmental obligations for the renovation of existing property, and construction of new buildings. Sustainability (*le développement durable*) was a key issue in the 2007 presidential election, and a wide variety of measures are being considered in all areas. For housing, the efforts that will be required over the coming years will include energy efficiency, and renewable energy.

FINDING THE ADVERTS

As with the rental of property, using professional real estate agencies implies a certain cost for the transaction. However, this can be weighed up against the protection of a professional contract with the agent acting on your behalf, should anything go wrong.

About half of all property transactions in France are dealt with by estate agents (*agents immobilier*). An estate agent cannot enter into negotiations unless they hold a *mandat de vente* (written power of attorney for sale) from the seller, or a *mandat de recherche* (written power of attorney to make a search) from you as the purchaser.

The seller usually has to pay the estate agent's commission, fixed by power of attorney, upon written completion of the transaction.

Anything not referred to in the power of attorney cannot be charged by estate agents. They may fix the amount of commission they receive, but their scale of charges must be on open display. The commission must also represent a percentage of the purchase price. The price displayed for a property must include the commission.

Many agents will be the sole agent for a property and so will have the *exclusivité* mentioned in the advertisement. However, both buyers and sellers eager to maximise their profit and minimise their costs can and do organise their own property sales. You are most likely to find direct advertisements from private home-owners in the *Le Figaro* (**www.explorimmo.com**), *Libération* (**www.libération.fr**), and *Particuliers à Particuliers* (**www.pap.fr**) on Thursdays.

UNDERSTANDING THE ADVERTISEMENTS

Advertisements for properties for sale use much of the same jargon and shorthand as those for rented property, already decrypted in the previous chapter. However, important extra information will also be included in sale advertisements, and you need to understand this before deciding if the property matches your criteria. The real examples given below will help you understand some of the most important extra points:

CLAMART – Secteur pavillonaire. Petit Résidence. Studio 30m².

In Clamart (92). In the part of the town which contains small individual houses (*pavillons*). In a small modern apartment block (*résidence*). A studio of 30 square metres.

Comment: a pretty minimimalist advertisement from an agency (often indicated simply by reference letters such as GEI, LF, etc., followed by a telephone number). The term *résidence* in this context normally applies to a modern apartment block without a *concierge*, but with a *digicode* at the front door and/or a second *interphone*. There will probably be no more than ten apartments in this building, which may have a small garden in front of or behind the building. *Pavillon* is a term used to describe small detached suburban houses.

Nation (5mn) 2P 34,5m² (loi Carrez) – 2é étg. Cuis.éqp., séjour, chambre, SdB, wc sép. Très clair. Parquet. Refait neuf.

Five minutes from Place de la Nation (in Paris), a two-roomed apartment of 34.5 square metres (certified in accordance with the *loi carrez*). Second floor. Fitted kitchen, sitting room, bedroom, bathroom, separate WC. Very light. Parquet flooring. Completely redecorated.

Comment: much clearer but still ambiguous on one important point: what does the five minutes refer to? A car drive, a métro ride, an RER ride, or walking distance – and in which direction? This is a major consideration. The *loi carrez* is the recent French law which requires certification of the square metrage of apartments (but not houses) as a basis for sale. If you buy a property and find that you have more than 5% less than what was stated, you are entitled to renegotiate the price. This vendor has already undertaken the necessary official verification and certification process. The fact that it is *refait neuf* might explain a slightly elevated asking price per square metre, depending on where it is situated. In theory, you will have no extra burden to bear in terms of renovation costs. However this should be checked carefully. (See also the decision-making checklist below.)

Butttes-Chaumont 3P 2 ch 52m² Parquet, moulures, à rafraichir. 114.337E

In the Buttes-Chaumont area of the 19th *arrondissement* of Paris. A three-room apartment including two bedrooms, of 52 square metres. Parquet and mouldings/cornices. Needs to be 'refreshed'.

Comment: You need to check on the lay out of this apartment. Many Parisian apartments have bedrooms leading one off the other, so that to get to the bathroom, for instance, you are obliged to cross somebody else's bedroom. It is obviously an older building in co-ownership, with the presence of both mouldings and parquet. But the most important point is that it needs to be redecorated. You need to find out just what is involved and then add an estimate figure to the cost of your purchase to get the real total cost.

15 min. de La Rochelle, Particulier vend maison de pecheur 1827 bord de l'eau. 190m² hab. terrain 1600m², 4 chbres, 2 cheminées, s.à manger, salon 40m², s.de bains, s.d'eau, toilettes, part.

15 minutes from La Rochelle, fisherman's house dating from 1827, in private hands, at the water's edge. 190 square metres of living space on a total area of 1,600 square metres. Four bedrooms, dining room, sitting room of 40 square metres, bathroom, shower room, separate WCs, €138,000. Direct from the owner.

Comment: A smaller house with plenty of features. One of the big advantages of this offer is that one individual (*particulier*) is looking to sell their property to another, hence there are no agency fees. You will still have to use a *notaire* to undertake the legal paperwork. There is no mention of work which needs to be undertaken. Even if the house appears to be in good condition, you should ask the current owners what they have spent on upkeep in recent years. Think also about the special environmental conditions created by facing the sea.

OWNING PROPERTY IN FRANCE

If you decide to buy property in France, either as your principal home or as a second home, the basic process is the same as regards the contracts you will have to sign and the charges you will have to pay.

The distinction between freehold and leasehold does not exist in French property law. Instead, a distinction is drawn between co-ownership and free-standing property.

◆ **Co-ownership** means that the property (normally an apartment block) is divided into units (*lots*). Each unit has a private area and a proportion of the communal area. The co-ownership regulations are known as *Le Règlement de Copropriété*. These regulations govern boundaries between private and communal areas, conditions for use of the building, etc. An assembly of the co-owners, the *Syndicat de Copropriétaires*, decides on changes to the regulations, and any major building works. The cost of any such works are divided amongst the co-owners.

◆ If you are buying your property independently, e.g. you are buying a house with a garden, you will have all the rights of ownership.

◆ In either case, your purchase will be subject to the complicated French inheritance laws (see below) and you should discuss these with your French legal advisors when you are planning your purchase.

DECISION-MAKING CHECKLIST

As you will have seen from the comments on the sample advertisements above, there are a large number of considerations to be made before making an offer on a property and signing any binding documents.

The checklist below is drawn from a variety of published sources in the specialist French property press and offer excellent food for thought before taking a decision. Obviously you need to weigh up the risks quickly, especially in the case of sought-after areas and types of apartments. But do not allow yourself to be rushed into a wrong and potentially expensive and disturbing choice.

1. **Check on the surface area**. The price of an apartment is estimated on the basis of a price per square metre. The *loi carrez* obliges all vendors in buildings owned by *copropriété* – but not individual house-owners – to detail the exact surface area of the apartment offered within a maximum error margin of 5%. All surface areas with an *HSP* (*hauteur sous plafond* – floor-to-ceiling height) of at least 1m80 (c.6 ft) must be included in this estimate. *Mezzanines* (split-levels artificially introduced into a room to create a double-surface area such as bedrooms), attics and staircases are not therefore included. However, cellars (*caves*) may be, depending on the age and style of the building. Garages, balconies, and terraces are not included in the surface area estimation, although they may well influence the price. Terrace

areas tend to be noted separately in the advertisements (e.g. ' + terrasse de 5m^2', which means you could eat out on the balcony if you wanted to hence the higher price for the apartment). If the surface area is in reality more than 5% less than the figure advertised, you are entitled to have the price reduced by legal ruling if necessary.

2. **Check on the communal charges**. The communal charges of a building owned by a *copropriété* (lifts, concierges, renovation, etc.) are shared out by the owners according to the size of their *lot* and is estimated in *millièmes* and *tantièmes*. This will have a direct effect on your annual bills. Every year the owners meet to vote on new works on the building and the budget for the year. You should make every effort to determine what has already been spent (which will also indicate if you are entering a spend-thrift environment), what has been voted but not yet paid for (which will be **your cost** if you buy the apartment before the work is actually carried out **even if you did not vote for it**), and what is planned for the near future. In the worst case scenario, the *copropriété* could have voted for a facade-renvovation (*ravalement*) which has not yet been executed but which will then take place, and could be planning to change the lift(s) in the building the following year. Both of these are very costly exercises. You can demand copies from the vendor of recent minutes (*procès-verbaux*) of the general meetings (*assemblées générales*) of the *copropriété*, and also enquire if a technical survey has been undertaken of the building. If you receive a negative response, there is nothing to stop you organising your own survey (*diagnostic technique* or *expertise*) of the building. If in addition to the cost of the facade and the lifts and any renovations you need or want to undertake, there is also a problem of subsidence requiring underpinning etc – think again.

3. **Check if the property is correctly valued**. Strangely, none of the many regular surveys actually ask this question, perhaps because the wily Gallic character assumes that you will haggle over the price in any case. However, the fact that detailed studies do appear regularly each year in the general press should encourage you to check the price per square metre – the basic cost element – of the property which interests you. Compare prices with similar size properties in different agencies. Many factors come into play when pricing a property, but you need to get a feel of the basic value of what you are buying.

4. **Check on the hidden costs**. Ask the vendors to tell you how much the building charges have been over the last two years. Ask also how much they have been paying in *impôts locaux* (local housing tax). The cost varies from area to area, according to the size of your apartment, the state of the building, and an official estimation of its market value (which may be out of date). You should also ask the vendor for copies of the bills for major works to the property, which in their eyes justifies an elevated price; find out just how much it really cost, and what precisely was done. A job half-done badly could be an expensive job to complete successfully.

5. **Check on precisely what the building is used for**. Are all your neighbours in a co-owned building simply living there and working elsewhere, or are they doing the opposite? If one or more is working there, who has the code to the building? Suppliers, clients, colleagues in other areas? Is it a small one-person independent outfit, or will you be regularly kept waiting for the lift because of streams of clients or because a delivery put it out of action once again? The more people who use your building and its facilities, the more wear-and-tear there is to repair. How safe are you in your own building?

6. **Check on environmental issues**. Take another look at the environmental issues discussed in Chapter 2. The local *mairie* will have plans for any developments, and will also be the place to find out about planned building projects which may change your gracious view into *face-à-face* with new neighbours. Local **schools** normally lead to higher prices, as families seek proximity, but they also mean noise and congestion.

7. **Check on asbestos, lead and pests**. For buildings in collective ownership, **asbestos** (*amiante*) checks on all common areas and private residential lots are obligatory, and a copy of the statement concerning your chosen building must be given to you no later than the day you are due to sign the *promesse de vente*. You should be able to obtain a copy well in advance for most buildings. For buildings dating from before 1948, an investigation of the risks of **lead** poisoning from paintwork or pipes is obligatory in Paris which is considered a high-risk zone. **Pests** such as cockroaches and notably **termites**, who are munching their way across some of the smartest parts of Paris, are becoming a major problem throughout France. Annual rodent and cockroach control exercises are the responsibility of the *copropriété* in a co-owned building, and you will find references to money voted for these works amongst others in the minutes of general meetings of the co-owners. For the termites now spreading across France, the vendor should attach an *état parasitaire* to the sale contract stating the level of infection dating from within three months. Once again you should be able to obtain this in advance of the signature date. If the building or property is at risk from any of these three dangers, then you will need to know the costs of dealing with the problems, and what if anything has already been voted but not yet paid by the

copropriété. Information regarding these problems amongst others and contact details for professionals qualified to deal with these problems can be found on the websites of both the housing ministry (**www.equipement.gouv.fr**) and the ministry of health (**www.sante.gouv.fr**).

8. **Check on technological risks** Vendors must now provide a number of technical certificates (*diagnostics*) before a sale can be completed. *L'état des risques naturels et technologiques* became obligatory in 2006, and must be annexed to sale documents by the *notaire*, when it concerns a building, property or land. It must be no more than six months old when delivered, and all buildings are concerned in a 'risk area' with a Emergency Recovery Plan (e.g. risk of flooding, subsidence). It should include details of any insurance claims on the property since 1982. The same rules apply to *le diagnostique de performance énergétique* (energy consumption report) since 2006. Basically it deals with the insulation of the property, and recommends improvements. Listed buildings (*monuments classés*) are exempted. Since 1 November 2007, *l'état de l'installation intérieure du gaz* (gas installation report) has also become obligatory. This applies to installations more than 15 years old. The report must be less than three years old. If a vendor fails to produce this report or inform the buyer of problems, then the vendor is liable for any resulting problems. A similar report on electrical installations more than 15 years old will soon become obligatory.

Since 2007, all of these reports – asbestos, termites and pests, lead, natural risks, energy consumption, and gas installations – are grouped together in one report, the *diagnostic technique,* which must now be annexed to the *promesse de vente*. If a vendor does not supply any of the necessary reports, they will be considered liable for any resulting problems.

SIGNING THE CONTRACTS

When you and the seller have reached an agreement, there is a choice of two kinds of pre-contractual agreements which are possible:

1. *Promesse de vente* – this is a unilateral agreement to sell, signed by both the seller and buyer. Under the terms of such an agreement, the seller agrees to sell you the property by a certain time, for a set price, and according to set conditions. The buyer is allowed time to reflect on his decision, but must nonetheless pay a deposit, normally about 10% of the full price. The advantage of this kind of agreement, which is very common, is that the seller cannot withdraw their acceptance of your offer if all the conditions of the agreement are met. The disadvantage is that if you as the buyer withdraw from the agreement, you lose your deposit.

2. *Compromis de vente* – once again, both sides commit themselves to a change in ownership of the property. However, certain 'get out' clauses can be included in the agreement, which are known as *conditions suspensives*. These conditions might include the granting of a mortgage (for which you normally have 40 days), or a town planning report (*certificat d'urbanisme*), etc. All of these clauses must be adhered to, or you are entitled to cancel the agreement and reclaim your 10% deposit.

Once the *notaire* (see below) has all the necessary information, a *projet de l'acte* (draft contract) can be produced. Copies are sent to the buyer and the seller for approval before the final contract is drawn up.

The *acte authentique de vente* is the conveyancing agreement between the two parties. It will reiterate clauses from th pre-contractual arrangement, and will also clarify any further details. The following information must appear in the agreement:

◆ Identification of both parties concerned.

◆ Identification of the property in precise terms and the title to the property (*origine de propriété*).

◆ The date when you as the new owner will take possession of the property and be entitled to use it (*propriété de jouissance*).

◆ A *certificat d'urbanisme* which restates any town planning regulations affecting the property, as discovered by the *notaire*. You should bear in mind the environmental issues pointed out in Chapter 2 when deciding on where to live. For rural properties if the neighbouring farmer is planning to install his livestock close to where you planned on installing your summer terrace or swimming pool, you may want to think again about the property. Also, rural sites are no guarantee against industrial developments (see 'Local considerations' in Chapter 2 concerning local housing tax).

◆ Any guarantees and estimates.

The *notaire* retains the original contract, and copies are given to the buyer and seller, known as *l'expéditions*. Once the sale has been registered at the *Bureau des Hypothèques*, no one else has any claim over the building. Finally the relevant section of the title deed is sent to the Land Registry.

SURVEYING YOUR PROPERTY

Structural surveys are not common practice in France as in the UK. Stringent building and construction regulations mean that there is usually no need. The seller, or in the case of a new house being built, the construction company, are obliged to issue guarantees on the property. Builders must also be insured for work undertaken for ten years thereafter, even in case of bankruptcy. The ten-year guarantee also applies to older buildings which have been bought and renovated by a builder and then sold off as apartments.

The *notaire* can include details of any guarantees on the property and a list of builders involved in your final agreement. A notaire or estate agent can carry out a simple survey if required. Otherwise, an *expert géometre* can check the total surface area of your new property, or you can arrange for a survey by an architect. If you are buying an apartment in a renovated building, be sure to check on precisely what the builder is charging you for, and do not be frightened to check the efficiency of sound-proofing and how well windows actually fit.

LOOKING AT THE LEGAL ISSUES

The role of the *notaire*

According to French law, every property transaction in France must be overseen by a *notaire*. The distinction in the French legal profession is between *avocats* who can appear in the courts (rather like barristers in the UK) and *notaires* who undertake contractual work (such as conveyancing and the writing of wills) rather like solicitors in the UK.

Notaires must be impartial as regards the two parties of a property sale and are responsible for legally validating the deeds involved, advising clients and drawing up the necessary contracts. They can and do also sometimes act as a tax consultant and also as an estate agent in certain cases.

The *notaire* is entitled to a legally determined sum as commission when acting as a sale negotiator. Normally this is around 8% of the purchase price. If the building is a new property the notaire's fee is reduced to no more than 3% (as an aid to the French construction industry). A building less than five years old which has never been occupied since construction also qualifies for this reduction in the *notaire*'s fee.

Notaire's fees (*frais*) will eventually include money paid on your behalf, taxes, dues and contingency duties. Overall costs are high, but vary from region to region within a set scale, and depending on the type and value of the property.

The *notaire*'s responsibilities when acting as intermediary for a sale are:

1. Verification of the seller including their right to sell the property.

2. Obtaining the relevant Land Registry papers, showing any planning objections to the property.

3. Contacting anyone with pre-emption rights to the property, and determining whether they plan to exercise these rights.

4. Contacting the *Conservation des Hypothéques* (mortgage/Land Registry) which must issue an *état hors formalité*. This shows any mortgages, securities, etc. on the property. Such debts must be payable and lower than the sale price to avoid redemption proceedings.

If you pay for the property through the *notaire*, they can withhold payment if it is discovered that the seller has used the property as collateral on a loan, until a *negative état sur formalité* has been issued.

Inheritance issues

It is extremely important that you take good professional advice when buying your property in France, as regards questions of ownership and inheritance. You must do this before you sign the contracts; afterwards, it will be too late. You should also bear in mind that the legal system is both very slow and very expensive in France.

The main thing to watch out for is that the *notaire* does not draw up a contract whereby you buy the property *en division*. The much more preferable option is to buy *en tontine*. There are other possibilities (e.g. an *acte de donation*), but you will need to discuss these with your legal advisors.

Problems with buying a property *en division*

If you and your spouse buy a property *en division*, you will each own half of the property. When one of you dies, the 'half' which belongs to the deceased person will pass automatically to their heirs. The situation then is that the surviving spouse may own half a house, with the right of abode for the remainder of their life.

If you have children, you cannot only leave part, but not half, of your property to your spouse. If there are more than three children, they automatically inherit three quarters of the deceased person's estate. Government tax reforms in 2007 abolished inheritance tax for the surviving spouse, or partner in the case of a PACS. You may now also make a **donation** to your beneficiaries of up to €150,000. **Before signing any documents, you must take good French legal advice in order to understand clearly the impact of the choices you are about to make.**

FINANCIAL CONSIDERATIONS

Financing your purchase

Your own personal situation will determine the variety of options open to you for financing your property purchase in France. Within France, the most common method of obtaining a mortgage is to apply to a high-street bank. A French bank will calculate the amount of money available for your mortgage according to your cash flow. A mortgage should be granted as long as your outgoings plus your mortgage repayments equal less than 30% of your pre-tax income.

Successive French governments in recent years have tried to boost the property market by permitting loans at very low rates. It is worth enquiring widely about the possibilities before taking a decision. Banks and financial institutions vary from the inflexible with anybody but the known and trusted clients, to more flexible and competitive in the face of opposition from high-street competitors. A great deal will depend upon your ability to negotiate and force the hand of lenders.

Paying tax on your property

When setting up home in France, you will be liable for the
following French taxes:

♦ **Government registration tax**. This tax is payable when you are
completing your purchase, and when added to the fees of the
notaire amounts to about 11% of the property's purchase price.
You will also be required to pay the equivalent of UK Land
Registry fees and stamp duty. The rates depend upon the size
of the property and its grounds, the type of buildings on the
land, and the age of the property. Once you have bought
property in France, it must be registered with the tax
authorities. If it is a secondary residence, contact the *Centre
des Impôts des Non-résidents*. Tax-registration should take place
before 30 April of any year.

♦ *Taxe foncière*. This is a local tax levied by the *commune* in
which your new property is situated, and levied on you as the
owner. Your name will be added to a register at the local
mairie. The register comprises lists of owners, tax rates paid,
and notional letting values of the property concerned. In some
cases you will be exonerated from the *taxe foncière* (see
Chapter 5).

♦ *Taxe d'habitation*. Unlike the two taxes above, this local tax is
not necessarily payable by the owner of the property, but by its
occupant. If you rent a property you will normally be liable for
this tax. The rate of tax payable is determined by the building's
amenities and size. The basic rate is calculated according to the
nominal letting value of property in the local area.

Insuring your property

You are required by French law to take out third-party insurance as soon as you move into your accommodation, or as soon as work has begun on your future home if it is still being built. This is known as *civil propiétaire*.

It is also highly advisable to take out insurance against fire, theft, etc. Comprehensive policies known as *assurances multirisques* are available, as are specific policies. The sum insured should reflect your insurable interest or potential loss according to the contract arranged. Co-owners should already be insured for the building itself and all communal areas.

RENOVATING YOUR PROPERTY

Owner-occupiers who are intending to in some way add to, transform or renovate their properties should take careful note before starting to knock holes in any walls, which may lead to situations which only gluttons for punishment would relish. Be sure to do things the right way and not the wrong way, as the French legal system is cumbersome, slow and expensive.

Basic rules regarding planning permission include a limit on the number of habitable or serviceable square metres which can be added. In addition, all changes in use of the property or exterior appearance require official approval from the local *mairie*.

What you can do without planning permission

◆ If you are planning to change the interior of your apartment, you can do so as long as it does not change the exterior of the building, or its volume or surface area. So, to add another shower room in the existing floor plan, for instance, is not a problem, and there is no need for planning permission.

◆ If you have a garden and you want to install a patio or terrace, you can do so as long as it is not more than 60cm (2ft) above ground level. The same goes for a greenhouse, potting-shed or garden-house, as long as it does not cover more than two square metres and is not more than 1.50m high. Anything over these limits requires planning permission.

◆ You can build a wall in your garden up to 2m high, as long as it is not a dividing wall from a neighbouring property.

What you can do with only a preliminary notification (*déclaration préalable*) at the *mairie*

◆ You can add less than 20 square metres to your surface living area (e.g. you convert an attic or a garage into living areas).

◆ You can build a garage of up to 20 square metres.

◆ You can build a swimming pool in your garden as long as it does not exceed 20 square metres.

What you cannot do without planning permission

All other building work over these limits, including the construction of a large pool or shed, or adding another floor to your property or a roof garden or terrace, require planning permission from the local *mairie*. This also applies if you purchase a larger property and convert all or part of it into commercial offices, as you have transformed the nature of the property.

For those people living in *copropriétés*, your plans also have to be approved by your fellow co-owners at the annual general meeting. The rules of the *copropriété* will expressly allow certain building works (e.g. a new bathroom), but other changes (e.g. a roof terrace or attic conversion) will have implications for the building as a whole which everyone has to agree to.

Financial assistance for renovation

There are a number of possibilities for obtaining state aid to renovate your property. Most aids are means-tested and will depend on how long you have lived in France and contributed to the system. However, providing that you are a full resident and paying your social contributions and tax in France, then there is no reason why you cannot successfully apply for these aids if you meet the criteria.

Information regarding all the benefits on offer can be obtained from the *Agences Départmentales d'Informations Logement (ADIL)* at www.anil.org.

A range of benefits exist for those who undertake major structural work in their new homes, and some of these are cumulative:

1. *Le prêt à l'amélioration de l'habitat* – this is available to both owner-occupiers and tenants. This loan at a rate of 1% is available for necessary improvements, such as heating or sanitary conditions. It is not means-tested, but you must already qualify for another family benefit. The loan is currently limited to €1,000, and 80% of the total cost of the works. Repayments take place over 36 months. For more details, you should contact your local *caisse d'allocations familiales*.

2. **Assistance from *ANAH (Agence Nationale pour l'Améliroation de l'Habitat)*** – this is not means-tested. Basically it applies to

vacant buildings more than 15 years old which are being made habitable. Normally it is paid only to owners, who commit to renting out the property afterwards. Generally the benefit is around 25% of the total cost of the agreed works, but can be higher. To find out more contact the *ANAH* at the local *direction départementale de l'équipement.*

3. *La prime à l'amélioration de l'habitat* – a means-tested 'bonus' available to owner-occupiers which varies from region to region. **This benefit is of particular interest to those adapting homes for people with disabilities**, amongst other more common measures regarding health and hygiene. The total amount of the bonus cannot exceed 20% of the real costs of the works, within a limit of just over €10,000. However, this bonus can also be added to another bonus worth 50% of the works necessary to allow access for, or conversion for use by, disabled people. The limit on this second bonus is €3050.

Applications for the *prime de l'amélioration de l'habitat* should be made to the section habitat of the *direction départementale de l'équipement* (except in Paris where applications should be made to the *préfecture*).

4. **The 0% loan** – This interest-free means-tested loan can be accumulated with other loans, but the total amount of the loan cannot exceed 50% of the total cost of the total of other loans. Conditions vary according to geographical regions, and the number of people who will be occupying the property. The loan can be used for a new or older building, and either for a principal residence or for a home intended as a future retirement home (according to certain rules). Generally you must be living in rented accommodation for at least two years before applying for this loan. This is not an easy loan to obtain. Contact your bank or the ADIL to find out more.

5. **The 1% loan** – This loan is available to employees in the
   private sector in companies of more than 10 employees which
   contribute to the scheme. The loan is not means tested, but is
   adapted according to your resources. The interest rate is
   actually 1.5%, and it can be used for new or older buildings.
   For buildings more than 20 years old, you are obliged to
   undertake building works worth at least 25% of the property
   purchase price. This loan is limited to principal homes, and
   can be accumulated with a standard loan. To apply for this
   loan, you need to contact your HR director if your company
   contributes to the scheme.

Looking at tax advantages

In September 1999, the French government decided on a kick-
start for the economy via the building and construction industry,
by reducing VAT on work by professional builders from 19.6% to
5.5%. This applies to all home improvements, maintenance and
renovation undertaken by professionals. The drop in tax rate also
applies to the materials they use, but this is a concession made
only to professionals.

If the property you purchase is an old building which has been
renovated by a developer and then sold off apartment by
apartment, then the lower rate of VAT applies to all works and
purchases for those works undertaken within the habitable areas
of the building. Certain *parties communes* such as a boiler for the
building or a lift are obviously not covered in the lower rate of
tax, but tax breaks are offered of up to 15% against the purchase
of this kind of equipment, for which VAT is 20.6%.

Do-it-yourself fans should note that they will still be charged VAT at 19.6% for any purchases they make to deal with household renovations themselves.

Since 2007, a Government tax reform allows new home owners to deduct up to 20% of the interest on their mortgage repayments, within defined limits and for the first five years of the loan (see Figure 3). Certain renovations which will increase the energy efficiency of your property, and may include renewable energy such as solar panels, are also tax deductible, as are works to enable handicapped access or as a result of technological risks.

	1st year €	2nd year €	3rd year €	4th year €	5th year €	Total €
Single, widowed or divorced person.	1,500	750	750	750	750	4,500
A handicapped single, widowed or divorced person.	3,000	1,500	1,500	1,500	1,500	9,000
A couple (married or PACS) with a joint tax declaration.	3,000	1,500	1,500	1,500	1,500	9,000
A couple (married or PACS) with a joint tax declaration, one of whom is handicapped.	6,000	3,000	3,000	3,000	3,000	18,000
A couple (married or PACS) with a joint tax declaration, with one child.	3,200	1,600	1,600	1,600	1,600	9,600
A couple (married or PACS) with a joint tax declaration, with two children.	3,400	1,700	1,700	1,700	1,700	10,200

Fig. 3. Tax deduction limits for interest on mortgage repayments.
(Source: **www.anil.org**)

Finally, if you have purchased a new property but still decide to undertake some form of reorganisation then you will be exempted from the *taxe foncière* for two years after completion of the works.

FINDING OUT MORE

◆ If you want to start your property search before even arriving in France, the development of websites now gives you easy access to visit the properties on offer at your leisure. The French magazine *Challenges* produced an exhaustive and excellent guide to the French property market in March 2001 which shortlisted the following websites as presenting the best value and interest for home-hunters:

www.123immo.com	www.immo-by-tel.com	www.pro-a-part.com
www.century21.fr	www.immostreet.com	www.seloger.com
www.explorimmo.com	www.minitelorama.com	www.smartimmo.com
www.fnaim.fr	www.nexdom.com	www.homevillage.com
www.pap.fr		

◆ *Agence National de l'Information sur le Logement (ANIL)*, **www.anil.org** – the national housing board. **This is an essential site for anybody buying or renting property in France**. An important part of the site is multi-lingual – just click on the button to switch into English. Other parts of the site, including the 'spotlights on . . .', are only in French. You can find contact details for your local *agence départemental* by clicking on the map.

◆ **www.directgestion.com** is a useful website for those people considering buying and renting out a property in France, and offers free advice from property business experts such as lawyers and architects.

◆ **www.batiweb.com** is a website with building industry contact and information for those considering building or renovating a new property.

Settling into Your Home

Setting up home in France can feel a bit like being a 'catch 22' situation. Without an address you cannot formally open your own bank account, but without a bank account you cannot make an official down-payment for an address. This in turn means that you cannot have a proof of residence (*justificatif de domicile*) because you will not even be able to open an electricity account.

Somewhere along the line, you *will* manage to square the circle. This is often at the moment that you find an apartment and landlord willing to accept a cash payment, or perhaps a cheque drawn on a foreign account. Once you have secured your new home, you need to move swiftly to put into place the other essential elements of your new home life.

MANAGING YOUR MONEY

There are four principal French banks: *BNP-Paribas*, *Crédit Agricole*, *Crédit Lyonnais* and *Société Générale*. Of the major UK banks, Barclays is the best represented in France with about 100 branches in Paris and across the country. In Paris *Société Générale* on the boulevard Haussman has an English-speaking international client service. HSBC bought the French bank *Crédit Commercial de France* (*CCF*) in 2000.

To gain access to banks in France, press the bell outside the street door. When the green light flashes, enter and wait until the door closes. Then press the second bell, and open the door when the second green light flashes. Follow the same system to get out again. Despite the security, the atmosphere inside is normally relaxed!

Bank opening times

French banks are generally open from 09h00 to 16h30 Monday to Friday. Many French banks in cities and large towns are now also open on Saturdays. Lunch hours generally run from 12h30 until 14h00. They are closed on all public holidays, and may close for *le pont* (the day between the holiday and the weekend). In smaller country towns, banks may close on Mondays if they are open on Saturdays.

Opening a French bank account

You will become accustomed to red-tape and paperwork in France. However, opening a bank account is one of the easiest steps to take. There are two options :

1. **A non-resident account (*compte non-résident*)** – previously there were many restrictions on these accounts. However, these restrictions generally no longer apply. But whilst you can negotiate loans to buy a car or a house, you may not have an overdraft facility (*découverts*). This facility would be appropriate if you buy a second home in France.

2. **An ordinary current account** – if you are resident in France or are working principally in France, then you will normally be able to open a current account entitling you to a cheque book and a *Carte Bleue*, the standard French debit card.

To open your account, take the following original items, plus copies of each:

◆ Passport, or residency permit (for resident accounts).

◆ Proof of address (*justificatif de domicile*). This can either be a copy of your rental agreement, or a telephone or electricity bill with your name and address on it.

You will sign standard account-opening forms and give a specimen signature to permit the payment of cheques written by you.

How the system operates

◆ Some banks may make you wait to receive your *Carte Bleue*. However, they will give you a cash card which will allow you to use the bank's cash machines. You can use your card not only to withdraw cash, but also to give you a statement of the balance of your account (*solde*), and also a statement of the most recent transactions on your account (*relevé*). Some banks also offer other services such as ordering cheque books, paying in cheques, etc.

◆ Cheques normally take about three days to clear once they have been paid into an account. This can take longer if they are drawn on an account (*compensable*) in a more distant town or city, or from another bank. Nonetheless, the date that will appear on your monthly statement (*relevé de compte*) is the date on which the cheque was deposited into your account.

◆ Cheques are used almost as frequently as cash in France for payment. To fill out a French cheque, write the amount in figures in the box or line provided, and then in words on the first (and second if necessary) lines of the cheque. Then fill out the name of the person or company to whom you wish to pay the cheque. Remember to sign the cheque in the space provided on the bottom right hand corner, and to fill in the date and town where you wrote the cheque. Many shops now have machines which automatically fill out the amount of the cheque, date, place and to whom it is payable.

◆ You can cash a cheque at any branch of your own bank. Simply make it payable to yourself. **A piece of official ID is normally required to endorse cheques, and is always required when cashing a cheque in the bank.** There are no cheque guarantee cards in France.

◆ Cheques can only be stopped in France in the case of loss or theft of your cheque book. They cannot be stopped because of unsatisfactory goods or services.

◆ A cash deposit into your account (*versement d'espèces*) will normally be registered much more rapidly than a cheque deposit. Banks usually have a separate counter (*guichet*) for cash deposits and withdrawals.

◆ Direct debits (*prélèvements*) can be used to pay for many services in France, including taxes, electricity bills, telephone bills and rent.

◆ There is no reason at all why you should close your bank account in your home country. It is probably a good idea to keep a reserve sum of money in your national currency in order to avoid conversion rates when you return home.

◆ You should also consider opening a deposit account in order to save for tax bills (which for the first year are a large lump sum) or to provide yourself with some form of security in time of trouble. The main accounts are *Livret de Développement*

Durable, formerly the *Codevi* (limited to a maximum of €6,000) with instant access; the *Plan d'Epargne Logement (PEL)*, with minimum savings periods of 18 months or five years; and the *Plan d'Epargne Actions (PEA)*, composed of shares and investment funds managed by the bank. Each of these has different implications, including tax exonerations, so you need to discuss them with your bank.

◆ Changing banks can be a very expensive process. Unless you are wealthy, French banks will react coolly to threats of a change of bank if you are dissatisfied with the service offered.

It is illegal to be overdrawn in France without a prior agreement with the bank, or to exceed your overdraft limit. There can be serious consequences if you break this rule. You may be placed on the Debtors List at the Banque de France, and be refused credit in the future.

Credit and debit cards

The principal French debit card is the *Carte Bleue Visa*, issued by all major French banks. This will give you the right to draw money from all cash machines in France, and is the most widely recognised and used of all cards. The *Carte Bleue* widely replaces cash. You will have your own PIN number, which not only gives access to cash machines, but is also essential for paying for goods in shops and restaurants. When you use the *Carte Bleue* the money is debited from your account (it is not a credit card).

Standard credit cards are generally accepted, with Visa being the most widely accepted. If the sign of your own credit card is not displayed at the entrance to a restaurant, you may wish to check it is accepted *before* spending any money. Many stores and commercial groups have account credit cards.

Some British credit cards without micro-chips are refused in France, although they *are* valid. If your card is refused, you should politely insist.

If you lose your card or it is stolen telephone 0892 705 705. Other emergency numbers can be found on most cash machines if the card is stolen whilst you are out. You must cancel the card immediately, and report the loss or theft to the police, and to your bank. All of this should be done as quickly as possible to avoid fraudulent use of your card. French banks will arrange replacement *Cartes Bleues* fairly rapidly.

Tipping

There are no hard-and-fast tipping rules, but generally the following people are tipped: porters, taxi drivers, doormen, room service, waiters, cloakroom attendants, hairdressers and lavatory attendants. Taxi drivers and hairdressers are normally given about 10% for good service; otherwise the amount is often rounded up by a few Euros.

In restaurants the service is usually included, in which case the bill will read 'TTC' (*toutes taxes comprises*). If you have received good service, it is customary to leave a tip nonetheless for the waiter. Never leave centimes as a tip. This is considered very insulting, and it would be better to leave no tip at all than to leave centimes.

You should tip the *concierge* of your apartment building at Christmas, depending on the level of service you have received from them. This should be in the region of €40, depending on your means. Should you live in a small garret at the top of the building, a smaller gift will be equally appreciated. Around Christmas, others will call on you for their 'Christmas Box' – postal workers, refuse collectors and the local firefighters. You are not obliged to give money to these people, and such collections are strictly speaking, illegal.

CLAIMING HOUSING ASSISTANCE

The *caisse d'allocations familiales* (*CAF*, **www.caf.fr**) administers various housing benefits for those with limited resources. You cannot receive more than one of these benefits at any given time, and your right to access any of the benefits will almost certainly depend upon the length of time you have lived and worked in France. All the benefits are means-tested. These benefits include:

1. *L'aide personnalisée au logement (APL)* – this never covers the total amount of your housing expenses but only a part. It is available to owner-occupiers who have undertaken to improve their property under certain conditions, and also to tenants. For owner-occupiers, the benefit is generally paid directly to your loan agency or bank, whilst for tenants the benefit is normally paid direct to your landlord. In both cases the sum is deducted from your loan or rent.

2. *L'allocation de logement familiale* **and** *l'allocation de logement sociale* – these benefits are available to tenants in a wide range of situations. You may be eligible for this benefit, depending upon your resources, if:

- you are already receiving another family benefit;
- or you have a child under 20 years old living at home;
- or you have been married for less than five years and have no children;
- or you are looking after a relative over 65 years of age;
- or you are unable to work.

A moving allowance is also available for those with limited resources. Applications should be made for this at your *caisse d'allocations familiales* when you move in.

GETTING CONNECTED

Electricity and gas

Probably the easiest way to deal with gas and electricity contracts administered by the state-run EDF-GDF company (**www.edf.fr, www.gazdefrance.fr**) is to take over the contracts of the previous residents of your property, be it rented or purchased. Contact your local EDF agency to arrange to have the meter read before you take possession of the property and take over the contract. Otherwise, go to the local EDF store with a copy of your rental agreement or your *acte de vente* if you are an owner, and a piece of official identity (e.g. passport or *carte de séjour*), and you can open your new account. If you do take this option, you will have to pay the rental fee, and arrange to be present on the date that the EDF set. Bills normally arrive quarterly, and can be paid at the post office using a *mandat (*postal order), or by cheque sent by post. Notices regarding meter readings will be sent to you or posted in your building. You must ensure access on the day of the reading. Normally *concierges* are willing to help if you live in an apartment and cannot be present.

Collective heating is controlled by the date, not the temperature. Normally it is turned on in October and turned off in April. In smaller and older properties, you may need to install extra electric heaters.

Water

As with electricity and gas, it is probably easiest to take over existing contracts when you purchase a new property. Tenants normally have their water charges included in the general charges they pay with their rent. Water is supplied by private companies. Arrange for a reading of the water meter when taking over a contract. Bills arrive about every three months.

Telephone

France Telecom, now also known as Orange, lost its national monopoly in France. However, in reality you still need to take out a France Telecom contract for line rental. It is now locked in price battles with its competitors (e.g. *Cegetel*, *Le 9*), many of whom offer very attractive rates for long-distance calls to the UK and the USA. You will need to contact each operator to discuss the offers available. If you take out a *Cegetel* or *Le 9* line subscription (*abonnement*), you simply dial 7 or 9 before dialling the standard number. You should also check out the integrated internet, phone and TV packages, and compare prices and services. The irony is that the first thing they do is disconnect you from the France Telecom network, so you need to decide if you want or need a France Telecom line and subscription. Generally the internet lines do work, but they can be difficult to access at certain times. A France Telecom fixed line is often still a good investment.

France Telecom now offer a **toll-free helpline in English on 0800 364 775** Monday–Friday 09h00-17h30. Phones can be rented or bought from France Telecom shops but can also be purchased from major stores such as FNAC or small phone shops. Phone directories (***Pages Blanches*** for individuals, ***Pages Jaunes*** for businesses and services, both available on line on **www.pagesjaunes.fr**) can also be found free of charge at your local France Telecom shop. The website offers street plans and even photos of many addresses.

France Telecom offer a number of cost-saving plans for overseas calls, the numbers most frequently dialled (*primalistes*), and so on. There is also an Internet *primaliste* with 50% off Internet calls at weekends and week-day evenings. Cheap rates for France Telecom phone calls are at weekends, French national holidays, and between 7pm and 8am (until 1pm for North America) on weekdays.

France is divided into five area codes, numbered from 01 (for Paris) to 05 (for the south-west). Dial the area code plus the eight-figure number to reach your correspondent. For international calls dial 00 plus country code plus city code plus telephone number. Call-back systems are readily available in France. Details of subscription rates and services can be found in 'international' magazines. Savings on international rates are often at least 30%.

Television

When you buy or rent a television in France, the shop will automatically send your name and address to the TV licence office (*Centre de Redevance Audiovisuel*). Your annual licence bill is now integrated on your pre-prepared annual tax declaration. You only have to pay a licence fee for one TV per household, so if you buy a second TV for the bedroom or the kitchen, it will be covered under the first licence.

DEALING WITH PROBLEMS

Structural problems

If you are the cause of a problem, such as a leak or a short-circuit, you are obviously responsible for repairing the damage or the problem. Contact your insurance company rapidly in order to establish what help they can offer you in the case of a major problem.

Tenants who are the victims of such problems should inform their landlords immediately. Landlords often have their own plumbers and electricians who deal with such problems for them, and send the bills directly to them. If you cannot contact your landlord and the situation is an emergency, you will have to arrange and pay for action yourself. Keep a copy of the bill and send the original to your landlord for reimbursement, once you have explained the situation.

The *syndic* of your building will have the names of companies they use in such situations, and whom they can recommend to you. But it is a good idea to try to arrange at least one other estimate in order to keep the costs involved at a minimum. You should note that calling out an electrician or plumber for an immediate visit, or at the weekend, will normally prove expensive.

Insects, pests and vermin

Unfortunately these may affect you no matter where you live.

Your local *mairie* very often will have a department which deals with insect problems such as wasp nests or cockroaches. Call to find out about this service, and check how much it costs. It is not too expensive, and can save a great deal of unpleasant trouble. Cockroaches (*cafards*) unfortunately tend to appear in clean homes as well as dirty ones. There are plenty of sprays and traps available for ridding yourself of this problem. Major infestations should be dealt with by professionals. Vermin such as mice can also be dealt with by traps and poison readily available in high-street shops. However, you obviously need to be careful about using these methods if you have children or pets.

Regular disinfections of your entire building should be organised by the *syndic*. Be careful to note when these are to happen, and arrange for access to your flat even if you do not have a problem. All flats in a building need to be disinfected for the process to be really effective. If you have a problem with vermin, warn your landlord and the *syndic* so that they can arrange for these measures to be taken.

Problem neighbours

Dealing with problem neighbours is often difficult and unpleasant. In the first instance, you need to try to speak to them about whatever is the source of the problem, be it noise or a leak. Try to remain calm and reasonable, even if your neighbours appear to be the opposite. If the problems persist, you will obviously need to speak to them once again. Keep a careful note of when you spoke to them, and a brief record of your conversations. Tenants with persistent problems are fully entitled to contact their landlord for help. Eventually putting your complaints in writing is a useful way of proving you have tried to resolve the situation. Keep a copy of the letter and place the original in your neighbour's post box. Sending a registered letter of complaint with proof of delivery (*lettre recommandé avec avis de réception*) is an elaborate but sure way of proving you have complained. The final resort for dealing with neighbours depends on whether they are tenants or owners.

- **Tenants** – speak to the *concierge* and find out the name of their landlord. You may need to ask your own landlord to help you to find the address. If a landlord receives repeated complaints about tenants, they may be forced to leave the property.

- **Owner-occupiers** – this is a more difficult situation. Ultimately, if you are in an apartment block, you would need to have a petition signed by the other residents of the building (many of whom will probably refuse even if they are sympathetic) before any definite action could be taken.

In both cases, the police can be asked to intervene. By law, excessive noise before 08h00 and after 22h00 is not permitted. If you own your property in an apartment block, you can also contact the *syndic* of the building for advice and help.

Avoiding problems with neighbours

If all of the above sounds rather drastic and worrying, then remember that there are certain basic courtesies which will at least mark you out as '*correct*' in French eyes and help you avoid problems.

Always remember to say good morning/evening, and generally 'mind your manners' in courtesy-conscious France. The French do not share the Anglo-Saxon notion of popping in to see the neighbours. You might consider a Christmas drink, but do not expect to establish a Saturday morning coffee-and-chat.

If you have building work in your apartment, apart from the common courtesy of warning your neighbours, make sure that your workmen clean up after themselves in the corridors and lifts. If you like throwing parties, place a little explanatory notice in the lift or entrance hall asking your neighbours to excuse the disturbance in advance. There is not normally a problem if you are polite. Avoid holding too many parties, and remember to keep the noise down in the apartment and also when your guests leave.

KEEPING IN TOUCH

During the first days in France, you may well be excited but you will want to contact the family and friends you left behind, and may well be suffering from loneliness linked to dislocation. Keeping in touch even when you have no permanent home is not difficult and is very reassuring for all concerned.

Using public telephones

Coin-operated telephones are now only found in a small number of cafés, hotels and restaurants. Otherwise, all public telephones are generally operated by phone-card (*télécartes*), sold in post offices and tobacconists (*tabacs*). Rates are cheaper after 21h30, on official holidays and Sundays. Long-distance rates vary according to distance. Local call rates normally offer fairly generous amounts of time.

Mobile phones

The French went from initial wariness to total obsession with mobile phones. The three French providers are Orange, SFR,

Bouygues and Virgin Mobile. If you bring a foreign-based mobile phone to France, remember the following rules for use :

◆ To make a call, dial as if you are a local subscriber. Dial your correspondent's number in the same way as you would do on a normal telephone. Include international dialling codes where appropriate.

◆ Calls made to other British-based mobile phones must be made using the international dialling codes, even if your correspondent is also in France. For instance, if you are in Caen and you want to call your friend in Paris who has a British-based mobile phone, dial 00 44, then your friend's normal mobile phone number but without the 0 at the beginning. **Be careful when using this system as you will be faced with very high phone bills as a result.**

The postal system

As in the UK, post offices offer many more services than simply the post. Main post offices are normally open 08h00–19h00 Monday–Friday, and from 08h00–12h00 on Saturdays. In Paris, the main post office in the rue du Louvre is open 24 hours. Stamps can also be purchased at tobacconists' shops.

Automatic franking machines inside post offices, including scales for weighing letters and small packages, dispense labels (*etiquettes*) for the appropriate value. Using these can help you to avoid the often considerable queues for assistance at the counter. Postage rates differ with destination and weight. In some major cities, these machines have a multi-lingual built-in option, including English.

If you wish to send a registered letter (*lettre recommandé*), there are a number of options:

◆ **with no proof of delivery and no declared value, but with a proof of despatch** – *sans avis de réception*

◆ **with proof of delivery (which will be sent back to you signed and dated), a proof of despatch, but no declared value** – *avec accusé de réception*

◆ **with declared value** – *avec valeur declarée.*

Chronopost is the French equivalent of Datapost in the UK, and next-day delivery is normally guaranteed throughout France.

France uses a five-digit postcode system, with the postcode written before the name of the town or city. The first two digits indicate the department, and the last three indicate the city. For instance, the eighth *arrondissement* of Paris is 75008 (75 for Paris, 008 for the eighth *arrondissement*).

Fax

All regular fax services are available throughout France, including both Group 3 and the faster but rarer Group 4. You can easily have a fax line installed in your home or office, but the machine must be 'approved' (*agréé*) by France Telecom. All the major fax distributors are present in France.

Most major towns and cities have shops where fax machines can be rented or purchased, from smaller phone-fax machines through to larger laser printer machines. If you buy or rent a machine, check on the cost and availability of after-sales service and supplies.

Internet

France participated fully in the internet boom of the 1990s. There are home-grown service providers (e.g. **voilà.fr** or **free.fr**) and a strong American presence (e.g. **AOL**) in the French market. You should have no problem connecting your existing equipment to French outlets. The France Telecom Internet service is **wanadoo.fr**.

'Cyber cafés' can be found in major towns and cities, allowing consumers to surf the net over lunch or a coffee. La Poste also offers free e-mail addresses. For more details ask at any post office.

LEARNING THE LANGUAGE

In order to get the most out of your time in France, you simply *must* study French and learn to speak it as well as you possibly can. If you do not, you will almost certainly find yourself considerably restricted and you will definitely feel left out. The French place a very high priority on their language, and their opinion of you as a foreigner will depend to a significant degree on whether you speak their language. Although they may criticise your less-than-perfect attempts to speak French, they will respect you far more for having tried, than if you insist on speaking English.

There is no easy formula that allows you to become fluent in French. Certain people have a gift for languages. Others tend to be natural mimics, and they have an advantage as they will soon catch on to key vocabulary and pronunciation. The only difficulty with the latter is that you may also pick up a local accent, but the French will find that all the more charming.

No matter which category you fall into – gifted linguist, mimic, somebody with rusty school French, or an absolute beginner – there are still a number of basic steps you can take:

1. Try hard to find time to study basic grammar, phrases and vocabulary before you come to France. If you have the opportunity, an evening class would be a very good idea.

2. Bring a good dictionary with you (not necessarily the most expensive), and also a good phrase book.

3. Sign up for lessons when you arrive. There are now literally hundreds of language schools throughout France. They provide tuition at all levels, from basic to advanced, and many offer courses in business French. Try looking in the *Yellow Pages* (***Pages Jaunes***) or the local phone book, or local expatriate community guides. Welcome offices, consulates, churches and clubs often have details or advertisements from schools and private tutors.

4. Put aside your inhibitions. Nobody, least of all the French, likes making mistakes in public. This is often what holds you back when you understand what is being said, and know how to reply but still cannot manage to say the phrase. When you let go of your inhibitions, you will often surprise yourself with what you actually do know. You may prefer to use a private tutor at first if you are shy of speaking French in public. This can be helpful by allowing you to build up your confidence with a sympathetic French ear.

5. You may also see offers of 'conversation exchange', whereby you trade an hour of English for an hour of French conversation. This could also be a good way to meet people and you could try joining a conversation group. A relaxed approach will help you gain confidence. Learning French in a relaxed atmosphere will help to avoid having a mental block on the language, with French only being used for unpleasant or stressful situations, from administration to problems in the home.

6. Use the French press. Try to listen to as much French TV and radio as possible, so that you start to become used to the sound of the language and the way in which it is used. Listening to news bulletins in French can be helpful, as the same phrases are used over and over again each hour. Also, try reading one of the more accessible French newspapers, such as *Libération, France-Soir,* or your regional newspaper (e.g. *La Voix du Nord, Midi-Libre, Ouest-France* or the free papers in the Paris *métro*) in order to develop your vocabulary. Choose small articles with headlines on topics you know something about, and try to really understand two or three articles a day. This will build up both your vocabulary and your confidence.

7. Use bilingual websites. Throughout this book, you will find recommendations for websites with information in English as well as French. Use the information in English to help you tackle the situation you are confronting, but then go back to the website and look at the same information in French. Once again, you will become familiar with vocabulary, phrases and style.

8. When you go shopping, read everything, paying particular attention to labels. Make an effort to go to some small local shops, and learn to ask for the items you buy. After a while you

will be able to carry on a simple conversation with the
shopkeepers, who are often happy to advise their loyal
customers.

Finally do not be afraid to make mistakes (*faux pas*). Use French
whenever you can, and try to forget the natural dread of saying
the wrong thing. A sense of humour is essential, as is the ability
to laugh at your own mistakes. Mastering the French language is
a question of confidence, no matter what level you are starting
from. Learning the language is like learning to walk – you stumble
every now and then. By and large, your efforts will earn respect,
an understanding smile, maybe a giggle which you should share in,
and a little patient help.

UNDERSTANDING FRENCH TIME

In France, the 24-hour clock is used. For example, 1.20 pm is
written as 13h20, 8.00 am is 08h00, and 5.30 pm is 17h30. We
have used the French format in this book to help you get used to
it. The French working day usually begins at 9h00 and finishes at
18h00. The long French lunch hour is still widely observed from
12h30 until 14h00. Even if only a shorter period is actually taken
for lunch, many offices will be closed to the public during this
whole period.

Early mornings are generally busy with the rush to the office or
school, but less so in the school holidays. It is a good idea to buy
yourself a French diary which lists the school holidays and French
bank holidays. School holiday dates vary from region to region,
and bank holidays considerably affect work patterns.

LISTENING TO FRENCH RADIO

Under French law, at least 40% of air-time every day must be devoted to French music on commercial music radio stations. There are a wide variety of stations available throughout France. The leading 'classic' radio stations are France-Info and France-Inter (current events, music and discussions), France-Culture (arts and literature), France-Musique (classical music and jazz) and Radio Classique.

The Parisian radio stations are, not surprisingly, the most trendy. Many, but not all of these, also broadcast on different frequencies across the country. The most popular stations for the eighteen to 30-somethings are Europe2, Nova, Voltage, and the gay radio station FG (only available in Paris), which is highly popular for young people of all persuasions. Nostalgie and Chérie FM churn out 'golden oldies', including French disco and ballads, and make a good preparation for your first invitations to French parties. RTL2 and OuiFM will appeal to rock fans and easy listening lovers.

For those who are pining for the cricket commentary or *The Archers*, it is still relatively easy to receive the BBC World Service and Radio 4 throughout France. You can also listen to many BBC radio stations via the Internet.

WATCHING FRENCH TELEVISION

Foreign TV sets do not work in France, so you will need to buy or rent when you arrive. There are six TV channels available throughout France:

♦ **TF1** is privately-owned. It generally has the 'big name' news presenters and TV journalists. Otherwise, the quality of programmes is variable, with many poor-quality game-shows and '*réalité*' shows.

- **France 2** is still under state control. This is the main heavyweight rival to TF1. There is a generally higher standard of varied programmes. **FR3** is also under state control, with regional news broadcasts.

- **Canal +** is a private pay channel. For part of the day everybody is able to receive their programmes and part of the day (normally the most interesting part), you must take out a private subscription for a receiver. It shows many good quality films and the popular satirical puppet show *Les Guignols*.

- **La Cinque/Arte** – These two stations share a frequency, Arte taking over at 19h00. The latter is a Franco-German company. An intellectual channel, with good documentaries, no game-shows, and films in original languages (*version originale* or *v.o.*) including English.

- **M6** is considered a 'lightweight' channel in comparison with the others. Nonetheless there is a good selection of films and reports (especially on Sunday evenings) and a much younger dynamic feel to the presentation. Foreign films are always dubbed in French.

On French TV there is a coding system with different symbols on the screen indicating the level of parental consent advisable for various films and programmes. The main programme for the evening normally begins about 20h45, after the news and weather broadcast.

Satellite and cable television is now widely available throughout France. Check to find out if your building is cabled (*câblé*) and ask neighbours about how and where to subscribe. The cable TV stations available include American and 'packaged' BBC programmes. Amongst the best cable TV channels are Paris Première (general arts, lots of v.o. English/American films, and Fashion Week specials), Téva (for v.o. American sitcoms), and channels such as Odyssey for general interest programmes. The French equivalent to CNN is LCI, the continuous news channel. MTV is available also, and the French equivalent MCM.

READING FRENCH NEWSPAPERS AND MAGAZINES

France has a very wide variety of newspapers and magazines. Regional newspapers are often given greater prominence in France than is the case in the UK. The principal national French newspapers are:

- *Le Figaro* – right-wing, conservative, but a good general read.

- *Le Monde* – independent, centre-left, regarded as 'the intellectual's newspaper' for both the right wing and the left wing. Takes some getting used to, but worth the effort.

- *Libération* – young, centre-left and trendy. Good arts coverage.

- *Le Parisien* and *France-Soir* – sensational headlines, most akin to the English tabloids but much softer.

- *Le Canard Enchainé* – the scourge of the political establishment, satirical but serious. A bit heavy going until you get into French politics.

- *Les Echoes* and *La Tribune* are the business newspapers (equivalent to the *Financial Times*); *L'Equipe* is the popular sports newspaper; *La Croix* is run by the French Catholic church. Magazines such as *L'Evenement, Marianne, Le Point, L'Express*, and *Le Nouvel Observateur* offer good broad-ranging weekly news coverage from a variety of political perspectives.

The foreign press is widely available every day in France, but at a more elevated cost. One way to save money is to take out a subscription to your favourite newspaper, which often leads to considerable savings. Telephone the newspaper of your choice before leaving to ask about subscriptions if you will be in France for some time. All major newspapers are available on the Internet.

FOOD SHOPPING IN FRANCE

Almost every village, town or city has its own market, offering fresh produce from fruit and vegetables, meat, cheese, to household products and clothes (although these will not always be reasonably priced in markets). Shopping at a French market is a real experience, lots of fun and a good way to brush up your language skills whilst choosing your produce. Your *concierge* and/ or your neighbours will be able to tell you where to find your nearest market.

Market streets will normally include the household suppliers for your daily dietary needs: the *boulangerie* (bakery), where you can also buy *pâtisserie* (cakes); the *boucherie* (butcher's); the *charcuterie* (cold and smoked meats, and pies); the *poissonnerie* (fish shop); the *épicerie* (grocer's store); the *fromagerie* (cheese shop); the *cave à vins* (wine shop/off-licence); and probably at least one *confiserie* (chocolate/sweet shop).

Remember that France works on the metric system, with one pound equivalent to 0.45 kg. If you tell a butcher or cheese merchant how many people you wish to serve, they will suggest what they think is the usual amount. Normally shopkeepers will serve you and then ask, *'Et avec ça?/Ça sera tout?'* And with that?/ Will that be all? If you have nothing more to buy, then the answer is simply, *'C'est tout merci'*.

At the charcuterie, if you are buying ham, you will be asked *'Combien de tranches?'* (How many slices). At the *fromagerie*, the shopkeeper will probably show you either the whole cheese or a ready-cut piece and ask you to choose the size of piece (*morceau*) that you want for hard cheeses. Soft cheeses such as Camembert are normally sold either in halves or whole; and certain small and rarer cheeses (e.g. goats' cheese, *chevres*) are only sold whole.

At the bakers, if you buy a baguette, you will be asked if you want it *'Coupé en deux'* (cut in half). If you buy a small loaf of bread the question will be *'Tranché?'* (Sliced?) If you do ask the baker to slice the loaf, it will be produced using a professional machine, presented in plastic with a seal, and cost a little extra. Finally if you buy flowers either at the market or in a *fleurist*, you will be asked if they are a gift (in which case they will be gift-wrapped automatically) or for the home – *'C'est pour offrir ou pour la maison?'*

1What do you do if you do not have the time, facility or inclination to shop at the market? Supermarkets are not lacking and there is nothing particularly special about the way in which French supermarkets function – everything is pretty self-explanatory even if you do not speak French. The most well-known hypermarkets are Auchan and Carrefour, both of which also sell clothing, computers and even package holidays. The Picard chain of shops specialises in frozen (*surgelé*) food.

DISCOVERING DEPARTMENT STORES

The five principal Parisian department stores (*grands magasins*) offering everything from household items to clothes are to be found distributed across Paris in the main shopping areas. The following Parisian flagship shops have now been reproduced elsewhere in the suburbs or in other city shopping centres.

- **Bazar de l'Hôtel de Ville**, rue de Rivoli, 75004 Paris. M° Hôtel de Ville, **www.bhv.fr**. The **BHV**, as it is usually known, specialises in home furnishings and DIY.

- **Galeries Lafayettes**, boulevard Haussman, 75009 Paris, M° Chaussée d'Antin/RER Opéra, **www.galerieslafayette.com**. Excellent choice of clothes.

- **Printemps**, boulevard Haussman, 75009 Paris, M° Havre-Caumartin/RER Opéra – the other great shopping experience. The great dome is best seen at Christmas when the Christmas tree is in place. Free fashion shows are put on during the Fashion Weeks. Very '*hype*' menswear department.

All of these stores have discount card schemes and both Galeries Lafayettes and Printemps in particular are full of concessionary mini-shops from all the major designers.

SHOPPING FOR THE HOME

If your budget does not stretch to shopping in one of these shops, home furnishings can also be found at Conforama. Castorama (**www.castorama.fr**) is another DIY/garden centre favourite. You should also check out the sites for Leroy Merlin (**www.leroymerlin. fr**), Habitat, (**www.habitat.fr**) and Ikea which has four shops strategically placed around Paris (**www.ikea.fr**). Another useful chain to discover is Mr Bricolage ('Mr D-I-Y') **www.mr-bricolage.fr**.

You should note that the BHV website offers some handy household tips (in French) about what appliances will and will not work in France. For plug adaptors (*adaptators*) try the local hardware stores (*drogueries*) or go to the accessories department of the major hi-fi and electrical appliance supplier Darty. FNAC, the all-purpose music/book/computer/ticket stores, also stock plug adaptors.

BARGAIN-HUNTING IN THE SALES

The *soldes* as they are known, are now regulated by the commerce ministry to make sure that sales start across France on the same day, avoiding the previous phenomenon of late starting towns suffering from shopped-out consumer apathy. The main sales are still the New Year sales in early-mid January, and there are also some summer sales. Obviously the best bargains go first, but this will only be the first mark-down (*démarque*). There will probably be second and third mark-downs (each should be indicated with the original price on the sale ticket). Sale items are not normally refundable or exchangeable.

MEETING PEOPLE

Meeting and making new friends with whom you can share your experiences and to whom you can turn for help (as well as offering it) is not always easy. One reason for this is that the French as a rule are reserved, taking time to get to know newcomers, whether foreign or French.

Although some French people may admire a perceived total embrace of their culture, many would find it puzzling and ill-advised. The French believe strongly in **networking**, whether through social, business or culturally-identified groups. Sticking together, at least at first, is normal for the French – so why should foreigners be any different? Do not be afraid to use the contact suggestions at the end of this book and/or details from your consulate to meet other expatriates in similar circumstances to you.

'**Anglophone**' is a word used in French to describe anybody who is English mother-tongue, a slightly more global term than 'Anglo-Saxon', which is principally reserved for the Americans and the British. Nonetheless the principal English-speaking communities in France are the Americans and the British, followed by the Irish and the Canadians, and a small but visible Australasian community.

CHANGING ADDRESS

You may find that the time comes to move home again, as your circumstances change. Moving home in France is not simply a case of finding and securing your new address, and then informing your family and friends where to find you. A great many other people and organisations, listed below, must also be informed. This information applies to both home-owners and tenants.

Moving home action plan

1. **Landlords** – Be careful to respect the notice periods stipulated in your rental agreements.

2. **Electricity and gas** – Contact your current EDF agency ten days before you move to have your meter read. The cost of

terminating your current contract will be sent to your new address. At the same time, contact your new agency to establish the new contract or arrange to take over the existing contract.

3. **Water** – as above.

4. **Telephone** – Contact your current and future France Telecom agencies. Arrange termination of your existing contract about eight days before the move. In certain cases if you are staying within the same exchange area, you can keep the same number if you wish. A recorded message can also be arranged on the old number for three months informing callers of your new number.

5. **Post** – Organise a *faire-suivre* at the post office to have all your post forwarded. This should be done no later than five days before the move. Generally it works well. However, you might wish to consider tipping your current concierge to check that all your post is forwarded.

6. *Carte de séjour* **and passport** – After you have moved, the new address must appear on your official documents.

7. **Driving licence,** *carte grise* **and car registration** – You have one month in which to make the change of address on your *carte grise*. If you change *départements*, your car must also be re-registered.

8. **Insurance policies** – You will need to inform your insurance companies of a change of address. You can either terminate your existing house insurance or transfer it to your new residence.

9. **Social security** – 15 working days before you move, contact your current and future *caisse d'assurance maladie* to arrange for your new card(s) and the transfer of your files. This is not the most efficient or speedy of services, so allow plenty of time...

10. **ANPE** – If you are registered at the local job centre, inform your old centre of your forthcoming change of address. Visit your new centre as soon as possible after moving in.

11. **Family benefits** – Inform your local *caisse d'allocations familiales* of your intended move 15 working days before the date. They should contact your new *caisse* for you.

12. **Bank** – Inform the bank of your change of address as soon as possible. This will allow them not only to send correspondence to the correct address, but also to print new cheque books for you. You may also wish to change branches.

13. **Tax offices** – Admittedly, they were probably not on your mailing list for change of address cards. However, they have a nasty habit of finding out where you are in any case. Inform your current tax office before you move of your change of address. The following year, you will send your tax declaration to your old tax office, but marked with your new address on the first page. You must also inform the TV licence centre of your change of address. **Correspondence from tax offices is <u>not</u> forwarded by the post office, but sent back to the senders. This can have serious consequences**.

14. **Municipal *crêches*** – You must enrol your children at your future *mairie* as soon as possible. You must also respect the one month notice period for withdrawing your children from their current *crêche*.

15. **Primary schools** – Before moving, ask the school for a *certificat de radiation* (this does not mean that your child glows in the dark, but that they have been struck off the school register). At the same time, contact the schools office of your new mairie to arrange an appointment. They will inform you which school

catchment area you now fall under.

16. *Collège* or *lycée* – Before moving, ask the school director for a *certificat de sortie* for your children. The appropriate files should then be transferred directly to the new school.

17. When you have completed all of the above, sit down, pour yourself a large drink and swear never to move home again in France!

FINDING OUT MORE

♦ **Barclays** is the only British high-street bank in France, with over 100 branches (*agences*). To find out more about their services, see their bilingual website, **www.barclays.fr**.

♦ **Britline, www.britline.com**, is the on-line English-language banking service offered by Crédit Agricole, originally intended just for Normandy, but now offering national assistance and coverage.

♦ **CIC Banque Transatlantique www.transat.tm.fr** (French only) is part of the nationwide CIC chain of banks. This bank specialises in wealth management. Main branches: 26, avenue Franklin Roosevelt, 75008 Paris, tél. 01 56 88 77 77; Finsbury Pavement, London EC21 IHX tel: 020 7496 1890; 1901 Pennsylvania Avenue, Suite 807, Washington DC 2006 (representative office), tel: 202 429 1909.

♦ **Société Générale International Private Clients branch,** English-speaking branch, 29, boulevard Haussman, 75009 Paris, tél. 01 53 30 87 30. The entrance is at the end of the main building (opposite Galeries Lafayette) facing the Opera.

- **www.britishinfrance.com** – more than 60 British and Franco-British or Anglo-American associations in and around Paris. A useful site even if you are neither British nor living near Paris, as the associations may be able to help you contact groups nearer to your home.

- **Local consulates** normally have lists of English-speaking and/or national associations in your region. Check your embassy website (see Chapter 2 for addresses).

6

Finding Employment

THE FRENCH ECONOMY

President Nicolas Sarkozy is a former Budget and Finance minister, and an enthusiastic advocate of liberal economic policy. His election slogan was '*travailler plus pour gagner plus*', quite literally 'work more to earn more', a direct attack on the 35-hour week regime and culture introduced by the Socialist Jospin government in 2000. He proclaimed his intention to become the '*le président du pouvoir d'achat*' ('the spending power president'), in response to widespread public dissatisfaction at the cost of living.

Sarkozy appointed a major think-tank commission on the French economy, and notably how to increase popular spending power, headed by former French Socialist presidential advisor Jacques Attali. Amongst their recommendations are the opening up of 'closed' professions such as lawyers, pharmacists and even taxi drivers, widening and standardising Sunday trading, allowing hypermarkets and cinemas to open up more freely across France, and reducing supermarket supplier paybacks in order to reduce prices.

A fiscal reform package has reduced the tax burden on high-level incomes, and notably on those subject to the famous wealth tax, *l'impôt sur la fortune* (*ISF*), and has heavily reduced the impact of inheritance tax. A new reform allowing tax relief on the interest on mortgage repayments has also been introduced to encourage home ownership in a country with a high-level of tenancy. In 2008, Sarkozy is intending to open access to the benefits of company profit-sharing schemes, allowing employees to benefit from these schemes at any time rather than waiting five years, as is currently the case.

In 1995, the Juppé government fell when it tried to reform public-sector retirement perks. For decades, the French public sector, *la fonction publique*, and its employees, *fonctionnaires*, representing some 25% of the French workforce, have resisted all attempts at reform. In 2007, after a series of strikes which were less intense than those of 1995, the government of François Fillon finally succeeded in partially aligning state and private sector retirement schemes. The fact that the strikes were shorter and less widespread than in 1995 was largely due to a change in public opinion, which favoured the ending of what many considered to be an outdated privilege. Sarkozy has also announced that he will not replace *fonctionnaires* as they retire, in a drive to reduce the number of state employees. Both measures are naturally unpopular with this workforce and further disruption and strikes could break out as he tackles difficult areas such as the health and education services.

Sarkozy wishes to make the French employment market more flexible. A new law planned for 2008 will introduce a fixed-term project contract of 36 months maximum with a defined purpose, which would come to an end when the project has been completed; extended trial periods for employees and management alike; the possibility to end a contract by mutual agreement, with a certain number of benefits for the employee guaranteed; and better paid unemployment benefit with guaranteed social rights, but for a shorter period. Reforms are also being prepared to help those who wish to create their own small businesses, with one-stop administrative declarations, and an end to the differentiation in social charges between companies with fewer than ten employees, and ten to twenty employees.

In December 2007, one French satirist noted that Sarkozy is the first French president not to include Work and Employment in the same ministry, probably because he realises that most French job seekers do not necessarily want to work! Sarkozy has repeatedly said that he would like to sanction job seekers who refuse two 'reasonable' job offers. French unemployment has been slowly decreasing, but is still stuck at about 8%. Sarkozy has already pushed through a number of reforms to encourage the French to work more. Overtime pay has now been made virtually tax-free, and employees can be paid for recuperation days (*RTT*s – see Chapter 7) which they have not been able to take.

Sarkozy is known for his close, some would say too close, links with France's leading industrialists. The head of LVMH, Bernard Arnault, was the witness at one of his weddings. The media mogul and investor Arnaud Lagardere has said that he considers Sarkozy to be like a brother; and the multi-millionaire businessman Vincent Bolloré lent Sarkozy his yacht for his post-election break and his private aircraft for his winter holiday. Sarkozy, who trained as a lawyer, draws inspiration from the private sector, and is very much a 'businessman's president'. He is determined to make France work, literally. On the other hand, increasing spending power is the Number One priority of the French. In

January 2008, an opinion poll (in *Libération*, 7 January 2008) showed that 62% of people did not think that his reforms had made any difference so far. An irritated president said the next day that he could give away money from empty state coffers, and that it was not the only issue to be addressed. For the French, the proof of the presidential pudding is in the eating, but Sarkozy the businessman also knows that he has to balance the state's deficit-ridden books and trade deficit if he is to succeed.

FOREIGN WORKERS IN FRANCE

Citizens of the original European Union (EU) member states are entitled to take any position in the private sector providing that security clearance is not required (which you may be granted in any case); but you are generally excluded from positions in *la fonction publique*, with possible exceptions for the health and education sectors. Certain other areas are open to foreigners, but think twice about entering all-French preserves as French unions do not tend to keep a welcome in the industrial hill-sides for what are perceived as neo-liberal Anglo-Saxon subversives, or quite simply interlopers in national territory.

Commonwealth citizens with residency rights in the UK should note that those rights are only valid in the UK, and do not exempt them from meeting French requirements for citizens of their own country. Residents of the Channel Islands and the Isle of Man should also note that these British dependencies are not full members of the European Union, and different rules also apply. Check with the British Consulate in Paris or the French Consulate in London for details.

US citizens

US citizens face a major struggle with French bureaucracy similar to the process for a European moving to the States. If you are planning to stay more than 90 days, or for purposes other than tourism then you must have a *visa de long séjour* (long-stay). If you do obtain one of these visas, you must apply for your *carte de séjour* **within one week of arrival**.

The basic rule for all visa applications – both employment and residential – is that you must start from the outside and work your way in. You cannot avoid returning to your point of origin outside France in order to successfully apply for your visas. You cannot convert a tourist visa into a long-term visa once in France. This applies to all non-EU nationals.

The US Embassy in Paris (**www.amb-usa.fr**) states very clearly in all its documentation that it cannot intervene with the French authorities on behalf of US citizens seeking visa exemptions and work permits after arrival. Wannabe Hemingways and fake Fitzgeralds take note...

US citizens who wish to take a full-time position in France are dependent upon the French employer to take initial steps towards securing both residence and work permits. The basic rule you have to remember is that a successful application by your employer for a work permit should normally lead to a successful visa application, after which you must complete the process by applying for your residence permit once you have arrived in France.

Authorisation for Americans to work in France rests with the *Service de la Main d'Oeuvre Étrangère* of the Ministry of Labour (127, boulevard de la Villette, 75010 Paris, tél. 01 44 84 42 86). However, you do have a vital part to play in your own application. The table opposite shows the parallel processes for your work permit and visa applications once you have found a potential employer.

Once you have passed all the hurdles outlined above, you will be issued with a *carte de séjour temporaire salarié*, valid for one year. It will specify in which departments the permit is valid and the professional activity in which your are employed. This card can be renewed two months before the expiry date, or upon presentation of a new work contract.

Five years continued residence in France allows a US citizen to apply for a *carte de résident*, valid for ten years and automatically renewable and valid for all professional activities. Spouses of French citizens are entitled to the *carte de résident*.

LOOKING FOR WORK
Looking for work is a full-time job in itself. In France, there are a variety of ways in which you can seek work.

Using job centres
The state-run job centres are the *Agence Nationale Pour l'Emploi*, (*ANPE*). You must register in person – written applications will not be accepted. Proof of permanent residence in France (e.g. *carte de séjour*) will be required, and they may also ask to see your passport. Job advertisements are displayed in the centres, and workshops, counselling and personal interviews are available.

Employer/French Government departments	Employee
1. Applies to French Ministry of Labour for permission to employ an American citizen. The authorisation will be sent to the chosen French consulate in the USA.	1. Informs the employer which French Consulate in the USA will receive the visa application in order to receive the Ministry of Labour approval.
2. Provides a copy of the signed employment contract to the French Ministry of Labour for approval. 3. If the contract is approved, the Ministry of Labour forwards a copy to the *Office des Migrations Internationales (OMI)* who transmit it to the designated French Consulate in the USA. **4. When the French Consulate receives approval from the *OMI*, the applicant will be informed and can proceed with the visa application (2).**	2. Provides documents required for French visa. The minimum requirements for a French visa are: a) a valid passport b) several passport-size photographs c) proof of financial resources to support the applicant and his or her dependents during their stay in France. This can be: ♦ bank statements ♦ written confirmation of regular transfers of funds from a US bank account to a French bank account ♦ letters from family or friends guaranteeing regular support ♦ a *certificat d'hébergement* (housing certificate) from a French family or friends with whom the applicant will be staying in France. **All documents need to be notarised including official translations into French of the documents supplied.**
	3. Once you receive your visa and enter France, you must apply at the *Préfecture de Police* for your residence permit (*carte de séjour*) within one week of arrival.
	4. The visa formalities are not completed until the candidate and family have undergone a medical examination by the doctors designated by the *OMI*.

Fig. 4. Administrative procedures for Americans intending to work in France.

APEC is the equivalent to the ANPE for *cadre* positions, open to both *cadre* and non-*cadre* applicants, although it specialises in candidates with *cadre* experience or profiles. There is no set moment when you can expect to be made *cadre*; it may happen immediately, or it may happen after some years. Further explanations are given below, but do not be afraid to explore *cadre* positions. You do not have to be registered at state job centres in order to reply to advertisements there.

Using employment agencies

Although employers are obliged to inform the ANPE of vacancies in their companies, they are much more likely to seek the help of recruitment agencies (*conseil de recruitment*) and head-hunters (*chasseurs de têtes*) to fill vacancies. Most agencies are accessible only by appointment. You therefore need to prepare and send your CV and covering letter (see the section on applying for jobs later in this chapter) in order to open these doors. There are now several agencies in Paris that specialise in bilingual appointments, particularly for secretarial and administrative work. Providing that you do have a good working knowledge of French, your greatest immediate asset in the search for work will be that you are English mother-tongue.

Using newspapers and magazines

The most important newspaper for job advertisements in France is *Le Figaro* every Monday. The separate '*économie*' section normally carries a wide variety of jobs of all levels and areas. These are repeated every Wednesday in the job newspaper *Carrières et Emplois*, which also includes jobs advertised in *Le Parisien*, and sometimes advertisements from *The International Herald Tribune*.

Le Monde on Mondays and Tuesdays carries a selection of well-paid jobs, and the business newspapers *Les Echos* and *La Tribune* *also carry similar job advertisements*. *Les Echos* has a reciprocal agreement with the *Financial Times* in the UK. This means that you may be able to start your job-search even before you move to France. *Libération* also has a small but developing jobs section each Monday, and magazines such as *L'Express* and *Le Nouvel Observateur* carry a variety of job advertisements. Regional newspapers are also an important source of opportunities. In Paris, two free magazines, *France-USA Contacts* (**www.fusac.fr**) also known as FUSAC, and *The Paris Voice* (**www.parisvoice.com**) have job sections of great interest to English-speakers.

Sending unsolicited applications

Candidatures spontanées, composed of your CV and a general covering letter, are the most important method of filling vacancies in France, accounting for 70% of appointments. This approach fits in with the general 'networking' approach which is highly prevalent. A well-presented CV and letter, followed up by a phone-call if appropriate, can secure you at least a first interview for a post that nobody else knew was even vacant.

Using the Internet

One sign of the changing times in France is that many agencies and firms will now accept applications by Internet, allowing you the chance to get out of the otherwise obligatory hand-written letter with the almost inevitable spelling errors. There is a vast choice of websites to choose from in well-connected France. Among the most important are: **www.anpe.fr** (well-designed and informative job centre site with access to all offers); **www.apec.fr** (the *cadre* job centre site); **www.monster.fr**, **www.keljob.com**, and **www.cadremploi.fr**. Many French companies now include job offers and on-line application procedures on their websites.

Using professional associations

Certain professions in France have very restrictive rules over practice, such as lawyers, accountants, and the medical professions. **Before leaving your home country** you should contact your own professional association to enquire if they have any information to offer you or correspondent associations in France who could offer you guidance on the work available to foreign professionals in a particular field. They may also have contacts with foreign nationals who have already integrated into the French system, who may be willing to offer advice, or even a position.

Using chambers of commerce

The Franco-British Chamber of Commerce and Industry (FBCCI) is the oldest foreign chamber of commerce in Paris. The American, Australian, Irish and South African chambers are all also very active and each chamber offers a wide selection of information and services. Each chamber organises regular social events to help new arrivals network with each other and with established members of the expatriate communities. These can be useful forums in which to introduce yourself.

The Franco-American Chamber of Commerce at **www.amchamfrance.org** and the Franco-British Chamber of Commerce and Industry at **www.francobritishchamber.com** both provide full details of the services offered to job-seekers and new arrivals by both chambers.

REPLYING TO JOB ADVERTISEMENTS

Job advertisements come in a wide variety of shapes and wording. Figure 5 opposite contains a number of standard terms. The explanation given beneath it will help you decode precisely what is being offered.

The basic format is to indicate the name of the company and/or its activity first, then to indicate the post that is being offered, followed by a brief description of the candidate profile the company is seeking. It is important to understand this brief profile – no matter how standard or banal it may seem – in order to compose the correct application letter indicating your suitability for the job.

Two common specifications given in job adverts are the level of education required of applicants, and whether the position is *cadre* or *non-cadre*. Both of these require explanation.

- *Bac + 3* or *Bac + 4*, etc. – this indicates that graduates are being sought who have at least the level of *baccalauréat* (A levels), plus three years of further education, or whatever number is indicated. Bac + 5, for instance, would require an initial higher education degree, plus perhaps a master's degree. A further specialised *cycle* may also be required for certain jobs. *Niveau bac* means A level education is the minimum.

- *Cadre* – this is basically an executive post, unique to France. Advantages include better salaries (in general) and better social security benefits later in life, and a certain 'snob' value. Disadvantages include long hours for no extra-pay. *Cadres* are not normally paid over-time, unlike *non-cadres*.

Decoding the final part of the advertisement is crucial. For the sample advert shown here, your complete application must include the following items:

---

*Importante société internationale de prêt-à-porter en pleine
expansion recherche*

Vendeurs/Vendeuses confirmées

*pour ses boutiques sur la Région Parisienne.
Jeune et dynamique, vous avez les sens du contact, une première expérience
professionnelle réussite dans ce domaine, et vous cherchez maintenant à
évoluer dans votre carrière.*

*Envoyez votre candidature (lettre, CV, photo et prétentions) à DRH,
Wear-Well S.A., Service Recrutement, 19, rue Eugene Leblanc,
92300 Levallois-Perret, sous réf. 24679.*

Fig. 5. Sample job advertisement.

◆ *Lettre d'accompagnement* – this *must* be hand-written in
impeccable French, well-presented, and no more than one side
of A4 paper. Standard forms of letter suitably adapted are
perfectly acceptable, but word-processed letters will simply be
ignored. Many firms in France still use graphology as a
selection test for candidates, especially for more important jobs.

◆ **CV** – your curriculum vitae or resumé must be neatly typed
and easy to read, in the French format and no more than one
side of A4 paper. Bring out the most important and relevant
elements in your experience which suit you for the job for
which you are applying. On average, most recruiters spend
about two minutes reading what has taken hours to prepare.
They need to see your suitability right away.

◆ Salary or **Prétentions** – some advertisements clearly state salary,
some give a salary range according to experience (e.g. €50–
55K) and some advertisements ask for your *prétentions*, as in
Figure 5. Basically, this is asking you to state what you are
willing to accept as a salary – which is a tricky business! You

therefore need to know what the 'average' salary is for someone of your experience, and for such a position. Looking at similar advertisements can help. **Only include your** *pretentions* **if you are asked for them**, or in certain cases when you make a *candidature spontanée*. Otherwise, *pretentions* will have a much more English meaning!

◆ **Photo** – despite being the land of *liberté, égalité et fraternité*, the French still tend to pre-select their candidates to a large extent on a rather superficial basis. On the other hand, for some jobs, as in the case of our advertisement in Figure 5, appearance is important. As with *pretentions*, only send a photo when you are asked to do so. Do not use a photo taken in a photo booth at a railway station. Go to a photo shop and arrange to have a set of four **black and white** passport size photos taken, in which you are dressed well and appropriately for the position for which you are applying. This should only cost about €6, and is money well spent. One photo should then be stapled to the top right-hand corner of your CV.

PREPARING YOUR FRENCH CV

Preparing your French curriculum vitae (or resumé) can be heart-rending, especially if you have spent your university career 'collecting CV points'. You only have one side of A4 on which to cram in the information in a relevant, readable, and eye-catching manner. There is therefore no point in telling potential employers how you captained a cricket team (which the French don't even understand), if it means taking up valuable space.

Figure 6 (on page 138) shows you the basic format for preparing your CV. Any of the decent guides available in France will help

Paul Williams
75, rue Aristide Briant,
75019 Paris
Tél. 01 47 97 14 39 (Dom.)

Etat civil
Situation de famille: Célibataire
Nationalité: Britannique
Né le 15 mars 1973 à Bristol (Grande-Bretagne)

Formation
1991 – 'A Levels' (équivalent du baccalauréat) en géographie, français et histoire contemporain.
1995 – 'Bachelor of Arts Honours Degree', University of Warwick (Licence d'Histoire Contemporaine en 3 ans).

Langues
Anglais (langue maternelle)
Français (parlé et écrit couramment)
Allemand (connaissances de base)

Expérience professionnelle
Depuis septembre 2000: Manager du département prêt-à-porter masculin auprès du Buyright Limited, Manchester, Angleterre.

– Responsable d'une équipe de cinq vendeurs dans un important magasin en plein coeur d'une des plus grandes villes d'Angleterre.
– Responsable de la commande des stocks.
– Participation à l'élaboration du plan général du management du magasin.

1999 – 2000: Assistant au directeur d'exportation auprès du Woolbridge Products Limited, Manchester, Angleterre.

– Réceptions et suivi des commandes (y compris les clients à l'étranger) et grande expérience du service facturation.

1996 – 1998: Vendeur, Woolbridge Products, Manchester, Angleterre.
1995 – 1996: Vendeur auprès du Riley Products, Sydney, Australie

Autres expériences
1991 – 1992: Voyages en divers pays de l'Afrique du sud.
1995 – 1996: Séjour en Australie et Nouvelle Zealand.
1993 – 94: Président du 'History Society' à l'Université de Warwick.
Permis de conduire

Fig. 6. Sample CV.

you to choose one of the variations on this theme which best suits your experience. Contrary to popular opinion, there is no one 'correct' way to present a CV in France. But what is definitely wrong is to produce the kind of detailed CV common in the United Kingdom. Points to remember are:

1. Your *état civil* (name, address, telephone numbers, marital status and number of children) always comes in a neat little section at the top of the page. Leave space on the right-hand side for a photo if necessary.

2. Start with the most recent or current employment and work backwards. Arguably you should adopt the same practice with your education.

3. Referees are not normally included on a French CV. They may be called for subsequently, but are not normally asked for in advance.

4. Companies and consultants receive thousands of CVs. To succeed, yours must stand out. Use a good quality paper, and if possible, a similar envelope. Ask French friends to check your spelling, grammar and punctuation. The French are very picky indeed about such things.

'Converting' your qualifications

If you or a potential employer has any doubt over the level of degree that you hold, a *lettre d'équivalence* can be requested from the *Ministère de l'Enseignment et de la Recherche* equating your degree to a French degree level.

WRITING YOUR APPLICATION LETTER

Even if you have the perfect CV and are amply qualified for the job, you may well fall foul of a recruiter with a badly written or badly presented letter. Standard form letters are acceptable. However, it is much better to take the standard form and adapt it to the job for which you are applying, bringing out the major points in favour of your application. The letter should not be simply a repetition of your CV. Figure 7 on page 141 is an example of a typical *lettre d'accompagnement* in response to the advertisement in Figure 5 on page 136. Examples of standard letters can be found not only in CV guides, but also in many good French-English dictionaries, such as *Le Robert*. Points to remember are:

1. The letter must never exceed one side of A4 paper.

2. Begin by stating that you are replying to the advertisement in X newspaper, and give the date of the advertisement. If a *réf.* (*référence*) is given in the advertisement, remember that it must appear in both the letter and on the envelope.

3. If the name of the person and their gender is not given, begin simply with '*Monsieur*'. Do not write '*Cher Monsieur*', as this would imply a degree of intimacy.

4. As with the CV, the letter must be impeccably written, on good quality stationery.

5. Finish the letter with a standard formula. Generally, men assure their correspondents of their '*salutations distinguées*', whilst women send their '*sentiments distinguées*'.

GOING TO THE INTERVIEW

The same basic rules apply in France as anywhere else in the world. Dress appropriately and smartly, arrive in good time, shake hands on meeting your interviewer – and smile!

75 rue Aristide Briant
75019 Paris

Wear-Well S.A.
19, rue Eugene Leblanc
92300 Levallois Perret

Paris, le 3 avril 200X

Monsieur,

Votre offre d'emploi pour un poste de vendeur auprès du Wear-Well parue dans Le Figaro économie du 30 mars, (réf. 24679), m'a beaucoup intéressé.

De nationalité britannique, et doté d'une forte expérience du domaine de prêt-à-porter, je suis actuellement à la recherche d'un poste en France qui me permettrait d'évoluer dans ma vie professionnelle.

Vous trouverez dans le curriculum vitae ci-joint le détail de mes études et de mes activités professionnelles. Le montant de mes prétentions s'élève à €1900 brut par mois.

Je suis à votre disposition pour vous fournir toute information complémentaire. Dans l'attente d'un entretien à cet effet, je vous prie d'agréer, Monsieur, l'expression de mes salutations distingueés.

Paul Williams

P.J.: Curriculum vitae

Fig. 7. Sample application letter.

As a foreigner newly-arrived in France, you can expect to be asked about your motivation for moving to France, as well as your experience. Prepare yourself as much in advance as possible for the questioning, as your language abilities will be under scrutiny. Allowances will be made for the fact that you are a foreigner, but you must understand at least 95% of what is being talked about.

7

Working in France

LOOKING AT EMPLOYMENT CONTRACTS

The two principal forms of contract for legal employment in France are the fixed-term contract, and the indefinite contract.

- *Contrats à durée déterminée* (***CDD***) (fixed-term contracts). These can only be applied in certain circumstances, such as a sudden increase in business, or for seasonal work (e.g. at Christmas), or to cover pregnancy or sick leave, or to replace an employee in a position which is being cut, or for which the new employee cannot yet take up the permanent position. They may not exceed nine months, but can be renewed a maximum of twice. After two renewals, the company is obliged to offer you a permanent contract. the company is obliged to offer you a permanent contract. The new project-based contract planned in 2008 will have a 36-month limit, and is not renewable.

- *Contrats à durée indéterminée* (***CDI***) (indefinite contracts). These are the most common form of contract in France. They are also the most preferable form of contract for foreigners moving to France, as they will provide you with longer-term residency rights.

Remember that your *carte de séjour* will initially be limited to the length of your work contract.

There is no standard model for a contract in France, and surprisingly, there does not even have to be a written contract.

However, the following points should normally appear in a written contract:

♦ name and address of both parties
♦ job title and description of duties
♦ place of work
♦ rate of pay and bonuses, etc.
♦ hours of work per week
♦ notice period required by either employer or employee
♦ trial period, normally from one to three months, which can be renewed once by the employer (both sides can terminate without notice during this period). Senior managers may have six-month renewable trial periods
♦ holiday entitlement
♦ collective agreement (*convention collective*) applicable to the position or company (this is important as it may modify standard working practices).

Details of where employer social security payments are made and of retirement fund centres may also be included.

Your acceptance for a position is subject to a general medical examination (*visite médicale*) by the independent firm doctor and being declared *apte* for the position.

You may be in a position of either having to accept a part-time or fixed-term contract when you first arrive (e.g. you may have a working spouse via whom you will acquire residency and social security rights and access to the property market); or you may be offered a long fixed-term contract of up to nine months, which will provide you with a chance to sample French life (if you are an EU national).

For part-time and fixed-term contracts, the following elements must also be included in your contract by law:

Indefinite contract, part-time	Fixed-term contract, full-time
1. Your qualification(s). 2. Pay. 3. Number of hours **either** per week **or** per month **or** annually, depending on how your job is organised. 4. Method for changing work hours 5. Number of complementary hours which the employer can request. This is generally limited to one-tenth of the time stated in the contract, and cannot bring the total over the legal limits. NB: This is not overtime (**heures supplementaires**).	1. The **precise** reason for the CDD. This does not allow the employer to force you into a CDD because 'there is too much work at the moment', etc. 2. If you are replacing somebody, the name and qualifications of that person. 3. Date limit of the contract, renewal date and deadline for renewal. 4. Minimum period if no fixed date is defined, i.e. at least three months. 5. All of the general elements outlined left must also be included. 6. All of the elements outlined in the previous two cases are required by law.

Fig. 8. French employment contracts.

SALARIES

The minimum hourly wage in France is usually known by the initials *SMIC* (*Salaire Minimum Interprofessionnel de Croissance*). It is currently €8.44 before social security contributions, making a monthly salary *brut* (before social security deductions) of €1280.07, and €1005.37 after social security deductions, on the basis of a 35-hour week. The *SMIC* is linked to the Cost of Living Index, which is reviewed every six months. When this index rises by 2% or more, the level of the *SMIC* is raised. Pay reviews must take place once a year by law. However, salaries above the *SMIC* do not have to be increased, even if the cost of living has increased. One of the unintended side-effects of the 35-hour week legislation has been to create a total of six different *SMICs* in different industries.

Salaries are normally quoted in contracts as a total annual figure before social security deductions, but may also be quoted on a monthly or hourly basis. Salaries are usually paid monthly, on around the 26th day of each month. This is to allow the transfer of money into your account to settle bills due at the beginning of the month (notably rent). Payment is normally by standing order to your bank account, except for lower salaries, which may be paid by cheque.

Bonuses

Most French firms offer bonuses of a 13th month's pay (*13éme mois*). This is normally paid as one lump sum at one point in the year, usually in December. Bonuses are not, however, obligatory. Other companies offer profit-sharing schemes (*participation des salariés aux résultats de l'entreprise*), which is an obligation in companies with more than 100 employees. Both of these, and any similar benefits, are normally mentioned in your contract. You should note that pay rises are not obligatory. Stock-options in France are still a limited commodity for the happy few.

If you are employed under a CDD, you are entitled to an end of contract bonus (*indemnité de fin de contrat*). This is equivalent to 6% of your salary, and in addition to any other bonuses. CDD employees do not generally receive other bonuses.

WORKING HOURS

Your general working hours should be marked in your contract. *Cadres* only have a notional working week to some extent and are expected to work the hours that it takes to get the job done without extra pay. *Non-cadre* employees should also note that in certain large firms, such as law firms, the lawyers will be classed as *collaborateurs* as they are officially self-employed, so that even if an office has a staff of 50, only 20 may be employees. This could have a significant effect on the length of your working week.

In the year 2000, legislation introduced by the Socialist Employment Minister, Martine Aubry, reduced the French working week from 39 hours to 35 hours over five days, but paid at the same rates as the 39-hour week. This caused major problems for all employers, and the worst offender for applying the new scheme was France's biggest employer, the State itself. Company social contributions were reduced to encourage recruitment, but employees found themselves picking up the extra social contributions.

When a right-wing government was returned to power under Jean-Pierre Raffarin, they immediately set to work to try to gradually limit the impact of the 35-hour legislation, viewed by many as a major constraint on France's chances of prosperity. François Fillon (then Social Affairs Minister, now the Prime Minister), increased the number of authorised overtime hours from 130 to 180 (the former level), paid at a lower rate.

In January 2008, President Sarkozy announced he would like to see the end of the 35-hour week within the year, but later retracted the statement, saying that if there was no minimum working week then there would be no overtime, and the French would lose out financially. New legislation introduced by Sarkozy and Fillon makes overtime an attractive financial proposition once again for both employers and employees; and it will become possible for employers to buy back unused recuperation days (*RTT*s), one of the principal side-effects of the 35-hour legislation.

Given the wide variety of variations that can and are concocted from these systems, you should make polite enquiries about the working week which is applied by potential employers. The exact organisation of working hours is generally negotiated company by company, and sector by sector, by the unions and management. The traditional long French lunch is rarer in Paris than in the provinces, but Government offices will still observe a total shutdown from 12h00 to 14h00.

HOLIDAY ENTITLEMENT, LEAVE OF ABSENCE AND *RTT*

Holiday entitlement is gradually built up on the basis of 2.5 days per month worked, to a total of five weeks' annual paid leave. This does not include public holidays. Normally this is taken in segments over the course of the year – one week in winter and spring, and a longer break in the summer months. Some companies still observe the traditional total shut-down in August, when seemingly the whole of France and his wife head for the hills, the coast or the airports. Extra days off may be allowed under the terms of *conventions collectives* (see below) for close family bereavements, weddings, or moving house.

Any existing holiday arrangements are normally honoured when you join a company, but be careful to check this. The 'holiday calendar year' normally runs from 1 June to 31 May. Some companies allow you to carry over some holiday entitlement, but you must be careful not to lose holiday time not taken.

One important side effect of the 35-hour week legislation has been the introduction of the *RTT* (*récupération du temps de travail*). These are days off each month in order to bring employees into line with the principle of the 35 hour working week. The method used varies from company to company, some insisting on long weekends whilst others are strictly limiting the amount of accumulated *RTT*s which can be taken at any one time so as not to disrupt office time.

OTHER BENEFITS

Insurance and pensions

In addition to the regular contributions you will make to the state schemes, you will probably find deductions on your pay slips for health insurance via the *mutuelle* to which the firm subscribes, and to an additional pension scheme.

These contributions, if they are levied, are obligatory. However, they are very worthwhile, and will cover most if not all of the shortfall in state reimbursements for medical treatment. Ask your personnel department or your colleagues how to apply to the *mutuelle* for supplementary reimbursement. Unemployment insurance (*allocation d'assurance chômage*) is automatically included in your social security contributions.

In 2000, the government launched a long-awaited and much-criticised reform which offered savings plans (*épargnes*) including plans for what look suspiciously like pension funds. These exist in many shapes and forms, from simple savings plans topped up by employers to share schemes for employees.

Collective agreements

Conventions collectives, as they are known, exist in many varied professions. They cover everything from compassionate leave to the right to union membership, as well as health insurance rights, loans and rates of pay. They may substantially alter the general conditions of work, and you should note if mention is made of a *convention* in your contract.

Food and travel

Many French firms offer either a luncheon voucher scheme (*ticket restaurant*) or a canteen facility. In Paris, the firm will normally reimburse half of the cost of your *Carte Orange* (travel pass) each month. This will be paid directly with your salary and will be indicated on your pay slip (*fiche de paie*).

Professional training

French firms with more than ten employees are obliged to set aside 1.2% of their gross annual payroll for *formation continuée.* This may be used for advanced training, but also for basic language training. In both cases it could be of great interest to you. However, the allocation is entirely at the discretion of the employer.

WORKER REPRESENTATION TO THE MANAGEMENT

There are three levels of worker representation, all of which may apply in the same company. This depends upon the number of employees.

1. *Déléguées du personnel* (employee delegates) – any company with more than 10 employees must have *déléguées*. They present employee concerns to the management over individual and collective working conditions, job roles, wages and application of employment laws.

2. *Comité d'entreprise* (work council) – both the *déléguées du personnel* and the members of the *comité d'entreprise* are elected by the employees, by secret ballot, with representatives for the *cadres* and *non-cadres* in a company. There must be more than 50 employees on the payroll for a company to have a *comité d'entreprise*. The *comité* normally also includes a senior management member, and a member of the personnel department. The *comité* discusses in more general terms the same concerns as the *déléguées*. However, it should also be informed also of general firm policies before they are implemented, and is entitled to view the company accounts annually. The *comité* normally has a budget of its own linked to the number of employees, which is used to enable employees and their families to undertake cultural and leisure pursuits at reduced rates. You may also find that your *comité* has offers available on the purchase of new spectacles, etc.

Union membership

The presence of unions is most heavily felt in nationalised and heavy industry. It is rarer in the private sector, and under the terms of certain *conventions collectives*, simply not allowed.

The leading union federations are fragmented and divided along political lines. Most unions are either run by or closely related to political parties. The power of the unions, however, comes from their strongholds in the public sector, particularly transport. The principal unions (CGT, FO, CFDT) are vociferous in their opposition to privatisation, and in defence of their members' *acquis sociaux* (basically this means 'perks').

It often seems that scarcely a day goes by without some form of strike (*grève*, sometimes also called a *mouvement social*), protest, demonstration (*manifestation* or '*manif*' for short), or one-day stoppage taking place in France. Generally, the unwritten French commandment seems to be 'strike, and thou shalt receive'. However, the French generally prefer to regard such behaviour as another form of the liberty of expression.

DEALING WITH CONFLICTS AT WORK

If at all possible, it is best to try to contain a problem before it gets out of hand. Speak to the personnel department, and if they cannot or will not help, then try your *déléguée du personnel*.

Questions raised by the *déléguées* during their confidential meetings with the management are recorded and viewed annually by the work inspectors (*inspection du travail*), who have the right to pursue an enquiry if they think it necessary. This may also help you in more serious disciplinary cases, or worst of all, in the case of dismissal.

Companies are obliged by law to display the address of the nearest inspection du travail, and a telephone number. You can go to them for free confidential advice. You can also find their telephone numbers in the **Pages Jaunes** (*Yellow Pages*).

Dismissal

Firing someone in France is almost as difficult for the employer as it is for the employee to find a job in the first place! Nonetheless, it does happen. Strict procedures must be followed, including written warnings. If the procedures are not adhered to, you have a strong case for compensation, especially if you have not been paid your full share of holiday pay, etc.

The two grounds for dismissal are *faute grave* (gross misconduct or incompetence) or economic, in which case you are entitled to 'first refusal' if your job is re-created subsequently. If you intend to contest your dismissal, you can take your employer to an industrial tribunal (*conseil des prud'hommes*). Winning your case would entitle you to compensation but not reinstatement. Most companies prefer to settle out of court. Legal aid does exist in France (*l'aide juridictionnelle*) for those on low incomes, including the income of your spouse or partner. For further information, contact your local *mairie*.

LOOKING AT CROSS-CULTURAL ISSUES

One phrase that often creeps into both French office conversation and job advertisements is '*culture générale*', which can be translated literally. Quite apart from points such as hand-shaking on arriving and leaving, linguistic problems and so forth, one of the main differences between British and French culture is the emphasis you place upon the rôle and importance of your work.

One French immigrant manager in the UK said recently, '[In the UK] *the assumption is that you'll be more productive if you work longer hours but I doubt it. People in France put work in a different place in their lives. It's important, but not central. We take our lunch breaks, for example, and even at a business lunch nobody talks about business. You talk about the food because food is also an important part of life*'. (*The Observer*, 2 July, 2000). Whilst this is a little exaggerated, it is generally true.

Both the French and the British place vital importance on the development of the working relationship, but they have different ways of going about it. The British prefer to call you by your first name but the French prefer to talk to you about your last holidays. The French are also renowned for talking about their personal lives in the office and their business lives at home, whereas the British are perhaps too prone to compartmentalise their lives.

The dangers of riding rough-shod over local sensitivities have been firmly displayed in France in recent years. Foreigners will quickly notice that the French government and press are quick to turn foreign companies in France into the scapegoats when French companies adopt new or unpopular courses of action. All the more reason, therefore, to take cultural sensitivity seriously.

The French are not keen, however, on out-of-office socialising such as you might find in the UK or USA, and the stalwarts of the local bar or office softball team are normally Anglo-Saxons. This reflects the fact that whilst the British in particular are considered too independent and individualistic in their professional practices, the French are once again notoriously individualistic in their private lives and private work domains. This difference might be summed up as the following:

French = obedient and conformist in public life, policy and method, but highly individual in private.

British = generally conformist but still highly individual in public life, but greater team spirit in private.

PAYING TAX IN FRANCE

> **The general advice given in this section is based on information available at the time of writing. If you have any doubt over your tax liability in France, you should seek professional advice.**

You are liable for tax in France if you reside more than 183 days in France in any one calendar year. A double taxation agreement between France and the UK prevents those who still have tax liabilities in the UK from being taxed twice on the same element of income. This is the *Convention for the Avoidance of Double Taxation and the Prevention of Fiscal Evasion with respect to Taxes on Income.*

If you do continue to pay tax in your home country (e.g. in the UK where you are taxed at source), then if you have taxable income you should declare the amount of tax you have paid and from what source of income, on your French tax declaration. **Take professional advice on this topic**, as some sources of revenue are more highly taxed in one country than in France and vice versa. You might therefore find yourself owing the French tax service an additional sum as they will consider you have not fully acquitted your obligations.

A similar double-taxation agreement exists between France and the USA. US citizens are required to declare their earnings throughout the world on their Federal income tax returns, and living outside the USA does not remove your obligation to file a tax return. However, living overseas can lead to deductions, exclusions and credits. The US Embassy in Paris offers advice on tax matters at the IRS office at 2, avenue Gabriel, 75008 from 09h00–12h00. You can call 01 43 12 25 55 from 09h00 to 15h30 (closed 12h00 to 13h30) or fax to 01 43 12 23 03, or e-mail: irs.paris@irs.gov. Information can also be found on the embassy website **www.amb-usa.fr** or the IRS website **www.irs.ustreas.gov.**

Making your declaration

Income tax (*impôt sur le revenu*) is paid in arrears. You will be required to complete a tax declaration, sent directly to your home in late April or early May each year. This will be for the preceding tax year, which in France runs from 1 January to 31 December. If you send your declaration in late, you risk a fine equivalent to an extra 10% of your tax bill.

The French Government now heavily encourages on-line tax declarations, and there is even a €20 tax deduction incentive for an on-line declaration. Details of how to complete the formalities will be supplied with your declaration. The declaration deadline is normally the end of May, if you send a paper tax return. An extra delay is allowed for on-line tax declarations. However, you should check carefully the date limit printed on your form. The Government has also now tried to simplify the system by including salary details which they have received from your employers, and also personal details. You need to check that these details are correct, and you can contest and correct any errors. In addition, you need to add details which may lead to tax deductions. Once you have made your on-line declaration, you do not need to send a paper version of the document. You must, however, keep all paper records and certificates available to justify your claim to tax deductions. These may be required if the Tax Office decide to investigate your claims. If you do correspond by post with Tax Offices, it is wise to use the registered postal system, a *lettre recommandée avec avis de reception.*

If you do not reach your tax threshold by the end of the calendar year (e.g. you start work in September), you will be exempted from income tax for your first year in France. However, you must prepare yourself for your first tax bill when it does arrive, as you will be required to pay this in one lump sum. This is normally in about October or November, and is roughly equivalent to one month's salary. It is advisable to open a deposit account at the bank to prepare for this.

After the first lump sum payment, you will have the choice of paying monthly (*mensuelle*), quarterly (*trimestrielle*), or annually (in one lump sum). You will also have the chance of paying by standing order, which the tax office will regulate, or by cheque. Paperless payments (on-line or by standing order) will earn you another €20 tax deduction.

The new tax demand will come into effect in January each year. In effect, you will be paying tax each year on the basis of your earnings two years previous to the current calendar year. For example, in May 2008, you declare your revenue for 1 January to 31 December 2007. In the summer or early autumn of 2008, you will receive a new *avis d'imposition*, based on the 2007 total, which will take effect in January 2009. If you have opted to pay monthly, your payments will be automatically adjusted over the last few months of the year to take into consideration your new monthly bill.

It is important to bear in mind when you leave France that you will therefore still have income tax to pay in France for a limited period after your departure. As and when you do leave France, you should visit the tax office to 'sign off' their registers, and make the appropriate arrangements.

Working out your declaration

1. On your December payslip for the year ending before the March declaration date (i.e. December 2007 for the May 2008 declaration), you will see a figure supplied by your employer marked '*Net imposable*'. This is the sum total to declare for the period you have been employed by this company. If you change employers during the year, you will need to take your December payslip figure and the same figure mentioned on your final payslip from your previous employer(s), and add all of these together.

2. Make sure you check all **personal details** recorded on your declaration, e.g. marital status, number of children, etc. This will determine the number of '**parts**' you will have and the attendant reductions.

3. If you have savings accounts or shares at the **bank**, they should supply you with a statement ready prepared stating what you owe and in which category on the form this belongs. Certain savings accounts are tax exempt as long as you keep to the terms of the account.

4. If you receive **shares** as part of your salary remuneration, you will be taxed not only on the dividends from the shares but also on the value of the shares at the date you received them. For stock-options, you must take professional advice.

5. If you make **donations** to a church or charitable association that is registered under *la loi 1901*, they can issue you with a tax receipt which will lead to a 50% rebate on the value of

your donation(s). These can be accumulated from several different charities.

Tax bands in France

In 2002 new tax bands came into force which saw tax rates come down for all tax payers, with the lower paid benefiting most. The rate went down by 5%, with a further 1% reduction planned in 2003. In total, if President Chirac's election promises are fulfilled, income tax will come down by 30% between 2002–2007. In 2006, the number of tax bands was reduced from seven to five. A variety of rebates and exemptions are granted on gross income which moderate the rate of taxation. Most salaried workers receive not only the standard deduction of 10% but also a further deduction of 20%. The lowest paid category must complete a tax return, and will almost certainly be eligible for a reimbursement of the CSG (one of the social contribution payments deducted from your monthly salary). Certain building works will also give you tax breaks; and if you have an adult child under a certain age living at home, they can be listed on your declaration if they are studying and you are paying for their general upkeep.

Reducing your tax burden

Generally, families are favoured by the French tax system. *Le quotient familial* means that taxable income is divided into units reflecting family status. Hence a single person is taxed on their whole income. A married couple are considered as two units, and their joint income will be divided by two. The first two children each count as a half-unit, and each additional child is counted as a full unit. Couples who sign a PACS receive the same tax status as a married couple two years after the signature of their PACS.

Amount declared in Euros	Current tax rates
Up to 5.687	0%
5.688 to 11.344	5.5%
11.344 to 25.195	14%
25.195 to 67.546	30%
More than 67.546	40%

Fig. 9. Tax rates.

Tax relief for families who employ (legally) a home help (*aide à domicile*) is now 50% of expenditure up to €10,000 (salaries and social charges included). The employees concerned can be cleaners, child-minders, tutors, or helpers for the disabled or elderly. It can be combined with a number of other advantages. Au pairs, music teachers and nurses are not covered. If your child attends a local crèche for which you will pay, you can accumulate this benefit with the *réduction pour garde de jeunes enfants à l'extérieur du domicile*, which is equivalent to 25% of your expenditure up to €2300 per child.

Wealth tax

Wealth tax (*impôt de solidarité sur la fortune* or *ISF*) must be paid by both French residents and non-French residents who have assets in France of more than a certain value. Currently this figure is set at assets of €760,000 and more. Tax rates are from 0.55% of the net value of the assets concerned in the first category (€760,000 – 1,220,000), to 1.8% of the net value for assets in excess of €15,810,000s.

Non-resident foreigners who are subject to this tax include those who have their family home or main residence in France; those who exercise their principal professional activity, including a salaried activity in France; and those who have their 'economic centre of interest' in France.

One of the first financial reforms that President Sarkozy undertook was to limit the impact of Wealth Tax. A new *Bouclier Fiscal* (fiscal shield) has been introduced which limits the total tax burden to 50%, including direct taxation at 60%, the ISF, the social contributions (CSG and CRDS), and property taxes. The Fillon Government has also introduced ISF tax breaks for investments in small- and medium-sized company start-ups; and increased the automatic tax reduction from 20% to 30% for the value of your principal residence. The major increase in property values in recent years has been one of the main causes in the increase in the number of people subject to the ISF. On the other hand, exonerations for stock options have been removed, and the revenue raised is intended to contribute to balancing the Social Security budget (which will require a lot of stock options to be distributed in France!).

Finding help on taxes

Most banks and the vast majority of newspapers and journals will publish free guides in some shape or form when tax declaration time comes around. The Finance Ministry offer a number of possibilities to help you complete your declaration: either by telephone on 08 36 67 10 10, or at **www.impot.gouv.fr**. You can order tax forms by Internet, and even make a declaration on line (although they still need hard copy in any case) on **www.minefi.gouv.fr/services/formulaires**. In the weeks leading up the declaration date-limit, you can also ask for help at your tax office, and also now in many local *mairies*. In the UK, the Inland Revenue EC unit can be contacted at Room 520, West Wing, Somerset House, London WC2 1LB. One of the best French-only websites to consult for in-depth up-to-date advice is **www.francetransactions.com**.

UNEMPLOYMENT IN FRANCE

Unemployment is dealt with by two agencies in France. The *ANPE (Agence Nationale pour l'Emploi)*, (**www.anpe.fr**) is the local job centre, where you must be registered if you are out of work and seeking to claim unemployment benefit. The **ASSEDIC** (**www.assedic.fr**) is the agency which actually pays you unemployment benefit, if you qualify.

Job seekers from Britain

You have the right to seek work in France for three months before you will have officially 'outstayed your welcome'. During that three-month period, if you are registered as unemployed in your home country for at least four weeks, you will retain your UK right to receive job seekers' allowance at British rates via the French unemployment service benefit service, the *ASSEDIC*. However, **this can take up to three months to be delivered by the French authorities.** In order to obtain your benefits, you need to complete and bring with you two EU social security forms:

◆ **The E303** – you must present this at your local **ANPE within seven days of your arrival**. You must also register at the ANPE at the same time.

◆ **The EHIC** – This will provide you with medical cover for the three-month period during which you are entitled to stay in France and seek work. To establish your health rights during this period, contact your local *CPAM (Caisse Primaire d'Assurance Maladie* – the local health authority), and ask for details of how to contact the nearest *Service des Relations International*.

Unemployment rights for French residents

If you are employed in France and are unfortunate enough to lose your job, you will start to appreciate the heavy social charges that you paid when you were in employment.

Qualifying for unemployment benefit

1. If you resign without good reason, are dismissed for a *faute grave* (serious misconduct) or refuse a suitable job offer, you will be refused unemployment benefit on the grounds that you do not wish to work.

2. If you resign in order to set up your own business, from 1 July 2001 a new law to encourage entrepreneurs will allow for resignations if you intend creating or taking over a business. If that business fails, a new law already in place since January 2001 now provides unemployment benefit for those who tried and failed, as long as they enrol at the *ANPE* within three years of the end of their last contract.

3. To qualify, you must have worked at least three months in the last year, and for two of the three last years. You must also be under 60.

4. You must register at the local *ANPE*, and be both capable of work and actively seeking employment.

The *allocation d'assurance chômage* (unemployment benefit) you receive depends upon how much you have paid into the system and over what period of time – i.e. if you have been working for four years on an average wage, you will receive more than if you have been working on the minimum wage for the last two years. Payments may take some time to come through initially, but are back-dated. Your *allocation* will diminish with time, as you effectively use up the fund you have created during the time you were employed by your and your former employer's contributions. After two years, your situation will be re-assessed and you will receive a reduced *allocation*. The next stage after that, known as the *RMI*, is the very basic minimum aid which is given out. It is not currently available to anybody under the age of 25. Once that has been exhausted, you are not entitled to any further benefit.

You must be careful to keep copies of job searches and applications during the time that you are *en chômage* (unemployed). This will be required by the *ASSEDIC* and the *ANPE* to justify your benefit payments.

The unions, government and *MEDEF* (the 'social partners' or *partenaires sociaux*) have sought to find a new plan for returning the unemployed to employment. The agreed system, which came into force on 1 January 2001, has been shunned by the largest and most hard-line unions, and was at first rejected by the Jospin government. The new *plan d'aide au retour à l'emploi* (*PARE*) works as follows:

◆ When you sign on, you will also sign a *PARE* and receive a fixed payment.

◆ The *PARE* contains: a reminder of your rights and obligations and those of the *ASSEDIC*; your signature of a Personal Action Plan (PAP); agreement to undergo an examination of your professional competencies if required.

◆ The PAP: determines suitable categories of employment in order to orientate your search; decides upon any training required to get you back to work.

◆ The PAP is activated. If after six months you have refused job offers, you can be reprimanded, lose your payments temporarily or permanently, or even be struck off the register of benefits altogether.

◆ After 12 months if you have still not found a job, you will be re-categorised and sent for training. An employer who takes you on will receive fiscal benefits for employing a long-term job-seeker, so your chances of employment are higher but your chances of a good salary are probably lower.

Help for the unemployed

Your social security rights, if they are already established, will remain intact throughout the time that you continue to receive unemployment benefits. Even after you have used up the right to the *RMI*, you will have social security rights under the French system for one further year.

The *service social* at your local *mairie* also has a fund at its disposal to help in cases of difficulty and emergency, e.g. the electricity is about to be cut off. The amount of aid available depends entirely on your local *mairie*, and may only be a token contribution towards clearing your debts.

The *ANPE* offers financial assistance in certain circumstances for travelling expenses incurred to attend interviews, and also for those who accept jobs far from their homes. If you are unemployed and you are forced to move to take up a new position, the *ANPE* also offers limited financial assistance for moving costs.

Redundancy due to economic cut-backs

If you are made redundant due to cut-backs in the firm, you will have 'first refusal' for your job should it be re-created subsequently. In terms of your financial situation, you can also request a *convention conversion* which will allow you to draw 80% of your final salary for six months. These conventions allow you to seek a job either in the same sector or a similar sector, as long as you have been employed by your previous firm for at least two years. It involves working closely with the *ANPE* training services, and does not stop you from accepting a new position if you find one during the six-month period.

For further details of the *convention conversion* speak to the *ANPE* or check their website, which offers full details of what is offered and what is involved at **www.anpe.fr**.

FINDING OUT MORE

Almost every topic covered in this chapter relates to a French government department. The quickest and easiest way to find out more is to go to **www.service-public.fr**, chose the appropriate ministry (social security, employment, finance), and refer to the appropriate government website. Most of these are only in French, but if you click on the English selection first, you will quickly be able to find which sites are bilingual.

British citizens moving abroad should also consult the Department of Work and Pensions website, and especially the on-line version of the SA29 leaflet *Your social security insurance, benefits and healthcare rights in the European Economic Area*, **www.dwp.gov.uk/international/sa29**. This is an indispensable guide for all health and benefits related topics.

8

Self-employment and Student Employment

Being your own boss in France is not as easy – or as cheap – as you might think it ought to be. Jean-Pierre Raffarin, who was Prime Minister from 2002 until 2005, was previously Minister for Small and Medium-Sized Business (*PMEs*), and professed a desire to create a France of entrepreneurs. In 2002 he announced a series of new measures to try to ease the process of creating your own business in France.

Nonetheless, becoming either a *travailleur indépendant*, a *professionel non salarié*, or a member of a *profession libérale*, (all of which are in fact the same thing), a *commerçant* (independent shopkeeper) or an *artisan* (craftsman) still involves certain basic and important steps at the outset to avoid pitfalls and nasty shocks.

PLANNING YOUR BUSINESS

There is a difference made in France between what might be termed 'active' and 'reactive' business creations. 'Active' business creations could be defined as an employee who decides to quit their job to start a new business, taking a considerable risk in the process. Previously the self-employed were left notoriously socially unprotected in a land of great social protection. Entrepreneurs are now, however, being encouraged, and one of the ways of doing this is to offer them protection should their business fail.

'Reactive' business creations could be defined as persons who are spurred into creating their own business by forced unemployment. They have not chosen their situation, but the state is willing to guarantee them a certain level of protection and to offer some form of financial aid to help them back to a reasonable level of prosperity. Although many foreigners may feel that they fall into the category of forced inactivity because they have moved to France with their employed spouses, it is unlikely that the state authorities would accept applications for state aid from individual foreigners who have not already been working in France and contributed to social security and unemployment funds.

Professional restrictions

Certain professions – most notably lawyers and doctors, but also accountants and architects, for example – may not simply open up their own business in France without the agreement of the appropriate professional association. Contact your own professional association before moving to France to find out if you fall into one of these categories.

You should also note that certain professions – accountants, lawyers, and doctors included – are not allowed to advertise their services under French advertising law. Any breach of this law can have very serious consequences. This may affect your ability to establish your own practice immediately upon arrival. Even if your natural instinct is to work independently, you need to establish a good reputation and a client base to make a success of your business. If you cannot advertise directly, you need to think carefully about how you are going to do this. To start with, the simplest and easiest option is to use somebody else's client base!

Finally you need to be sure that you have the correct qualifications to operate professionally in France. This is particularly true for English teachers. You must hold one of the official teaching certificates for teaching English as a foreign language (TEFL). Courses for these certificates are offered very widely in Paris. Without one of these certificates, you will be hindering yourself considerably, in a very crowded market.

BUDGETING FOR YOUR BUSINESS

For the first two years after establishing your business, you will be assessed for social charges on the basis of set figures for health insurance, pensions and family allowance contributions. Your *CSG (contribution sociale généralisée)* and *RDS (recouvrement de la dette sociale)* payments are also included in the set figures for the first two years of operating.

In the third year of operating, you will suddenly find that you are facing higher social charges, and a significant separate CSG and RDS contribution. Since your contributions are based on your net profit from the previous two years, you may find yourself heavily out of pocket if you do suffer a sudden downturn in business.

You must take all of these factors into account when you are preparing your business plan as you search for funds for your new business. You must also bear this in mind even if you do not intend seeking funds because you are not intending to hire premises, etc, and you only intend to stick to a small-scale one-person independent operation.

OBTAINING FUNDING FOR YOUR BUSINESS

There are a number of different means of seeking funding now available to entrepreneurs in France. All of these come with different restrictions and requirements, but all also require you to put together a solid business plan.

The variety of loans also distinguishes between the 'active' and 'reactive' categories explained above. None of the loans listed below appear to be mutually exclusive, and so it may be possible to accumulate loans from different sources providing you meet the criteria and provide a solid business plan to the loan agencies concerned.

Loans more appropriate for 'active' business start-ups

- *Le prêt à la creation de la enterprise (PCE)* – these loans are for businesses less than three years old. The loans range from €2,000 to €7,000, for a five-year period, for start-up expenses such as publicity and general commercial requirements. A bank loan is also required to access this loan. More details can be found on **www.Oseo.fr**.

- *Réseau Entreprendre* – backing projects likely to create at least 13 jobs in five years, and providing interest-free loans repayable over five years. The full list of the 18 networks can be found on **www.réseau.entreprendre.org**.

- **Business Angels** – the Angels have landed in France, and operate in much the same way as the *Réseau Entreprendre*. Details of how to contact Business Angels in France can be found on **www.businessangels.com** and on **www.pme.gouv.fr**, the website of the Ministry for Small and Medium Sized Companies (*Petits et Moyen Entreprises*).

- **Capital risk investors** – a useful starting point is *AFIC* (*Association Française des Investisseurs en Capital*), tél. 01 47 20 99 09, **www.afic.asso.fr** , and *UNICER* (*Union des Sociétés de Capital Risque de Proximité*), tél. 03 20 68 35 86, **www.unicer.asso.fr** (see also comments below).

Loans aimed at 'reactive' business start-ups

- *ADIE (l'Association pour le Droit à l'initiative économique)* – a network of local associations providing loans up to €10,000. Limited to the unemployed, and/or those with difficulty in obtaining bank loans. Tél. 0800 800 566, or contact **www.adie.org**.

- *Le Dispositif Eden* – destined for the young unemployed (age limits 18–26), but now also for the over-50 age group thanks to the Raffarin reforms, this action plan includes exemption from payment of social charges for the first 12 months, a set of free advice session 'vouchers' with designated specialists (*chéquiers-conseils*) either just before you launch your business or in the 12 months following the start-up; and loans of up to €6,098 for one-person operations, up to €9,145 for multi-partner projects, and €76,225 for a group of former employees who buy up their former company should it shut down. For further details, consult the website of *L'Agence pour la Création d'Entreprise*, **www.apce.com**. This is a multi-lingual website with some sections in English.

- *Fonds France Active (FFA)* – aimed at the same public as the *ADIE*, the *FFA* will guarantee limited bank loans under certain conditions specified on their website. See **www.franceactive.org** for current details.

Other sources

♦ **Admical** – the website **www.admical.org** provides a list of those company foundations which also provide business start-up funds as well as charitable or arts sponsorship.

♦ **Former employers** – your future ex-employer can make you a loan at a reduced rate and turn this into a company tax break by deducting up to half the amount loaned as an aid to a former employee seeking to create their own business.

♦ *Fonds de Garantie à l'initiative des Femmes (FGIF)* – acts rather like the *FFA* by standing guarantee for loans from two to seven years, for up to €27,000 for female business entrepreneurs. More details, including contact details for applications, can be found on **www.franceactive.org**.

♦ *Fonds d'Investissement de Proximité (FIP)* – this is one of the new Raffarin reforms. The idea is to seek out capital risk investors from within your own circle of friends and family. These investors will each receive a tax reduction of 25% of the amount invested, up to a limit of €10,000 for a single person or €20,000 for a couple.

♦ **Tax breaks** are also offered to investors in companies that are not registered on the Stock Exchange (*non cotée*). This tax break is equivalent to 25% of the sum invested, within an investment limit of €12,000 for a single person, and €24,000 for a couple. Tax payers who are subject to the Wealth Tax (*ISF*) also now have the opportunity to access a 50% tax break on a further business creation investment, for an amount up to €10,000.

When you are planning your business, take professional advice before counting on using any of these measures. They all naturally have restrictions as well as advantages.

TAKING THE FIRST STEPS

Your first steps fall into two different categories: administrative and financial. Some steps are optional but highly advisable, others are obligatory. The administrative steps will mainly be taken care of for you once you have taken the initial step of registering your business. However, these are important steps as they are not only the most costly, but are almost all linked to providing you and your dependents with social protection including healthcare and pensions.

Visiting the local tax office

This is not an obligation, but a wise precautionary measure. The tax inspector (*inspecteur des impôts*) will be able to tell you if you can open up your business as a self-employed person. They will also set out your financial obligations, including those for VAT (known as *TVA* in France).

Registering your new business

You must register your new business with the appropriate authorities, including the *Union de Recouvrement des Cotisations de Sécurité Sociale et d'Allocations Familiales*, more commonly and easily known as *URSSAF*. To register your business, contact the local *Centre de Formalités des Entreprises (CFE)*. Check the website **www.urssaf.fr** to find your nearest office.

The *Chambre de Commerce et de l'Industrie de Paris (CCIP)* also offers CFE facilities. For further details see **www.ccip.fr**, and the bilingual site **www.parisdeveloppement.com**. Their **Foreign Investment Department and Paris Development Agency** with information in English and business creation information is at 2 rue de Viarmes, 75001 Paris (tél. 01 55 65 33 93, fax 01 55 65 33 90). One of the new Raffarin reforms has been to establish an on-line CFE facility via the *Agence pour la Création de l'Emploi*, **www.apce.com**.

Another Raffarin reform has been to extend the period of time during which you can declare your business as based in your home, from two years to five years. Over 3,000 French companies now have 'head offices' (*siège social*) outside France in order to pay lower social charges. Many of these are based in the UK. Whilst this complies with EU law, the French Ministry of Finance has sought to fight back legally against the evasion of French social charges. No matter where the 'head office' of the company is, it is local French law which applies, just as it will be French services that you draw upon to support you and your dependents.

To avoid paying excess social charges (which are very heavy in any case), the best time to register your new business is at the beginning of a quarterly period (e.g. 1 April). Once you have made the initial *déclaration du début d'activité non salariée* (un-waged activity), the *CFE* will automatically undertake the next steps for you. These are:

1. The *déclaration d'existence* to the tax inspector, and the enrolment for the *taxe professionnelle*.

2. Your enrolment at the *Caisse d'Allocations Familiales* (family allowance centre), run by *URSSAF* itself.

3. Your enrolment at the *Caisse d'Assurance Maladie des Professions Libérales* (local health authority for non-salaried professions). They will offer you a choice of compulsory medical insurance schemes, of which the largest is the Mutuelle de Mans, (see their website **www.mma.fr** for local contact details).

4. Your enrolment at the *Caisse d'Assurance Vieillesse* (for pensions). Most professions have their own individual *caisse*. However, if you do not fall into an established category, you will be enrolled at CIPAV, 21 rue de Berri, 75403 Paris, Cedex 08, tél. 01 44 95 68 20.

5. Your registration at *INSEE* is the national statistical office. Your registration here acts as a form of business registration, which will lead to your business receiving the necessary SIREN and SIRET numbers.

Once you have completed this process, you will receive a *récépissé de création d'entreprise*, valid for one month. Under the new Raffarin reforms, this will include your definitive SIREN and SIRET numbers, which will allow you to proceed immediately with your banking matters.

PROTECTING YOURSELF IN CASE YOUR BUSINESS FAILS

Two extremely important new changes to social legislation became law in 2001. For precise details, enquire at your *CFE* and at the *ASSEDIC* (who actually pay out unemployment benefit), **www.assedic.fr**. Basically, for the first time they provide continued limited unemployment rights for those who choose to enter self-employment, changing the traditional French approach that resigning your job also meant resigning your right to unemployment benefit.

◆ Every entrepreneur can enrol for unemployment support as long as it is within 36 months of the end of your contract, prior to the creation of your business. This includes all business entrepreneurs, including those who have not managed to achieve financing for their start-ups.

◆ Entrepreneurs who resign from their existing paid contractual employment to start up their own business will have the same rights. The rules regarding validating that your resignation was for the right reason have not yet been defined.

Both of these changes clearly only affect those people who have already been employed in France and have contributed to the French social security system, and so are 'activating' the 'points' they have acquired under the system. As these are new rules, it remains to be seen whether it would eventually be possible to transfer to France rights acquired in other EU countries under their social security schemes, although this should be a theoretical possibility.

One other advantage which it is possible for employees to apply for, but which is at the discretion of their employers, is the *congé de création d'entreprise* for employees who have worked at least 36 months (not necessarily consecutively) in the same firm. Further details can be found on the employment ministry website, **www.travail.gouv.fr**.

MAKING THE RIGHT FINANCIAL CHOICES

◆ **Registering for** *TVA* – this is an optional step, which you can take at your tax office. Companies will expect you to charge them *TVA* (VAT in the UK), and you will be able to reclaim *TVA* on purchases if you are registered. On the other hand, you are not obliged to charge *TVA* to individuals – hence you can be more competitive in your pricing policy. You should discuss the pros and cons of this choice with the tax inspector when you first visit the tax office.

◆ **Joining an *association agréée*** – this is another optional step to take, but very worthwhile. An *association agréée* offers not only advice and support, but can also offer an important reduction (*abattement fiscal*) in your tax burden. Conditions of membership are simply falling in to one of the self-employed categories, conforming to basic accounting rules and paying an annual membership fee of around €150. This *abattement fiscal* is achieved by having your annual accounts checked and counter-signed by the association before your tax declaration. In effect, it is worth 20% of your profit figure, as you will only be assessed on 80% of your profit (if it is less than €106,900) by the tax authorities if your accounts have been counter-signed by an association.

◆ **Making banking arrangements** – you must have separate bank accounts for private and business accounts. If a bank is aware that one of your accounts is being used for business purposes, you may be required to pay higher bank charges. If necessary, to avoid these higher charges, open your business and personal accounts at different banks.

◆ **Accounting** – you must keep correct accounts which conform to basic French accounting procedures. The easiest way to do this if you already have a computer is to buy an inexpensive personal computer program, which will eventually correspond to the standard French tax form (number 2035).

WORKING ALONE OR IN PARTNERSHIP

One consideration you may wish to make is whether to be truly *indépendent* or to work with a business partner (*associé*). This is a complex issue which requires professional advice, as certain investment and tax issues might favour a 'company' partnership of self-employed workers. Certain clients may also prefer the apparent security of dealing with a company rather than an individual. Amongst the options to explore are:

◆ Forming a company without any partners, *une entreprise unipersonnelle à responsabilité limitée* (or *EURL*).This is an alternative to being a *travailleur indépendent*. The minimum capital for an EURL has been reduced by the Raffarin reforms from €7,500 to €1. However, bear in mind that the smaller your declared capital, the more difficulties you might encounter with your suppliers.

◆ The 'means of business' – e.g. office premises, furniture, etc. – can be placed in common ownership, whilst each professionel libéral maintains their own clientele. There are several ways of achieving this, for which you should seek professional advice (e.g. from an *association agréée*).

◆ Associations in France, which are controlled by the law of 1901, can also be of use in making certain economies, as can *Groupement d'Intérêts Economique* (*GIE*). It costs nothing to establish an *association 1901*, but in general they are designed to be non-profit making. Any profit will be taxed on the basis of company tax rates. An *association 1901* is not allowed to distribute profits amongst its members. Once again, seek professional advice on this point.

None of these steps should be taken without professional advice. A good *association agréé* should be able to put you in contact with the appropriate professionals to discuss the best way forward.

MULTIPLE EMPLOYMENT

Pluriactivité, as it is known in France, has a number of important implications, which make it a generally unproductive option. This is principally because of the level of social charges involved.

1. **Several self-employed activities** – this will affect which *caisse d'assurance maladie* and which *caisse de vieillesse* you contribute to. If you have chosen to advise a public authority, you contribute to their funds. If you belong to a profession which has an 'order' (e.g. doctors or lawyers), you will contribute to their funds. In other cases, you have a fairly free choice according to the areas of activity.

2. **A self-employed activity and a non-waged, '*non-libéral'* activity** – you will be obliged to contribute to the same funds as above for the activity which brings you the highest revenue.

3. **Self-employment and paid employment** – one of the new Raffarin reforms has been specifically aimed at this category. For the first year, an entrepreneur who remains in salaried employment will only have to pay social charges on the salaried activity. After the first year, you will be obliged to make payments to the *caisse de vieillesse* in both systems, even if your self-employment is a subsidiary activity. However, you will have rights under both systems. The same applies for the *caisse d'assurance maladie*. But only those services and rights offered by the *caisse* of your *principal* activity will be available to you.

MAKING THE FINAL DECISION

If you are considering self-employment in France, you are probably already aware of the attractions of such a choice, most notably the entrepreneur's freedom of action. However, listed below are the three main considerations you must make before taking the plunge.

♦ **Professional restrictions** – Are you allowed to practise in France, and how will you build up your clientele if you are not allowed to advertise? Do you have the right qualifications to succeed in the French market?

♦ **Heavy social charges** – on average, an employee costs a company in total double what they receive in their bank account each month. Being your own boss means paying the boss's share of the bill too. French social charges are amongst the highest in Europe. Worse still is the fact that after two years of operating, you are assessed on your profit figure two years ago. If your sales suddenly drop, your difficulties will be increased by social charges which could rise to as much as 90% of your current revenue.

♦ **Employment versus self-employment** – you should also bear in mind that a period of one or two years of paid employment in France will bring with it a considerable number of benefits and safeguards when you do decide to launch your own business. These include unemployment protection but also market knowledge, professional contacts and a stronger financial position and credit rating.

FINDING OUT MORE ABOUT SETTING UP A BUSINESS

- **American Embassy** (US Foreign Commercial Service), 2 avenue Gabriel, 75008 Paris, tél. 01 43 12 25 32, fax 01 43 12 21 72, **www.amb-usa.fr**.

- **American Chamber of Commerce**, 156 boulevard Haussman, 75008 Paris, tél. 01 56 43 45 67, fax 01 56 43 45 60, **www.amchamfrance.com**.

- **Australian Business in Europe**, 4 rue Jean Rey, 75015 Paris, tél. 01 40 59 34 92 / 33 00, **www.abie-france.net**.

- **British Embassy Commercial Section**, 35 rue du Faubourg St Honoré, 75008 Paris, tél. 01 44 51 31 00, fax 01 44 51 34 01, **www.britishembassy.gov.uk/france**.

- **Franco-British Chamber of Commerce**, 31 rue Boissy d'Anglas, 75008 Paris, tél. 01 53 30 81 30, fax 01 53 30 81 35, email: fbcci@fbcci.com, **www.francobritishchamber.com**.

- **French Embassy in London**, Economic and Commercial Section, 21/24 Grosvenor Place, London SW1X 7HU, tel. 0207 235 7080, fax: 0207 235 8598. See the separate website **www.invest-in-france.org/UK** for advice and help in English if you are considering setting up a business in France.

- *Greffe du Tribunal de Commerce de Paris*, **www.greffe-tc-paris.fr** – the Commercial Court of Paris responsible for company registrations offers an excellent bilingual site explaining what you need to do, where, how and when.

- **OSEO**: **www.oseo.fr** – government agency for the promotion of small- and medium-sized companies, offering nationwide coverage and practical and financial support.

- *APCE (Agence pour la Création d'Entreprise)*, the official government agency to aid entrepreneurs in France and to encourage business start-ups, **www.apce.com.**

- **Paris Chamber of Commerce and Industry**, 2 rue de Viarmes, 75040 Paris, Cedex 1, tél. 01 45 08 36 00, fax 01 45 08 35 80, **www.ccip.fr**. Publications in English available.

- *Chambre de Commerce Française de Grande-Bretagne*, 21 Dartmouth Street, London SW1H 9BP, tel: 0207 304 4040, fax: 0207 304 7034, email: mail@ccfgb.co.uk, **www.ccfgb.co.uk**. Publishes a guide in English on setting up small business in France.

- **Internet businesses: AFA** (*Association des Fournisseurs d'Accès à des services en ligne et à l'internet*), **www.afa-france.com**; **3SCI** (*Syndicat des Sociétés de Services et des Conseils en Informatique*), tél. 01 47 07 02 99.

- The French Government web directory is at **www.service-public.fr**. See **www.pme.gouv.fr** for the website of the small and medium-sized business ministry's website.

WORKING WHILE YOU ARE STUDYING IN FRANCE

Students are amongst the most sought-after workers on the current French job market and in the new working environment of France. Government restrictions limit the right to work for both student French nationals and foreign students alike. (See **www.campusfrance.org**, in English.) Foreign students normally find that a command of English and another foreign language will give them a cutting edge over competitors.

Every situation is different, so it is hard to generalise in this field of work. But the main points to note are:

- **Hotels and restaurants** – if you can stick the smell and the pace, you will have a good chance of finding a position in this industry. Some 51% of the employees of the 'Quick' chain of restaurants and up to 65% of employees at Pizza Hut are students with CDI (fixed-term) contracts. This contract status is a handy extra when it comes to applying for apartment rentals. The downside is that the fast food environment is hard, and not the most desirable CV material. The hotel industry is suffering from a lack of good staff.

- **Working with temporary agencies** – working as an *intérimaire* has its advantages as well as its pitfalls. The work on offer will to some extent depend upon your abilities as well as what the agencies have to offer. But at least if you find that you really cannot bear where you are working, you know that you can ask your agency to place you somewhere else.

- **Call centres** – although the English term has crept into the French language, these are officially known as *centres d'appels*. Advertisements regarding *télémarketing* or seeking *téléopérateurs* or *téléacteurs* will mostly involve working for a call centre. The number of such centres has exploded in recent years. A limited product training is normally provided, but conditions and contracts vary greatly. You may be offered a *contrat vacataire*, which is designed to allow an employer to take on temporary workers to complete a particular project, e.g. launching a new product which requires telephone canvassing or a user hotline. These contracts are pretty basic and swiftly ended by the employer as they please, and pay may be by the hour and/or linked to the number of calls you deal with. It should be noted that *contrats vacataires* do not contribute towards securing residence rights for new arrivals.

- **Working on the Internet** – this is the *luxe* of student employment. You need to be appropriately educated and up to pace to make it in this world, but if you are, this is where the money is for students: longer contracts, better salaries, and better CV material.

WHO CAN WORK, WHEN, AND FOR HOW LONG?

The Raffarin government was keen to respond favourably to the recent increase in the number of foreign students in France, and has announced that they will speed up the positive approval of student work visa applications without actually changing the process.

- Students registered at language schools are *not* entitled to work whilst they pursue their studies.

- You must be registered and studying at an official French university or institute of higher education which has both obliged and entitled you to be enrolled into the French social security system under the special student *régime* (see Chapter 12). This does not mean that you will be exempt from French social charges (*cotisations*) but it does mean that your extra contributions will start to accrue other advantages for you within the social security system.

- Students are allowed to work a maximum of 964 hours per year. You should check with your campus counsellors on any precise current restrictions to the number of hours relating to work in term-time and vacation periods.

◆ American students are obliged to justify their need to work when applying to the French Ministry of Labour for the *autorisation provisoire de travail*, normally valid for three months and renewable upon production of evidence of continuing studies. Students over the age of 18 may work for up to 830 hours per year, on the basis of a 35-hour week, for no more than three consecutive months. Students who receive grants and/or have sufficient financial means to continue their studies are not normally granted a work permit. American students must also produce a valid *carte d'étudiant* and contract from their employer with full personal details and details of working hours and pay. These provisions generally apply to students from non-EU countries, but you should check with your embassy for precise terms and conditions. For current details of the regulations, check the American Embassy website on **www.amb-usa.fr**.

◆ Students from EU countries do not require work permits, but are subject to French legal restrictions. Commonwealth citizens should remember that British residency rights do not equate to British citizenship rights within the European Union. You will be governed by the regulations pertaining to your nationality status.

Where to look for work

Most of the French newspapers and magazines listed in Chapter 6 also include job offers specifically aimed at students. French students produce their own magazine, *L'Etudiant*, which has its own important employment service (**www.l'etudiantfr/jobsstages.fr).** **Other notable sites include www.recrut.com and www.net-work.fr.**

A word of warning

No matter who you work for in France, you and your employer are subject to French law in France. Your contract and work conditions must conform to French law. Foreign firms have been criticised repeatedly for failing to observe basic French regulations when employing students and temporary workers.

The official French government website, **www.droitsdesjeunes.gouv. fr**, will help you draw the line between working hard for your money and working for next to no money at all.

WORKING AS AN AU PAIR

Au pairs and nannies

Nannies have formal qualifications in childcare and as such are much better paid. Their duties are much more restricted specifically to childcare, and accommodation is not normally provided. Both nannies and au pairs are often expected to travel with their employers.

An au pair is generally a young person with no formal qualification in childcare, who lives as one of the family. The legal age limits are 18 to 30 years old and au pairs are paid a small sum of 'pocket money' (normally €270–300 per month) in return for looking after the children, **light** housework, and several evenings baby-sitting per week. Accommodation and meals are normally provided by the family. Au pairs normally take a language course during the daytime. This is obligatory for non-EU residence permits.

EU nationals who can enter and leave France easily are able to take their chances by accepting non-declared unofficial positions with families. However, an illegal status leaves you open to abuse – and this does happen. Non-EU nationals who are willing to work as au pairs should definitely not accept illegal contracts. Not only are you not covered if you have an accident cleaning an apartment or minding the children, but you are living and working illegally and could face deportation.

Looking for work

There are a number of agencies that place au pairs and nannies in France, both in the UK and in France (principally in Paris). It is quite possible to find a position before arriving in France, through British magazines such as *The Lady*.

In Paris, the magazines *France-USA Contacts* and *The Free Voice* carry regular advertisements. Some agencies are better than others at placing you with a family, take the fee and never contact you again. Try asking around for the names of the good and bad agencies.

Check noticeboards for small advertisements and place advertisements seeking work in the same places. There are generally more jobs available than au pairs to fill them, so you should not have a problem finding a position.

Conditions of employment

Au pairing falls within one of the 'grey' areas of French employment. The official title of an au pair in French law is a *stagiaire aide familiale*. There are set guidelines, but making sure that these are applied is not always easy. Establishing a good relationship not only with the children but also with '*Monsieur et Madame*' is vital to a successful stay.

Generally, you will be employed from September till June, although you may well be asked to stay and help in the summer holiday months. Your employer **should** make a *Déclaration d'Engagement* to the social security office. In reality, few employers will do this voluntarily as they fear paying extra taxes to cover your statutory rights. If you are an EU citizen, make sure you take the EHIC form with you to France to cover emergency health care.

Legal requirements for American au pairs are listed below. **Rules and requirements also applying to EU nationals are in bold**:

1. **Age limit of 18–30 years old**.

2. Fair knowledge of French and/or studying French.

3. Minimum stay of three months, maximum 18 months. You can change families during this period, but the maximum stay is 18 months.

4. Summer au pairs staying one to three months are not required to take French classes, but must have completed one year of college-level studies in French.

5. The recognised objective of au pairing is to share in a French family's life and culture. Foreign families are not normally authorised to hire au pairs.

6. **Room and board must be provided, with meals shared with the family and a private bedroom.**

7. **The au pair's daily schedule should not exceed more than five hours' work per day, and should be arranged to allow time for study including classes. Au pairs should have one day off a week,**

and once a month this should be a Sunday. An au pair should never be prevented from attending church on Sunday even if this is a working day.

8. American citizens must obtain their au pair visa in the US from the French consulate with jurisdiction over their place of residence *before* entering France. You cannot convert tourist visas. This means following the same procedure outlined in Chapter 6 for obtaining a *visa de long séjour*, with a contract as a *stagiaire aide familiale* approved by the French Ministry of Labour. Your work permit itself is finally granted once you arrive in France after your contract has been approved by the Ministry of Labour.

You may be required to travel with the family, in which case they should cover your expenses. If you are based in or near Paris, the family may pay half of your travel pass, but this is not obligatory.

Au pair contracts
EU nationals from one of the new member states may not stay in France more than three months without a valid residence permit (*carte de séjour*). To obtain this, you need a formal work contract with social security declarations and contributions.

Americans with student visas can obtain au pair status after arrival in France after registering at a French university and obtaining a residence permit. Student au pairs can still only work for French families under a valid contract approved by the French Ministry of Labour.

French families and au pair agencies can obtain contracts at the French Ministry of Labour section dealing with foreign workers at the address given in Chapter 6. This needs to be completed and returned accompanied by a medical certificate not more than three months old signed by a doctor, either in French, or translated into French. If you are a student planning to work as an au pair you must either produce your student card if you are already studying in France, or produce evidence of your student status if you are applying in the US for your visa. Completed applications including these documents will be approved and stamped by the Foreign Workers section, and one copy stays with the family and one with the au pair.

The American au pair must then provide the stamped copy together with evidence of registration at a French language school (evening classes are not acceptable) together with all other documentation required in order to obtain the *carte de séjour* within eight days of arrival in France. Once the carte de séjour has been obtained, and following a final visit to the Foreign Workers section, you will be granted a renewable temporary work permit of six months.

SEASONAL WORK

The major department stores normally advertise for extra help throughout the traditional busy periods up to and after Christmas and during the sales (*soldes*). Every year, the *CIDJ* (*Centre d'Information er de la Documentation de la Jeunesse*) organises a special two-day summer recruitment fair to help students find a summer job. The term 'job' is now used in French, but normally implies low/minimum pay for menial work.

You need to start early on the summer job search if you are planning to work. For more information on this area and all areas of student employment, call in at the *CIDJ* of your university or go to **www.cidj.asso.fr**. The *CIDJ* also offers advice on rules and regulations covering the employment of students from outside the European Union.

Non-EU students are still subject to visa formalities but work for up to three months during the summer vacation period is generally allowed. The Council on International Educational Exchange (CIEE) has negotiated reciprocal rights between France and the USA allowing students in full-time American university education or study abroad programmes to obtain temporary work permits. Further details can be obtained from the following addresses:

- Work Abroad, CIEE, 205 East 42nd Street, New York NY10017, tel: 212 661 1414.

- Work in France, CIEE, 112 ter, rue Cardinet, 75017 Paris tél. 01 57 57 28 50 or 20 41. The CIEE website can be found at **www.ciee.org**.

9

Retiring in France

If you decide to spend your twilight years in a place in the sun in France, there are a great many preparations to be made. It is difficult to establish hard and fast rules, as everybody's personal circumstances are so different. Nonetheless, the basic administrative steps that must be taken – securing a residence permit and enrolling in the French social security system, not to mention making arrangements for pensions payments – all require careful attention. Do not be fooled by the notion of 'free movement' of workers and citizens within the European Union. Moving is not a problem; staying can be, if it is not handled properly.

There are also important considerations to make when purchasing property in France. The basic outlines given in Chapter 4 apply. However, you must plan carefully for the future when purchasing. The system of purchasing that you choose will have very serious consequences when questions of inheritance and ownership arise after death.

THE PENSION SCHEME IN FRANCE
If you are already working in France and paying into the French social security system, retirement age is 60 for both men and women. This is when you become eligible for state and supplementary pensions to which you have contributed during your working life.

Your insurance record takes into account periods of absence from work (including sickness, work accidents, maternity leave or unemployment). Pensions are then calculated on the following basic formula:

$$\frac{\text{basic wage} \times \text{period insured}}{160}$$

To receive a full pension, you must now have contributed for at least 40 years. The maximum state pension possible is equal to 50% of your average earnings in your 25 highest paid years. A reduced pension is equivalent to 1/160 of the full pension × number of quarters' insurance you have paid. State pensions are indexed to take account of rises in the cost of living. Supplementary pensions depend on the number of points you have accumulated during your working life up to the age of 60. Added to the state pension, the complementary pension normally brings a retirement pension income up to about 80% of your final salary at retirement, for those who have contributed continuously to both schemes. Currently the minimum annual state pension is €6511, and the maximum state pension is €16,638.

You need to apply for your pension entitlements about three to four months before the date you plan to retire. For this you will need to complete a *demande de retraite personnelle*. Contact your local health authority (*caisse primaire d'assurance maladie*) for further details.

CLAIMING YOUR PENSION

If you intend to draw your UK pension whilst living in France, the British SA29 document states clearly: 'Every EC country has its own rules [on how to claim pensions]. You must follow these rules before a pension can be paid to you. The age that you can start to get your Retirement Pension may also be different in other countries.' (SA29, published by the Benefits Agency, August 1998).

Claiming a UK retirement pension abroad

If you are entitled to a UK state pension and are within four months of retirement, you can ask for a retirement pension forecast from the Contributions Agency (see below). The pension forecast will tell you the current level of your pension, and whether or not there are any ways of improving that level. You can receive a UK retirement pension, and also widow's benefits in any EU country. The amount you receive will be the same as in the UK, although you must take into account exchange rates. You will also benefit from annual increases in the pension rate if you live within the EU.

You can choose to have the money paid to you either:

- directly into your bank account abroad
- or into a UK bank or building society
- or sent to your address abroad.

Claiming pensions from more than one EU country

If you have been employed in more than one EU country (e.g. France and the UK) you will have paid insurance into both systems. As long as you meet the rules of both countries, you will be entitled to a pension from each system.

Each country will work out the pension due to you under their own national system. They will also look at the amount of pension due to you from the other country concerned. This can help you to get a pension, or even a high pension, under their own national system. They do this by working out how much pension you would be entitled to if all your contributions had been paid into one national system. Whilst the paperwork is exchanged, you will be paid your pension from each system. Once the information exchange has been completed, the two countries work out how much you would be entitled to for the total sum of your contributions had they been made entirely within each national system. Then each country pays an amount to you in proportion to your contributions to its system.

For example: if one third of your insurance payments have been made in France, then France will pay one third of the total pension, with the UK paying the balance of your final entitlement.

Paying tax on your pension

Pensions are taxable in France, but on a much lower scale than for those in active employment or self-employment. If you are moving to France from the UK, contact your local tax office in the UK to make arrangements for qualifying as a non-resident, and therefore being exempted from British tax duties. In France, you must then contact your local *centre des impôts* to register for French income tax.

OBTAINING A RESIDENCE PERMIT

The new ruling exempting EU citizens from applying for a *carte de séjour* also applies to those retiring to France. However you should bring with you the documents listed in Chapter 2, and you will be asked to produce the following documentation:

◆ A *justificatif des ressources* – normally this will be a bank reference which has been translated by an approved translator.

You will certainly need proof of all the money at your disposal (including pension entitlements). Enquire at the nearest French Consulate *before* coming to France in order to establish what precisely will be required.

◆ You may also be required to produce a medical certificate. Once again, check this with your local Consulate before coming to France, or the *Préfecture* when you arrive. Evidence of medical insurance is now obligatory, and you should read the following section carefully when preparing your move.

The French legislation makes clear that even though *cartes de séjours* are no longer required by retired EU citizens, unless you are able to produce proof of medical insurance and proof of sufficient financial means not to become a burden on the French state, you will in fact be illegally resident in France.

Working after your retirement

Under the French system, there are strict limits on paid employment after retirement. If you worked in the private sector, the amount of your total revenue (salary + pension + complementary pension from your *mutuelles*) must not exceed your last monthly salary *brut* (i.e. before social security deductions). The social security contributions (*cotisations*) that you make on your post-retirement salary do not open any new social security rights. Other restrictions apply in different sectors within the French system.

You should take advice whilst considering your retirement move to France. There are also implications regarding your health cover which you need to explore with your own national health system, and if possible with the local health fund (*caisse régionale*) in your area in France.

TRANSFERRING HEALTH AND WELFARE RIGHTS

Important new legislation came into effect in November 2007 for non-remunerated EU citizens, including retired EU citizens who have taken early retirement.

Access to the French social security system is now limited to those retired people with five years continued residence in France, and/or who have already reached full retirement age in their country of origin. For the initial five-year period, the French legislation expects EU citizens to draw upon health cover entitlement deriving from their home country, or the country where they have principally been employed and accrued their social security rights. More realistically, the new system which has been introduced apparently to comply with EU legislation, means that you almost certainly must take out private health insurance for the initial five-year period if you have taken early retirement.

After five years continued residence, you will be entitled to join the French national health and social security system under the scheme known as the *Couverture de Maladie Universelle*. Applications for this health cover will be under the responsibility of your local *Préfecture*, and your local health service (*caisse primaire d'assurance maladie*, or *CPAM*).

Exceptions will be made to the legislation, allowing for earlier access to the CMU, in one of the categories known as *accidents de la vie* (life accidents), such as divorce, separation or the death of a partner; or a new medical condition which you develop **after** your

arrival in France, which your private insurer refuses to cover. If
you move to France with a known specialist medical condition,
you must be covered by your private health insurance.

◆ If you have already reached retirement age, or will have
   reached retirement age when you move abroad, you need to
   obtain **Form E121**. To apply for this form in the UK, write to
   The Contributions Agency, International Services, Department
   of Social Security, Longbenton, Newcastle upon Tyne NE98
   1YX. The International Services helpline is 0645 154811, fax:
   0645 157800. From France, dial 00 44 191 225 4811 for the
   telephone line, or fax: 00 44 191 225 7800. You should make
   arrangements to obtain Form E121 as early as possible before
   you leave for France. The EI21 is valid indefinitely. When you
   arrive in France, take it along to your local *caisse primaire* (or
   régionale) *d'assurance maladie*. At the same time you must take
   either your *carte de séjour*, or the receipt (*récipissé*). You will
   then be enrolled under the French social security system. The
   E121 establishes your rights not only to healthcare, but also to
   pensions.

◆ It is highly advisable to join a private health insurance scheme
   even if you make all of the appropriate arrangements for
   transferring your rights under the state systems.

If you transfer your rights into the French system, and
subsequently return to the UK and/or fall ill whilst there, no
private scheme in the UK will admit or readmit you over the age
of 65. You will thus be left with minimal coverage at the time of
life when you are most likely to need it, or the prospect of a heavy
bill for private care. You should also bear in mind that you will

not be eligible for any assistance from the UK government if eventually you need to be admitted to a private nursing home or residential home in France.

Chapters 4 and 10 also contain information relating to disability which may be of interest either now or in the future. The Jospin government introduced a very popular measure which is also available to foreigners permanently residing in France with a *valid carte de séjour*, called the *Allocation Personnalisée d'Autonomie* or *APA*. This benefit is not officially means-tested, but your means are 'taken into consideration'. As resources for this benefit are very limited (it is run from regional not national funds), not every application will be successful.

Applications are made to the *conseil général* of your *département*. To apply you must be over 60, and losing your capacity to remain independent, and thus requiring assistance for the essential acts of everyday life. Amongst the documents required are French bank and tax details. This all presumes you followed the correct procedures when you moved to France.

You will be assessed in your own home by a medical team appointed by the *département*, but your own medical advisors or family may be present when you are visited. If you are awarded an APA the award will take into account your needs, your revenue and the cost of meeting your needs. When considering your revenues, other social benefits are not counted in the total figure.

The maximum level of assistance which can be awarded is €1,208.94 per month in the first category of applicants, and

€518.55 per month in the fourth category. However, the amount awarded is variable and takes into account all the factors mentioned above.

BUYING YOUR RETIREMENT HOME

Chapter 4 gives you a basic outline of the process involved in purchasing property in France.

Choosing where to buy

When you are choosing where to buy your retirement home in France, you need to consider a number of factors, especially if you are looking at property in rural areas:

◆ What transport links are near to the property? You may *think* you want to be a million miles from anywhere and anyone. In reality, if something goes wrong, you do not want to be too far from the emergency and medical services, not to mention essential shops. Also, what will happen when you are no longer able to drive your own car?

◆ If your idea of hell is other people, you may discover that hell is in fact not having other people around. Certain parts of France are very sparsely populated indeed. Whilst this means that you may be welcomed to an area because you are intending to renovate a derelict property, it may also mean neighbours are very few and far between. French provincial social life revolves mainly around the family. Even if you have a lot of visitors (as is often the case), this may not really compensate for the lack of society to which you are accustomed. Regional associations may be able to help fill this gap, but not all regions offer the same possibilities.

Buying a property in France, especially in a rural area, is normally a lot easier than trying to sell it again afterwards. French buyers are normally on the look-out for properties that can be easily renovated to make holiday homes. The type of property you purchase may not fall into this category. Also, there is the problem of a potential buyer securing a mortgage. Obviously certain areas of France and their property markets are more popular than others. What you may have to remember is that if you bought your house for a 'bargain' price, you may well have to sell it at a similar rate if you ever want to be free of it in years to come.

Looking at inheritance issues

Your property and possessions in France are subject to French law. It is extremely important that you take good professional advice when buying your property in France, as regards questions of ownership and inheritance (succession). You must do this before you sign the contracts; afterwards, it will be too late. You should also bear in mind that the legal system is both very slow and very expensive in France.

The main thing to watch out for is that the *notaire* (solicitor) does not draw up a contract whereby you buy the property *en division*. The much more preferable option is to buy *en tontine*. There are other possibilities (e.g. an *acte de donation*), but you will need to discuss these with your legal advisors.

Problems with buying a property *en division*

If you and your spouse buy a property *en division*, you will each own half of the property. When one of you dies, the 'half' which belongs to the deceased person will pass automatically to their heirs, including any children from a previous marriage. The surviving spouse may then own half a house, with the right of abode for the remainder of their life. **If you have children, you can only leave part of your property to your spouse**. If there are more than three children, they will automatically inherit three quarters of the deceased person's estate. Inheritance tax is then payable immediately for children, but under the generous new arrangements introduced in 2007 (see Chapter 4), surviving spouses and partners are now exempt from inheritance tax, even if they continue living in the house. The house cannot be sold to pay the inheritance tax without the consent of the surviving spouse, nor if one of the children is under 18 years old. The inheritance tax threshold for children inheriting from their parents has now been raised from €50,000 to €150,000, and levels have also been raised for other relatives and beneficiaries.

DEALING WITH BEREAVEMENT

After dealing with the 'here', you also need to be prepared for the 'hereafter'. Like most other things in France, dying is not as simple as you might think! Quite apart from the emotional aspect of dealing with the death of a loved one, there are numerous administrative tasks to be undertaken. These concern not only winding up a deceased person's estate, but also putting your own affairs in order.

Immediately after the death

1. The death certificate (*certificat de constatation de décès*) must be signed and certified by a doctor.

2. Within 24 hours of the death, the death must be registered (*declaration de décès*) at the *mairie* of the place where the death occurred. For this, you need an official piece of identity, the

death certificate, and an official piece of identity (*carte de séjour*, birth or marriage certificate) of the deceased.

3. After registering the death, you will be given the *acte de décès* which is the official death certificate required by banks and administrative offices, etc. You can ask for several copies of the certificate straight away to avoid delays in dealing with the next round of paperwork.

Arranging the funeral

The undertaker (*pompes funèbres*) can arrange all of the certificates as part of the services offered. Before you go ahead with the funeral service, you will need a burial permit (*permis d'inhumer*). The earliest that this can take place is 24 hours after the death, and the latest six days after the death. Burial is still by far the most common form of funeral in France, and crematoria are relatively rare. Nor are they as 'user-friendly' as in the UK or the USA.

The burial must take place in the local cemetery of the village or commune where the deceased lived, unless they had purchased a burial plot (*concession*) in another cemetery. If you wish to arrange a burial in another commune or village, you will require the authorisation of the local *maire*. On average the cost of a burial is in the region of €3,000 to €4,600. In addition to this, you will be faced with a bill for the purchase of a burial plot and tombstone. If you want the burial to take place in your home country, you will need to make enquiries as to the likely costs involved for transportation. Although financial assets are officially frozen initially (see below), most banks or financial institutions will release approximately €3,000 to the immediate family for funeral expenses.

Informing creditors and debtors

The following people must all be notified of a death within a week:

♦ All banks, savings plans, etc., where the deceased had an account. Joint accounts will need to be converted into personal accounts.

♦ Any credit organisations where loans had been taken out.

♦ All insurance companies, and especially life insurance companies.

♦ The local health authority (*CPAM*), the local pensions unit (*caisse vieillesse*) and any other welfare units that were issuing benefits to the deceased. If the deceased received a complementary French pension, then that *caisse* must also be informed.

♦ The landlord, if the deceased was renting property. If the deceased was renting their property to somebody else, then the tenants must be informed to whom they should now pay their rent.

♦ If the deceased lived in an apartment in a copropriété, the *Syndic* must be informed.

Wills and inheritance

Normally you will only need to use the services of a *notaire* (equivalent to a solicitor) if there is any dispute over the will amongst the legatees, or if the deceased was the owner of property. If the deceased was not a property owner, and left only furniture, bank accounts, etc., then as long as there is no dispute amongst the legatees, there is no need to involve a *notaire*.

If the deceased owned property, you must use the services of a *notaire* to take the necessary steps. The principal rôle of the notaire if one is involved, will be to issue the *attestation de propriété des biens immobiliers*, which will permit the legatees to inherit the property legally. Like the undertaker, the *notaire* can also undertake other administrative tasks for you which can make life easier at a difficult time. These include dealing with social security offices, the tax offices and tenants. Their other functions are:

◆ checking on any unknown claimants on the deceased's estate

◆ checking the terms of a will or an *acte de donation* between a married couple

◆ checking that each legatee has received the correct portion left to them under the terms of the will and French law.

If you are permanently resident in France, all your assets worldwide are governed by French law. If you retain assets in your country of origin, or another country, you should consider making a will in each country concerned in order to settle your affairs in precisely the manner which you wish. One possibility would be, for instance, to make a British will and a French will and to annexe one to the other in order to make absolutely clearly that these are your instructions for all your estate. However, there could be tax issues involved here so **take good professional advice** in **both** France **and** the other country concerned.

If there is dispute over your will, you should be aware that if your assets are in two separate countries, the law of the first court to hear a case contesting your will takes precedence over the law of the other country concerned.

Transferring your estate to your family

If you make large financial donations to members of your family, either to assist them or to begin to transfer your estate towards them, you must be careful not to become liable for the *droit de donation* tax. New legislation introduced in 2007 allows you to transfer up to €150,000 to a child from each parent. Donations between married couples and partners in a PACS or civil partnership have a tax-free limitation of €76,000. If you opt for one of the legal systems whereby you invest your property in a company (*société civile immobilière*) you must conform to the regulations governing such institutions. These include holding annual general meetings and keeping company accounts. Any gifts to children of shares in the company should be made at least ten years before your death to attain favourable tax rates.

Your *notaire* will be able to advise you on the full tax implications of any proposed movement of funds, and you must take advice from a qualified professional competent in French law before taking any decisions.

Tax issues

Tax is one area where you may well be pleased to benefit from the expertise of a *notaire*, if you are not happy dealing with the tax office yourself. A *déclaration de succession* is no longer necessary if the beneficiary is in direct succession (i.e. a child of the deceased), or is the surviving spouse or partner in a PACS or civil partnership, and the amount of the inheritance is less than €50,000 *brut* (before any deductions). To be exempt from this formality, the beneficiary must not have previously benefited from a *donation*. Any other beneficiaries who are left estate worth €3,000 *brut* are also exempt from making a *déclaration*. You will be well advised to take the advice of a *notaire* nonetheless regarding these arrangements.

Officially each beneficiary should make an individual declaration if they are over the prescribed tax limits. However one declaration can be made on behalf of all the beneficiaries by a defined nominee, normally a *notaire*. This must be made within six months of the death at the tax office of the deceased. Normally any payment due must be made at the same time as the declaration.

For the surviving spouse, the tax declaration will have to be made at the usual time of the year (March), taking into account revenue acquired between the date of death and the end of the year. The surviving spouse and any children still benefit from the same number of 'parts' as if the deceased were still alive. For further clarification, speak to your local tax office in France.

There are taxation treaties between France and the UK and the USA. These will help you avoid double taxation for any inheritance. However, you will be obliged to make declarations to the tax authorities in both countries, who will then assess if you are still liable for any final balancing payments to the secondary country because of different tax systems.

COPING ON YOUR OWN

Health and welfare rights for widows and their children

If you had French health and social security rights by default of your late spouse's rights, you and your children will retain these rights, under the following conditions:

1. The period is one year from the date of death, or until your last child reaches the age of three.

2. If you have at least three children, you will then still keep your rights.

3. If you receive single parent payments, or benefit from a *pension de réversion* or the *assurance veuvage* (see below), your health expenses will automatically be reimbursed.

If you do not fall into either category above, then you must make a personal application to social services to be registered.

Claiming UK widows' benefits

You can continue to receive widows' benefit when you move abroad. Arrangements for transferring this benefit are similar to those for transferring pension payments. Once again, you will benefit from annual increases to the benefit. To arrange for payment, you must contact The Benefits Agency, Pensions & Overseas Benefits Directorate, Department of Social Security, Tyneview Park, Whitley Road, Benton, Newcastle upon Tyne NE98 1BA (tel: 0191 21 87777).

You may be able to claim this benefit if your husband dies whilst you were both living abroad if your husband had the necessary National Insurance record in the UK, or if you return to the UK within four weeks of his death. All of the above rules also apply for the payment of widowed mothers' allowance from the UK social security system. However, you cannot claim both widows' benefits.

Claiming French widows' benefits

If you are widowed in France, and your late spouse was

contributing to the French social security system as an active worker, you will be entitled to a number of financial aids:

- *Le capital-décès* – a lump-sum payment based on social security contributions and the employment record up till the time of death of your spouse. It is designed to act as an emergency measure to cover immediate difficulties due to a loss of salary from the deceased. The deceased must not have ceased active employment for more than 12 months at the time the death occurred. Normally the amount is about three times the last monthly salary of the deceased. Applications for this sum should be made at the local *caisse primaire d'assurance maladie* of the deceased. The *capital décès* is available by order of priority to surviving spouses and partners, former spouses and partners, and children of the deceased.

- *L'allocation de parent isolé* – a limited period minimum revenue payment for single parents. The amount paid is the difference between your own resources and the minimum amount guaranteed under this benefit.

- *L'assurance veuvage* – this is assistance for widows under the age of 55 who are raising children. As with the *pension de réversion* (below), it is means-tested.

- *La pension de réversion du régime de retraite de base* – this is a means-tested way of deciding if you are entitled to continue claiming a reduced basic state pension earned by your late spouse. It is currently equivalent to 54% of the last pension paid to the deceased. You must be at least 55 years old to be considered for this benefit. If you do not qualify on the first application, you can reapply. If you are awarded this pension, and even if you remarry, you will continue to receive this pension for the rest of your life. This also applies even if your financial situation improves. Apply for this at the *caisse de retraite* of your late spouse.

◆ ***La pension de réversion du régime de retraite complémentaire*** – this is not means-tested. Generally speaking, the surviving spouse is entitled to receive 60% of the complementary pension that the deceased received, or would have received if they were still working at the time of their death. Contact the *caisse d'assurance vieillesse* concerned to apply for this pension.

DRAWING UP A RETIREMENT ACTION PLAN

You need to plan your move to France carefully. You will certainly need to take sound professional advice, and not to rush into a situation which it is quick and easy to set up, and difficult and/or expensive to escape from afterwards.

1. Make sure you have up-to-date bank statements and other proofs of your financial resources ready for your residence permit application. See the checklist in Chapter 2 to make sure that you have all the necessary documents for this application. In addition, make enquiries to your local French Embassy or Consulate as to the documents and steps required if you decide to continue some form of paid activity.

2. Contact the appropriate social security agencies to arrange for the transfer of pensions and benefits. Make sure that you have applied for the Form E121 in good time. Discuss the implications of your move to France with the social security services if you are considering some form of paid activity.

3. Check out private healthcare options available to you.

4. Contact your local tax office to arrange to be declared non-resident. You must then contact your new local tax office in France in order to register.

5. **Seek legal advisers in both France and your home country** (if appropriate) who can help you with property contracts, wills and tax issues. This will be a wise investment for the future. Make sure you **use professionals who know and understand French law**, and can explain clearly to you in your own language what your options are, and what each option entails.

6. Consider carefully the pros and cons of a particularly property and its location before signing anything. Do not rush into anything, and be practical about the future.

FINDING OUT MORE

♦ UK Contributions Agency International Services, Department of Social Security, Longbenton, Newcastle upon Tyne NE98 1YX, tel: 0645 154811, fax: 0645 157800; or from abroad, tel: 44 191 225 4811, fax: 44 191 225 7800 – for information on National Insurance contributions, healthcare and retirement pension forecasts.

♦ UK Department of Social Security, Pensions & Overseas Benefits Directorate, Newcastle upon Tyne NE98 1BA, tel: (+44) 0191 218 7777, fax: (+44) 191 218 7293 – for information on benefits and healthcare.

♦ **www.dwp.gov.uk** – the website of the UK Department of Work and Pensions. If your computer is equipped with *Acrobat Reader* software click on, '*Your social security insurance benefits* *and health care rights in the EEA'*, and then select the SA29 document. You will be able to access on-line (and download) the latest information relating to UK pensions and benefits for British expatriates.

◆ **www.thepensionservice.gov.uk** – the website of the UK Pension Service, specifically designed to reply to all questions relating to retiring abroad. Easy to use, well written, and up-to-date, current information is available in The International Pension Centre section.

◆ **www.europa.eu.int/comm/employment_social** – the European website concerning the transfer of social security rights and pension entitlements within the European Union. This is a useful site, but you must be sure to check the date of the information offered. Cross-referencing with the DWP website, and the SA29 leaflet, is strongly advised.

◆ **www.ameli.fr** – this is the French national website (in French) which will allow you to locate your nearest *caisse primaire* (or *régionale*) *d'asurance maladie* (local health fund or authority).

◆ **www.cnav.fr** – **Caisse National d'Assurance Veillesse**, (the national old-age pension fund) 110 avenue Flandres, 75951 Paris, cedex 19. Tél. 0821 10 12 14 (information on retirement), or +33 821 10 31 60 from overseas (both pay services charged at €0.12 per minute) (information on payments), or 0826 826 700 for a recorded information service. In Alsace, you need to contact the regional centre at 36 rue du Doubs, 67011 Strasbourg, cedex 1, tél. 0821 10 67 67 or +33 821 10 39 60 from overseas. Calls to all CNAV numbers are charged at €0.12 per minute.

10

Accessing Health and Welfare Services

For British citizens, it is essential that you obtain a copy of the Department of Work & Pensions pamphlet 'Your social security insurance, benefits and health care rights in the European Community' Number SA29. You should also contact the Department of Social Security Overseas Branch, Newcastle upon Tyne, NE98 1YX, to check on the pamphlets that they have available. Separate leaflets are available from the Northern Ireland Social Security Agency International Services at 24-42 Corporation Street, Belfast BT1 3DP.

You can find SA29 on-line on the British Embassy website: www.amb-grandebretagne.fr. You can find the SA29 on-line on the Department of Work and Pensions website: www.dwp.gov.uk/international/sa29.

There used to be a joke amongst British expatriates that the standard remedy for any medical problem in France was to prescribe suppositories. This is not only untrue, but distracts from the reality that French healthcare is generally of a very high standard. Critics might retaliate, however, that this is because the French are a nation of hypochondriacs, which at times is hard to dispute.

The cost of sometimes over-generous healthcare has certainly been a bitter pill to swallow in recent years. French doctors will not generally prescribe just one drug to cure a complaint, but several.

Attempts to limit stock-piling of half-used medicines have provoked outrage, but are gradually being pursued as the French come to terms with their huge social security bill.

President Chirac established two health-related national priorities for his presidency; the fight against cancer; and the social inclusion of, and aid to, the disabled. In 2007 President Sarkozy has announced that he is also targeting aid to victims of Alzheimer's Disease as a new national health cause. An on-going campaign of 'national solidarity' was also launched to increase and improve residential care for the elderly, especially following on from the murderous droughts of recent years. In an effort to try to begin balancing the Health Service books, the introduction of generic drugs, a more efficient approach to managing healthcare, and small patient cost contributions, have all been phased in. Finally in January 2008, France introduced a total smoking ban not only in offices, but in all public spaces, including cafés, bars and nightclubs.

JOINING THE SOCIAL SECURITY SYSTEM

If you are living and working in France, you are obliged to join the French *Sécurité Sociale*, covering pensions, sickness and healthcare, and unemployment. Generally, you will need certified copies of your birth and marriage certificates, as for your *carte de séjour*. Check with your employer and/or your local social security office.

The website **www.cnamts.fr** (in French only) will allow you to find your local *caisse primaire d'assurance maladie* or *CPAM* (local health authority), where you need to be registered. Click on the section '*votre CPAM*', and then use the pull-down menus to either enter your *département* number (the first two numbers of your

French postcode), or to select your *département* by name. Remember that *département* names are not the same as regional names such as Normandy or Alsace.

◆ If you are in regular employment in France, you should automatically be registered courtesy of your employer. Both you and your employer must make regular contributions to ensure that you and your dependants are adequately covered. This rule applies to all foreigners who have obtained their *carte de séjour*, visa, etc.

◆ If for any reason the enrolment (*inscription*) to the *Sécu* (as it is generally known for short) is not organised by your employer, you should go to your local *caisse* (each *arrondissement* and commune has their own local branch). You will need to take with you a piece of official ID, a *relevé d'identité bancaire* also known as an *RIB* (bank account details, available from your bank) and your pay slips. These last documents are essential to show that your employer has been making the necessary contributions on your behalf to the Social Security service.

◆ If you are in paid employment in France, and are therefore enrolled in the French Social Security system, your spouse, partner (if they are totally dependent on you financially) and your children under 16 years of age, or up to 20 years of age if they are studying, are all covered by your social security payments for standard medical treatment and reimbursement.

◆ If you are self-employed, you pay a percentage of your taxable income as your contribution which will then be deductible for income tax purposes. Self-employed workers are not covered in the same way as employed workers by the *Sécurité Sociale*. It is therefore important that you join the appropriate scheme as soon as possible after arriving in France. See Chapter 8 on self-employment. If you take up residence in France as a self-employed worker, but you return to work in the UK for a period, you should also read carefully the information laid out in the SA29 document concerning the documents you will require for healthcare when you are in the UK.

- If you are a UK national sent to work in France for less than 12 months, you will normally remain insured under the UK National Insurance scheme. You or your employer should obtain the appropriate forms (E101 and EHIC) from the DSS Overseas Branch, Newcastle upon Tyne NE98 1YX, before coming to France. These prove that you remain insured under the British system, and entitle you to emergency medical care. You should also check the current information that is given in the SA29 document, and which covers a variety of different options which may be applicable to your personal circumstances. This information also concerns what will happen if your contract is extended beyond the initial period.

- For those working as au pairs, your employer is obliged to make the necessary declaration and payments on your behalf to the social security administration service (URSSAF). This will provide you with basic rights and coverage.

- If you are unemployed and come to France to look for work, see Chapter 7 on working in France. Jobseekers should note that since 2007 they are now in the same category of unwaged residents as early retirees and students. This means that officially some form of private healthcare will be required when you arrive in France. Contact your local social security office for help and advice on this issue.

- If you are a student and an EU citizen, you will need to obtain form EHIC. See Chapter 11 on education in France for full details. Students with EU nationality form the third category of unwaged residents affected by new legislation introduced in 2007. In practice, you should not experience any problems if you are enrolled at an official institution which will take care of your enrolment in the French student national health scheme. If you are attending a private institution, you should clarify the situation when preparing your move.

Introducing the *Carte Vitale*

The *Securité Sociale* is notoriously slow in issuing numbers, cards known as the *carte vitale* and reimbursement. You may have to wait some time until you receive your card demonstrating your eligibility to use state services, and for reimbursement. Medical treatment will only be reimbursed after proof that you have worked 200 hours in the previous three months. This can include time worked in the UK. Form E104 available from the DSS in Newcastle upon Tyne will need to be completed and submitted by your French employer.

In 1999 the *Couverture Médicale Universelle* guaranteed minimum health care to all 'stable' French residents. In parallel to this move, efforts have been made in recent years to reduce the paperwork involved in the reimbursement process by the introduction of the *carte vitale* which is now issued to all subscribers to a *CPAM*. Once your rights have been validated (i.e. you have joined the system), they remain valid throughout the

time that you are a legal French resident. The end date on your
card will simply indicate when the card needs to be renewed and/
or brought up to date.

Each person in the household over the age of 16 who is registered
with the *Sécurité Sociale,* or derives their rights from their spouse,
partner or parent, will receive their own individual *carte vitale.*

If your card carries specific prescription charges exoneration
rights, etc., then the end date indicated will refer to the moment
when your rights and needs in this respect will be reconsidered by
the *Sécu.* If you lose this card or it is stolen, or for some reason
you never receive it, you have to make a *déclaration sur l'honneur*
in writing to your *caisse* in order to be issued with a new card.

What is the *carte vitale* and how do you use it?

The *carte vitale* is a card with a personalised record on a
microchip (*puce*), which allows doctors and other health service
professionals to register their acts and charges on a central
system. The plan was that in 2002 the brown *feuilles de soins* (see
below) would disappear and reimbursement would become a
paperless process. However, you should not count on this
becoming an immediate reality. The cost and practical
implications of depriving the French of two of their favourite
hobbies – procuring medicines and medical treatment, and filling
out forms – are proving colossal, and there is much resistance
from health service professionals to the costs they themselves are
facing in converting to the new system.

For all of these services, the *carte vitale* will send the required
information through to a central data bank, which will

automatically register the demand for reimbursement for the cost of the transaction, which you must still pay in full.

You should note that the *carte vitale* is not a form of payment and you are still required to settle the full fee at the end of your appointment and to be reimbursed subsequently. The difference is that you do not have to send the forms through the post to the *Sécurité Sociale*, so there is less paperwork and less chance of lost and unreimbursed claims.

Updating your *carte vitale*
You can make updates to the information on your *carte vitale*. There are almost 150 sites in Paris (e.g. hospitals, local *caisses*, pension withdrawal centres and family support centres) which have computer terminals (*bornes*) that allow you to check the accuracy of the information on your card. They do not give access to medical records.

- If you move home, you may well move to a different reimbursement centre/local *caisse*. You will need to make contact with your new *caisse* to ask them to update your card with your new address and perhaps also new bank details.

- If you acquire some form of exemption or medical assistance, this should be registered on your new card also.

- Children acquire their rights from their parents already in the system. New mothers need to present both a demand in writing for the *inscription* of their children, plus the birth certificate (*extrait d'acte de naissance*) and the *livret de famille* (see below), at their local *caisse*. All reimbursements concerning the children will then be made onto the same bank account as for the mother or father (as you wish).

WORKING ABROAD FOR A FIXED PERIOD

Medical records

If you inform the UK DWP Contributions Department that you are going to live or work abroad for a limited period (e.g. because you or your partner have been seconded), they will automatically inform the National Health Service Central Register. They will amend the Central Index of Patients which helps to determine funding for each Family Health Service Authority (FHSA).

The FHSA will in turn withdraw your medical records from your GP about nine months after your departure. Your records will be held either until you return or re-register with a new doctor, or until they are destroyed. Records are normally held for at least six years.

If you are going abroad for a limited period and plan to return to your current home area, it may be useful to inform your GP of both your departure and your anticipated return date. This will avoid your records being withdrawn unnecessarily.

Maintaining British social security rights

DSS pamphlets explain in detail how to go about maintaining your British social security rights (if you have them) whilst working abroad. It is very important that you check the most recent publications and take advice based on the information which they provide. This can affect your eligibility for state benefits upon your return to the UK, and your pension rights later in life. Voluntary contributions can also be made in some circumstances, but these will not automatically entitle you to French social security benefits. They will simply guarantee your right to apply for British benefits. Contact your local DSS office for more details.

IMMUNISATION

Standard immunisations are always worthwhile, although there are no particular dangers associated with life in France. Frequent contact with former French colonies in Africa may possibly mean that certain diseases are more common in France than in the UK or the USA, but the extra risks are minimal. All vaccines are available on prescription in France from pharmacies, and can be administered by qualified doctors. If you arrange immunisations yourself, you can ask your doctor to write you a prescription in order to obtain reimbursement from the *Sécurité Sociale*. However, you will generally have to pay a fee to the doctor, so it is best to ask them to write the prescription when they administer the immunisation.

GOING TO YOUR FAMILY DOCTOR

In France you are not limited to registering with one doctor in your area. You are free to consult as many doctors as you wish, as often as you wish, wherever you wish. The French frequently take advantage of this system to ask for second or even third opinions, but it is not really advisable unless you doubt the competence or approach of your doctor. You should also note that visits to doctors who are not registered with your local health authority as your general practitioner (*médecin référent*) will be reimbursed at lower rates. However, if your general practitioner sends you to see a specialist or another medical practitioner (e.g. a nurse), then the reimbursement system will take this into account when calculating the level of reimbursement.

Sticking to one doctor allows them to get to know you and your problems better. The government now financially encourages doctors and patients to build 'exclusive' relationships, to cut back on the amount of money spent reimbursing multiple doctors' appointment fees. Your chosen doctor may also be designated as your *médecin-référent*, which means that they will coordinate all your medical cover and also prescribe generic medicines (see below).

Each time you visit the doctor, you will be asked to pay a consultation fee (*honoraire*), currently of €22 – the price depends on the system the doctor works within (see below). Make sure that the doctor completes and signs a brown *feuille de soin*, which you will need to reclaim this cost. The level at which you will be reimbursed for standard doctors fees is currently 70% for doctors who are *conventionné*. There are also small charges for medical acts such as cleaning and dressing a wound, administering injections, etc.

For those doctors who now accept the *carte vitale*, an automatic registration of your visit activates an automatic claim for reimbursement from the *Sécurité Sociale*.

OBTAINING MEDICINES

At the chemist's shop (*pharmacie*), indicated by a green cross, hand over the prescription (*ordonnance*) and the *feuille de soin* to the pharmacist. Once your medicines have been prepared, you will be asked to pay in full. If the pharmacist is not equipped with a *carte vitale* card reader, then they should enter the cost of the drugs should enter the cost of the drugs on the reverse side of the *feuille de soin*, and also stick on the small labels (*vignettes*) from the medicine boxes. Without these labels, the cost of the drugs will not be reimbursed.

The level of reimbursement for medicines varies from nothing up to 100% if you have obtained an exemption certificate proving that the treatment is essential to your well-being. Chemists' shops provide a rota of weekend cover, which is posted clearly in shop windows along with details of late-opening chemists.

The chemist may advertise and/or ask if you wish to operate the *tiers payant* system. This means that you only pay one-third of the cost of the drugs, with the balance being reimbursable via the *Sécurité Sociale*. Many chemists are now equipped for this system with *carte vitale* card readers. This option is only open to salaried employees within the French social security system, not to self-employed workers.

Finding the medicines that you need

Most medicines are available in France, but may be marketed under a different name from the one you know. It is very worthwhile checking this with your regular pharmacy, or even the drug company, before moving to France. Another good idea is to take the packaging listing the ingredients with you, so that the doctor can check the components against a similar product in the 'Bible' they always consult before prescribing.

Over-the-counter drugs are available in more or less the same way as in the UK. Chemists will advise you as to cost and value of the products you require. Paracetamol and aspirin are both known under the same names.

In 1999 the Health Ministry introduced a 'right of substitution' allowing pharmacists to suggest (but not impose) generic copies of the medicines prescribed. These medicines must contain all the same molecules and properties as the brand-named medicines marked on your prescription. If you accept these cheaper medicines (the average saving is 30%), then the actual medicine handed over the counter to you will be noted in writing on the original prescription beside the first-named medicine. Doctors are being encouraged more and more to prescribe cheaper generic drugs.

Weekend and evening pharmacies

Each pharmacy will take it in turn to stay open on Sundays and Bank Holidays. Details are normally displayed in pharmacies.

Obtaining exemption certificates

If you have a disability or disease which requires regular and/or expensive medication, you may be eligible for an exemption certificate (*pris en charge*). Normally this will cover 100% of all fees associated with treatment, including medicines.

You will need to speak to your family doctor or hospital specialist to arrange this. It is not an easy process, and can take a long time. There is a list of 30 diseases recognised as automatically offering exemption, and the minimum length of period for treatment is now considered to be six months.

The availability of such help can also vary from area to area, according to the local health authority budget. You will certainly need thorough medical documentation and a recommendation from a French doctor, and will be summoned to 'demonstrate' your disability or disease by a local health authority doctor (*médecin conseil*). Exemptions are also sometimes granted for a limited period after an accident and during the convalescence period.

Renewals of exemption certificates are always undertaken case by case. With the *carte vitale* system, you should theoretically be reviewed automatically, but it would be as well to keep a close eye on the end date of your exemption, and to make sure that your doctors have sent all the necessary documentation to your local *caisse* and *médecin conseil* at least three months before the expiry date of your exemption period.

GETTING REIMBURSED FOR MEDICAL TREATMENT

In major cities, the *carte vitale* system is now largely in operation, leading to automatic reimbursement of medical fees and prescription charges.

If you are in an area which is still operating under the old system, once you have a complete *feuille de soin*, fill in the personal details, including social security number and means of payment (direct debit or cheque), and send it to your local *caisse*, where your file (*dossier*) is held. Keep a copy of each *feuille de soin* sent. In either case after several weeks, you will eventually be reimbursed, and will receive a statement of how much you have been received for each expense. You will also need to send a complete *feuille de soin* to your local *caisse* if you have lost your card, and are waiting for a new one.

The DSS form EHIC available from British post offices will provide British citizens with emergency healthcare cover for up to three months from the date of issue. However, the level of cover is limited to emergencies. Reimbursement can take place in either France or the UK. Private health insurance will provide a fuller cover for a visit of several months.

Under new French legislation, certain charges are no longer reimbursed by the health service, nor by complementary health schemes. These are all part of the efforts to balance the health service books.

♦ €1 of your standard consultation fee will not be reimbursed.

♦ For some more minor surgical acts and scans, which cost more than €91, a total of €18 is now at the charge of the patient and will not be reimbursed.

♦ From 2008, a new annual *franchise médicale* (medical threshold) has been introduced for all patients, with the exception of those under 18, pregnant women from the sixth month of their pregnancy until 12 days after delivery, and certain beneficiaries of the CMU. The following amounts will not be reimbursed to patients for the services listed: €0.50 for every box of medicines, €0.50 for every paramedical act, and €2 if you require medical transportation. The total limit of the patient threshold or contribution for these services each year has been limited to €50 per patient. Once you go beyond the €50 limit, you will be fully reimbursed. This scheme is intended to help finance research and support for victims of Alzheimer's Disease. If you require regular paramedical acts or transport, a mechanism has been devised to limit the daily cost.

TAKING ADVANTAGE OF ADDITIONAL HEALTH INSURANCE

The remaining part of your expenditure on treatment or medicines can be reimbursed by joining a *mutuelle*, which is the standard French private health scheme. If you are in paid employment, you will almost always find that you are automatically included in such a scheme. Contributions are deducted each month along with regular social security contributions, and will be indicated on your pay-slip.

Almost every trade and profession has its own *mutuelle*, and it is very worthwhile belonging to such a scheme. Benefits can also include extra sick pay, a 'top up' to retirement pensions, and the ability to use private clinics if necessary, or if you choose. In principal, *mutuelles* will cover the remaining costs incurred. They will also cover some dental and eye-care costs.

Some *mutuelles* offer the possibility of linking your reimbursements from the *Sécu* directly to the reimbursement system offered by your *mutuelle*. For further details of this kind of service, you will need to make enquiries with your own *mutuelle*. Otherwise, you will need to send each statement of reimbursement from the *Sécu* to the *mutuelle*, along with your *mutuelle* membership details.

Students are required by law to join one of the special student *mutuelles*. See Chapter 4 for further details.

GOING TO HOSPITAL

Every large town has at least one *hôpital conventionné* which acts as the local general hospital, and includes the casualty unit (*urgences*).

You have a free choice as to whether to enter a public hospital (providing you do not arrive in emergency!), or a private clinic. However, there are certain differences as regards reimbursement for the cost of your healthcare. Private hospital treatment will only be reimbursed by the *Sécurité Sociale* at the same rate as treatment in a *hôpital conventionné*. If you choose a private clinic, you will be given a form which must be validated by your local health authority centre, where your file is held. Once this has been validated, you hand this back to the clinic at your admission.

Your local *caisse d'assurance maladie* will settle the largest part of your hospital bill (80%) if you are in a public hospital. Remember that private clinics will charge more for their services, and that you will only be reimbursed on the basis of a stay in a public hospital. The outstanding 20% (or more for private treatment) is at your cost. When you need hospital treatment is thus the moment that you will most appreciate financially the benefits of a *mutuelle*.

In all cases you will be asked to pay the *forfait journalier* (about €16 per day), which is basically a 'board and lodging' fee. You will normally also be offered the chance to hire your own telephone, and sometimes also a TV. Rooms are normally shared, except for those cases which require isolation.

There are numerous situations where your entire medical bill (i.e. not just the usual 80%), except the *forfait journalier*, will be paid entirely for you by your local *caisse*. For instance:

◆ Important surgery.

◆ If you are in hospital more than 31 days.

- Delivery of a baby (for 12 days) – nor are you obliged to pay the *forfait journalier*.

- If your admission is due to a work accident – once again, the *forfait journalier* is not charged.

- If you are receiving invalidity payments or benefit due to a work accident.

- If you are suffering from a serious illness which requires expensive medical care (as recognised by your local *caisse*).

You may also find that certain minor operations and clinical tests will take place during the course of one day, in which case you will be assigned a bed and admitted only for the day (*hôpital du jour*).

DENTAL CARE AND EYE CARE

The same rules apply for visits to the *dentiste* or the *ophtalmologiste* (optician) as apply to visiting a doctor. The optician will simply provide the prescription for your glasses or contact lenses, and you must then go to one of the many specialist shops in order to choose your frames or lenses. *Conventionné* dentists' fees are reimbursed at the same levels as doctors' fees in the same category.

POINTS TO REMEMBER

1. It is very important to check if the medical practitioners and services you use – doctor, dentist, optician, hospital, physiotherapist, etc. – are *conventionné*. There is nothing to stop you using private medicine, but you must be able to bear the cost.

2. About 20% of doctors are *non conventionné*. Their fees are reimbursed much less by the *Securité Sociale* and *mutuelles*. Practitioners who are *conventionné à honoraires libres* charge variable prices. The *Securité Sociale* will reimburse at their *conventionné* fixed rate, and the *mutuelle* normally covers the rest of the cost. For instance, if your *non-conventionné* doctor *à honoraries libres* charges you €28 for a consultation, the *Sécu* will reimburse you on the basis of 70% of €22, not 70% of €28.

3. Make sure that all practitioners complete a *feuille de soin* and return this to you after each consultation. Also make sure that pharmacists similarly complete their part of the feuille, and attach the *vignettes* from the medicine boxes. Where your *carte vitale* is accepted and used, pharmacists normally retain the *feuille de soin* now and send it directly to the *Sécu*.

HEALTH IN THE WORKPLACE

The French commitment to healthcare includes the firm doctor (*médecin de travail*). You will be expected to undergo a medical examination by this doctor, paid for by the firm:

◆ When you join the company.
◆ Regularly once a year thereafter.
◆ After a prolonged absence due to illness.
◆ After pregnancy leave.

You also have the right to ask to see this doctor on request, and you may also be obliged to see the doctor at the request of your company. These doctors also carry out 'spot-checks' on your working conditions.

SICK LEAVE AND SICK PAY

Under French law, absence due to illness during the first year of your contract is not paid leave. Application of this law is, however, often at the discretion of the firm.

If you are obliged to take time off work due to illness, ask the doctor for a sick note (*arrêt de travail*). You should complete and sign this paper, and send one copy to your employer, two copies to the *Securité Sociale*, and keep one copy for yourself.

The note will specify the length of absence permitted, and will also designate the hours in which you may go out to buy provisions, etc. This is from 10h00–12h00 in the morning and from 16h00–18h00 in the afternoon. If you intend to recuperate from your sickness elsewhere than your home, then you must have the prior agreement of your local *caisse*. If you are admitted to a hospital, you must also include a copy of the *bulletin d'entrée* given to you when you are admitted. **You must send off this note to your employer and your caisse within 48 hours.**

Be warned – the *Securité Sociale* regularly undertake random investigations to see if you are obeying the terms of the note. If you are not there when the Inspector calls, the *Securité Sociale* can and will refuse to reimburse the firm for part of your salary during your absence. You could also face disciplinary proceedings. You are obliged to provide all details regarding the place where you can be visited during your *arrêt de travail*. This includes providing entry codes to your building.

Your employer will continue to pay you during your absence, but will recover part of the cost from your *caisse d'assurance maladie*.

Your entitlement depends upon having completed a certain number of hours of work. If your inability to work lasts less than six months, your eligibility will depend upon your having worked 200 hours in the last three months. If your inability is more serious and requires a longer period off work, eligibility for sick pay requires you to have worked at least 12 months, with at least 200 hours' work in the last three months.

Accidents in the workplace

If you have an accident at work or travelling to work, you should inform your employer within 24 hours. You must then ensure that the following steps are taken:

a) **By your employer** – your employer must declare the accident at your own *caisse* within 48 hours; give you a form certifying the accident, ref. 6201, which will exempt you from paying medical fees in advance; and send an *attestation de salaire* to your *caisse* if you are signed off work due to the accident.

b) **By your doctor** – the doctor who treats you should issue a medical certificate (ref. 6909) indicating your state of health and the consequences of the accident; send sheets 1 and 2 within 24 hours to your local caisse, and give you sheets 3 and 4 of the declaration.

c) **By you yourself** – send sheet 4 (*certificat d'arrêt de travail*) to your employer; and take sheet 3 of the medical certificate to every subsequent doctor's appointment, etc.

Sick pay is subject to income tax, and basically you will receive half your normal daily pay. Maternity pay or monies paid as a result of a work accident are not subject to income tax. Payments are made every 14 days.

DEALING WITH FAMILY MATTERS

Pregnancy healthcare

If you are a British citizen and pregnant at the time of moving to France, you should speak to your doctor and local health authority to find out what steps you need to take to ensure your health and benefit entitlements.

You must declare your pregnancy before the end of the third month to your *caisse d'assurance maladie*, and to the *caisse d'allocations familiales* or *CAF* (Family Benefit centre). To do this you must hand in the *premier examen médical parental* form duly signed by your doctor. You will receive a *carnet de maternité* which contains vouchers allowing you to receive the services to which you are entitled.

Figure 10 on page 234, translated from the French National Health Service Pregnancy Guide, explains clearly the steps you need to take and when, in the event of a pregnancy. As you will also see, the French National Health Service offers a generous package of free and subsidised medical support during pregnancy.

These rights are limited by the number of hours worked and the amount of money you have paid – or your husband or partner has paid – over the preceding months. You will have to pay as usual for all the services you receive, but will receive reimbursement at 100%. To do so you need to stick your vouchers to the *feuille de soins* each time that you send in a claim for reimbursement, unless the practitioners are equipped with the *carte vitale* card reader.

Time-line	Medical services	Formalities to accomplish
First quarter	First consultation reimbursed at 100% and first Echography scan reimbursed at 70%.	*Déclaration de grossese* (pregnancy declaration) at the CAF. Check out local childcare facilities. Contact your *Mairie* for details.
4th month	Second consultation reimbursed at 100%, plus a full blood test for the father also reimbursed at 100%.	The first of eight free ante-natal sessions will be arranged.
5th month	Third consultation reimbursed at 100% and second Echography scan reimbursed at 70%.	If you have not already done so, contact a midwife (*sage-femme*) or gynaecologist for future appointments.
6th month	Fourth consultation reimbursed at 100%.	From the first day of the sixth month of the pregnancy, all medical charges for the expectant mother are reimbursed at 100%. This applies until 12 days after the delivery. None of the statutory contributions (€1 or €18) are withheld.
7th month	Fifth consultation reimbursed at 100%.	From now on, 7 free ante-natal sessions are reimbursed at 100%.
8th month	Sixth consultation reimbursed at 100% and third Echography scan reimbursed at 100%. Pre-anaesthetic consultation.	
9th month	Seventh consultation reimbursed at 100%. All costs linked to the delivery of your child will be fully reimbursed, if you use a *conventionné* hospital (or will be reimbursed at *conventionné* rates). All costs, including the *forfait journalier*, are free in the 12 days following the delivery. This also applies if you are admitted in the four months before the expected delivery date. Transportation fees can be reimbursed if they have been prescribed.	...Lift off!

Fig. 10. Pregnancy timeline. (Source: **www.ameli.fr**)

The current cost is about €160 for a delivery by a midwife (*sage-femme*). Extra costs are incurred for a night-time delivery, for Sundays and Bank Holidays. All costs are reimbursed at 100%.

Maternity leave pay

Once again, the number of hours and level of contributions made is one of the deciding factors in whether you receive paid maternity leave. You must also have been enrolled in the *Sécurité Sociale* at least ten months by the expected date of delivery of your baby.

To obtain maternity pay, you must send the *attestation de salaire* (salary certificate) signed by your employer to the *caisse d'assurance maladie* as soon as you begin your maternity leave. You must then send a similar form to the *caisse* at the end of your maternity leave. The pay is calculated on the basis of your salary for three months before you stopped work, and works out at 84% of your daily wage. At the end of your maternity leave, you must also send a certificate from your employer to your local *caisse* stating that you have returned to work.

If you are already receiving maternity allowance when you leave the UK, you may be able to persuade your British social security office to carry on providing that benefit.

Maternity leave entitlement

For a first or second child, the normal leave period is six weeks before delivery and ten weeks afterwards. From the third child onwards, it is eight weeks before delivery and eighteen weeks afterwards. For twins, it is 12 weeks before delivery and 22 weeks afterwards; and for triplets (or more) it is 24 weeks before delivery and 22 weeks afterwards. In the case of premature delivery, the total leave period is not reduced. In cases of medical necessity, a doctor may prescribe an extra two weeks.

Paternity leave

The new and popular paternity leave is reimbursed in exactly the same way as maternity leave pay. Employers are obliged to accept requests for paternity leave.

You automatically have the right to three days' leave when your child is born. To apply for paternity leave as well, you need to send a registered letter to your employer with receipt (*lettre recommandé avec accusé de réception* – see Chapter 5) at least one month before the start date of the paternity leave requested. A second registered letter, either from you or your employer, must be sent to your *caisse*, together with a salary certificate (*attestation de salaire*) and a copy of the birth certificate (*extrait d'acte de naissance*), or of your updated *livret de famille* with details of your new child, or of an official statement from you recognising fatherhood of the child (*acte de reconnaissance*).

You may take up to 11 days, but leave must be taken in one go (i.e. not a few days here or there). Weekends are included in the time calculated. It must be taken within four months of the birth. If you have had twins, triplets or more, your paternity leave entitlement rises to 18 days.

Registering the birth

You **must** register the birth of your new child **within three working days** – i.e. if your child is born on a Thursday, you have until the following Tuesday at the latest. Otherwise, you cannot register your child's birth without making an application to the courts. The registration should take place at the *mairie* of the place where your child was born, and the following documents are required:

♦ The *déclaration de naissance* completed by the hospital, doctor or midwife (*sage-femme*).

♦ A piece of official identity (driving licence, *carte de séjour*, passport) for the person registering the birth.

♦ The mother's *carnet de maternité* (see above).

♦ The *livret de famille* if you have one. You will only have this if you were married in France.

♦ Your passports (if you and your wife have separate passports).

♦ You should also register your child's birth at your own embassy to ensure the nationality rights of the child for the future. Contact the Consular services to find out how to do this.

Once you have registered the birth, you need to send a copy of the birth certificate (*extrait de certificat de naissance*) or the *livret de famille* to your local *caisse*. You should also add one of your 100% exemption vouchers. The *caisse* will you send a guide for medical 'surveillance' of your child up until their sixth birthday. You will also receive vouchers for the obligatory examinations which must be undertaken. These should be taken to the examining doctor on each occasion together with the *carnet de santé* (personal health note-book) of the child.

If you are not married, when it comes to registering the child at the *Mairie*, either person can declare their parenthood, or both.

The first parent to declare their parenthood will give their family name to the child, or both names can be recorded in the order which you wish. This can be done even before delivery. Your local health office (*caisse*) must also be informed to which parent the new child is officially linked, in order to update the parent's social security file, and create a new entry in the system for the child.

Maintaining foreign citizenship rights

Regulations change frequently, and it is important that you check with your own embassy as to the requirements for the correct registration of the nationality status of your children.

For American citizens, registration is by appointment only at the American Embassy (tél. 01 43 12 46 71). You should read the information on the American Embassy website for up-to-date requirements for this process (**www.amb-usa.fr**). You will need to request a registration pack which must be completed before the appointment and bring the originals or certified copies of the following documents, and also your child:

a) French birth certificate, *extrait de l'acte de naissance intégrale.*

b) Evidence of parent(s)'s US citizenship (e.g. passport, naturalisation certificate).

c) Parents' marriage certificate and *livret de famille* if the wedding took place in France.

d) If either of the parents has been previously married either the decree of dissolution or divorce, or the death certificate of the previous spouse.

e) Two recent passport sized photographs of the child for their passport.

f) Fees in cash or travellers' cheques – check the exact amount required when you make your appointment.

If the child has only one parent with US citizenship, the parent must have lived in the US for at least five years, two of them when they were over the age of 14.

A child born in France with two **Australian** parents has automatic Australian citizenship. Registration should occur either at birth or upon demand of a passport. Children with only one Australian parent need to apply to the immigration department of the Australian Embassy.

British parents are not obliged to register their new-born children at the Embassy. A child may have a British passport providing at least one parent is British, and both parents agree in writing. Remember that all British citizens of no matter what age are now required to have their own passport, and children may no longer be registered on their parents' passports.

Any child born with at least one parent who is a **Canadian** citizen is entitled to Canadian citizenship. Certificates of Canadian citizenship can be obtained at the Paris Embassy.

Support groups for English-speaking mothers

There are two principal Paris-based support groups for English-speaking mothers:

- Message (**www.messageparis.org**) – a network of English-speaking mothers and future mothers in and around Paris. Meetings and activities for mothers and children, specialising in early parenting.

- The Junior Service League of Paris (JSLP) (tél. 01 58 45 27 64) – a wide-ranging women's social welfare network and group including health and child welfare, and training courses for child-minders.

These organisations, and regional Consulates, will be able to put you in touch with regional associations.

Child benefit and family allowance

The current levels of family allowance (*allocation familiale*) are €120.32 for two children €247.47 for three children, and €154.15 extra per child for more than three children. For children aged 11–16, the amounts are increased by €33.64, and for those aged 16–21 and still at the charge of their parents, the amount is increased by €60.16 per child. However, if you only have two children, these increases only apply for the second child.

To apply for these benefits, you need to register at your local *centre d'allocations familiales (CAF)*. If your child is born in France, and you have declared the pregnancy (see above), the CAF should contact you automatically. Details of state assistance to which you may be entitled can be found on **www.caf.fr**. *Allocation Familiale* is means-tested, taking into account the salaries of both parents if they are working.

A number of other benefits are available from the CAF under certain conditions for parents who are forced to give up work to look after children:

◆ *Prime à la naissance* – the Birth Bonus is means-tested, and distributed in the seventh month of pregnancy. Multiple births will lead to multiple bonuses, if you qualify.

◆ *L'allocation de présence parentale* – valid initially for a six-month renewable period, within a limit of three years, the APP is available to parents to care for sick or disabled children.

◆ *L'allocation parentale d'éducation* – valid if you have given up your employment to look after your child up to the age of three years.

◆ *L'AFEAMA (aide à la famille pour l'emploi d'une assistante maternelle agrée)* – the level of aid offered depends on the total family income. The level of support is reduced when the child is three years old, when the child could enter a public school.

One parent benefit and child benefit from the British authorities normally ceases if you move abroad permanently. However, if you or your child stay in the UK, you can receive these benefits. Any UK insurance contributions you have paid **may** help in persuading the French authorities to pay you the French *allocations*. Contact your local Child Benefit Centre to find out more.

SEXUALLY TRANSMITTED DISEASES
Your nearest hospital will be able to put you in touch with services and clinics for sexually transmitted diseases (*maladies sexuellement transmises* or *MST*). For free AIDS information ring the SIDA Info Service on 0800 840 800 (24 hours a day, seven days a week).

SUPPORT FOR DISABLED PEOPLE
There are numerous support groups in France to help disabled

people and those who care for them. Your doctor should be able to direct you towards the appropriate association. You should also apply to the *bureau de l'aide sociale* of your local *mairie* for a Disabled Person's Card which will entitle you to certain discounts and assistance. See also Chapters 5 and 12 for further information on housing adaptation loans and travel assistance. Two benefits for people suffering from handicaps are operated by the *Caisse d'Allocations Famililes (CAF)*. The *Allocation aux Adultes Handicapés* is a means-tested benefit, aimed at severely handicapped people. A similar aid for the education of handicapped children, with similar conditions, the *Allocation de l'éducation de l'enfant handicapé*, is also operated by the *CAF.* Contact your local *CAF* to find out if you may qualify for these benefits.

If you are receiving severe disablement allowance in the UK and you want to go to another EU country, including France, you must contact the Pensions and Overseas Benefits Directorate, Department of Social Security, Tyneview Park, Whitley Road, Benton, Newcastle upon Tyne NE98 1BA. The decision as to whether you continue to receive this allowance will depend upon your age, how disabled you are and how long you have lived in the UK.

If you are receiving any form of disability working allowance or carer's allowance, and you move to France, you will not be able to continue receiving British support. Visiting France may also affect your UK allowance. Contact your local benefits authority to see what help they can offer in transferring your rights gained by British National Insurance contributions to the appropriate French authorities.

Services of interest for those with disabilities who are living in France include:

◆ France Telecom provide a range of products called *'Arc-en-Ciel'* (rainbow) which are designed to facilitate communication for the disabled. These include telephones with flashing lights for the hearing impaired, and a system known as the *boîtier dialogue* which allows communication via Minitel for the hard of hearing or speech-impaired at an increased speed. Ask at France Telecom agencies for details.

◆ The RATP provides details of RER and métro stations and bus lines that provide easy access for passengers with disabilities. More details can be found on their website at **www.ratp.fr**, (click on the wheelchair to access the special pages for handicapped travellers), or by telephoning Infomobi on 0810 64 64 64. The French national railways service, SNCF, offers a variety of travel discounts and arrangements for disabled travellers. **To qualify for these advantages, apply at the *bureau de l'aide sociale* of your local *mairie* for the appropriate card**. Similar offers may be offered by other travel companies, so do check. The French government website at **www.franceguide.com** has an extensive section of tips and links for disabled travellers. You should also check out the website **www.mobile-en-ville.asso.fr**. This association website publishes guides for those who use wheel power – pushchairs, prams, roller-blades and wheel-chairs – to explore Paris and the surrounding suburbs. They are also drawing up a 'Handimap' of Paris for the City Council.

- **FAVA** (tél. 01 42 45 17 91) is the Franco-American Volunteers Association for people with learning disabilities, providing programmes for children and adults.

SERVICES FOR ENGLISH-SPEAKING PATIENTS

Many French doctors do speak some English. But unless you are reasonably fluent in French and familiar with medical terms, you could experience difficulties, especially if the illness or problem is serious. Help can be found at the following places:

- English-language Consulates have lists of English-speaking doctors.

- Private health insurance companies and travellers' associations (e.g. American Express, the Automobile Association) often have help-packs they can provide to their customers.

- The American Hospital in Paris, 63 boulevard Victor-Hugo, 92202 Neuilly-sur-Seine Cedex, tél. 01 46 41 25 25. Emergency Service number: 01 47 47 70 15, patient access department: 01 46 41 27 27. This expensive hospital may be accessible to you via your *mutuelle*, but otherwise do not count on receiving much reimbursement from the *Sécu* for using this hospital.

- The Hertford British Hospital in Paris, 3 rue Barbés, 92300 Levallois-Perret, tél. 01 46 39 22 26, 01 46 39 22 22 for emergencies, fax 01 46 39 22 26. A small modern hospital within the French Social Security system with English and English-speaking staff.

- Sunny Bank Hospital, 133 avenue de Petit Juas, 06400 Cannes, tél. 04 93 06 31 06. Private Anglo-American hospital.

- The Paris English-language group of Alcoholics Anonymous, tél. 01 46 34 59 65.

- A cancer-support group is based at the American Hospital, tél. 01 46 41 25 25.

- SOS Help – English language telephone crisis line linked to the Samaritans and Befrienders International. Tél. 01 47 23 80 80 every day 15h00–23h00.

- SPRINT – **www.sprint.france.free.fr** – is an association of English-speaking therapists for children with special needs.

FINDING OUT MORE

- **British citizens** should check the two relevant government websites: Department of Work and Pensions leaflet, **www.dwp.gov.uk** (you will need *Acrobat Reader* software for the on-line version of leaflet SA29; Department of Health, www.doh.gov.uk/travel advice.

- **www.cnmats.fr** – the national site of the French health authority, which allows you to locate your local health authority website and addresses (in French only).

- **www.caf.fr** – the family benefits unit, for everything from maternity and paternity leave information to child benefits, to housing benefits (French only).

- **www.amelie.fr** – this website mainly acts as a springboard for more detailed health agency sites. All of these sites are in French only. The *Centre des Relations Internationales* of the *Sécurité Sociale* is at 175 rue de Bercy, 75586 Paris, cedex 12 (next to the Gare de Lyon) tél. 01 40 19 53 19.

DISABILITY AND HANDICAP

Travel guides for disabled and handicapped travellers are available in the UK from:

◆ RADAR, 12 City Forum, 250 City Road, London EC1V 8AF. Tel: (020) 7250 3222. **www.radar-shop-org.uk**.

SAMU (ambulance service)	**15**
Police	**17**
Sapeurs-Pompiers (fire brigade and ambulance service)	**18**

0800 23 13 13	Free drug information service
0800 05 41 41	Free child-abuse help line
0800 306 306	Free helpline for the homeless
0800 840 840	Free AIDS information service in French
01 46 21 46 46	SOS Help – English-language telephone crisis line. Every day 15h00-23h00

Fig. 11. Emergency telephone numbers in France.

11

Enrolling for Education

Generally, academic levels are very high in France, and teachers, pupils and students are expected to show a serious commitment to their work. The Socialist government of the Chirac era placed an increased emphasis on modern languages and the arts within the school curriculum, but the more recent Right-wing governments have increasingly insisted on a 'back to basics' programme centred on mastering the French language, 'reading, writing and arithmetic'. From September 2008, there will be lessons on personal hygiene and politeness, and Saturday Morning School will also be abolished for elementary classes. President Sarkozy has also provoked strong reactions by insisting on a more patriotic approach to education, including increased emphasis on the role of the French Resistance in the Second World War. More generally, the emphasis is being placed on providing extra help to pupils struggling with basic literacy, and extra-curricular catch-up classes are being introduced.

The French education system remains one of the bastions of militant union action. One of the curiosities of France is that even pupils sometimes go on strike! Students and teachers regularly set the example for this. Change is not something which comes easily in France, and whilst the younger generation of *professeurs* (or *profs*) (high school teachers) and *instituteurs* (or *instits*) (junior school teachers) are open to new ideas, the older generation tend to hold the eternal view of French education. Funding remains a major problem for all levels of the education system, and is at the heart of most of the problems in the academically successful, but physically needy, French universities.

THE ACADEMIC YEAR

France very much beats to the rhythm of the academic year. This begins in mid-September with *la rentrée scolaire* and ends in late June. A mid-term break occurs around All Saints Day (*Toussaint*) at the beginning of November, followed by a two-week break for Christmas and New Year. There is then another mid-term break in February, and two weeks for Easter holidays (not necessarily linked to the date of Easter itself). Holiday dates vary from region to region.

THE SCHOOL DAY

In state schools, children attend school from 08h30–11h30, and then from 13h30–16h30 from Monday to Saturday, with Wednesday and Saturday afternoons free. Variations occur according to the level of education of your child; Wednesdays are completely free for smaller children, whilst Saturday mornings and Wednesdays are obligatory for older children at *lycée*. Some private schools have adopted the more simple five-day week, as have some experimental *collèges*. From September 2008, Saturday Morning School will be abolished for all pupils in the *écoles élémentaires* (pupils aged 6 to 11 years old). The school week will be adapted to provide 24 hours of class time, and two hours of extra-curricular support classes.

NURSERY EDUCATION (AGE TWO TO SIX)

School is not compulsory in France for children until they are six years old. Nonetheless, 93% of three-year-old children in France are enrolled in the voluntary *écoles maternelles*.

Enrolling your child

Enrolment takes place at your local *mairie*, on the published dates (normally around March), and can be performed as soon as the child reaches the age of two years. At enrolment, you will be informed of the school catchment area you fall into. It is possible to choose another school if you wish, by following a typically long procedure. Documents needed to enrol your child are:

♦ The *livret de famille* (if you were married in France) or a *fiche d'état civile* of the child.

♦ A proof of residence (*justificatif de domicile*), e.g. electricity bill with your name and address.

♦ The *carnet de santé* of your child, proving they have received all necessary vaccinations.

Once you have received the enrolment certificate (*certificat d'inscription*) from the *mairie*, you need to make an appointment straight away with the school headteacher. Children are accepted on a 'first come, first served' basis, with priority for older children. Schooling for children under three years old depends on the availability of places.

The classes offered in the *école maternelle* are roughly equivalent to Early Learning in the UK for French Year One; the UK Reception Class for French in Year Two; and the UK Year One for the French Year Three (for five–six-year-old children). Classes equate to US nursery schools for French Years One and Two, and US Kindergarten for French Year Three.

PRIMARY EDUCATION (AGE 6 TO 11)

When your child begins their compulsory education at the age of six, they will enter the *Cours Préparatoire* known as *CP*, and then progress to *Cours élémentaire première année* known as *CE1*; then *CE2*; then the *Cours moyen première année*, or *CM1*, followed by the *CM2*.

If your child is already enrolled at an *école maternelle*, they will automatically be enrolled at your local school. Enrolments must take place no later than the month of June preceding your child's entry into the school at the *école élémentaire*. For popular schools, the sooner you apply the better your chances are of enrolling your child at the school of your choice. The same processes must be gone through if you wish to choose a school in a different sector. If your child is not already enrolled, you must follow the process outlined above.

In the *écoles élémentaires*, (for 6–11-year-olds) the course of study may change according to the area you live in. Basically children are taught to read and write, along with learning basic maths and a few less academic subjects. As children grow older, they are rigorously taught the grammatical rules of the French language, including spelling and the use of tenses.

A great deal of time is spent learning poetry, which is considered good practice for the child's memory. Sciences of observation will take up to about an hour a week depending on the teacher. Most schools now spend a few hours a week on English, arts and crafts, an extra sport and a computer class. A lot depends on the human and other resources available in a school as to what is offered.

The use of the Internet in schools and teaching is strongly encouraged, but depends on school resources. Physical education usually includes two hours per week of general fitness classes and all children learn to swim.

SECONDARY EDUCATION (AGE 11 TO 15)

From the 6ème to the 3ème (11 to 15 years old), children attend a **collège**. Similar procedures exist for enrolling your child in a *collège* as for other state schools. If you choose a *collège* outside your district, your choice requires more justification than at earlier stages. Acceptance depends upon, amongst other factors, the availability of places in the *collège* chosen.

At *collège*, pupils have a different teacher for each subject, and classes generally last about 50 minutes. Maths and French are still the most important subjects, and are really still considered as the keys to a child's success. History and geography are taught as one subject, and physics and natural sciences are each attributed equal importance.

When students enter *collège* in the *6ème*, they choose a foreign language to study, normally English or German. In the *4ème*, they choose a second foreign or regional language to study, and in the *3éme* there is an opportunity to choose an optional course in either Latin or Greek.

Repeating a year

When a student reaches the end of an academic year they change from one cycle to another – at the end of the *6ème*, *4ème* and *3ème* – the *conseil de classe* ('class board') composed of the teachers concerned decides if they are ready to move on to the next class. If they think not, then they can recommend that the student repeat a year (known as *redoublement*).

If you disagree with the decision, you must act swiftly to lodge your complaint (within three days). You will need to see the headteacher to request an explanation for the decision. However, if you still disagree with the decision, you can force the issue to another 'commission' including other parents, and at which you will be allowed to speak briefly. However, the decision here is final once it is taken.

Planning for the future

In February of the *3ème*, families are requested to fill in a form indicating the proposed career orientation they wish their child to take. Final applications and decisions are taken in May of the *3ème*, with input from the school. At the end of the *3ème* (aged 14 to 15), students take a 'global' examination known as the *brevet*.

The result of this examination, together with the annual report, is used to decide upon the future education of the student. However, it is not an entry examination to *lycée*, but simply a knowledge test for the end of this section of the child's education.

The choices made at this stage affect the type of *lycée* to which your child will next progress, and the sort of qualifications they will leave school with. The choice of *lycées* are:

◆ *générale et technologique*
◆ *professionnelle*.

The final decision is taken by a small commission, which informs parents at about the end of June which kind of *lycée* their child has been recommended for. More than 25% of students currently choose to orientate themselves towards professional life by opting to work towards either a *brevet d'études professionnelle (BEP)* or a *certificat d'aptitude professionnelle (CAP)*, both of which are two-year courses at *lycées professionnelles*. Normally this will lead to an entry into working life almost immediately after leaving school.

THE FINAL SCHOOL YEARS (AGE 16 TO 18)

The final school years are *seconde*, *première* and *terminale*. The latter is when the final *baccalauréat (bac)* examination is taken. For these final years, your child will be educated at a *lycée*. It is here that final choices will be taken which affect the kind of *bac* for which your child will prepare, and consequently, the kind of higher education which they will normally continue with.

Seconde

More than 60% of students currently enter the *seconde* in the general/technology classes. This leaves scope for taking final decisions over which type of *bac* to study for. Only those seeking careers in music or dance, or a technical qualification (*brevet de technologie, BT*) have specifically orientated courses. Those preparing either the *BEP* or *CAP* can study a further two years to take a *bac professionnel* before finishing their studies.

Première and *terminale*

The choice must now be made which of the variety of *bacs* your child will study for. The general *bac* leaves the option open for entry into higher education. Other choices will be required if your child wishes to pursue a vocational course at university. The courses attended in these final years will depend on the option chosen. There are seven compulsory subjects plus physical education and two optional subjects.

At the end of the *première*, there are written and oral French tests for *bac* candidates. The marks from these are included in the overall success or failure of the candidate. The final examinations are taken in summer of the *terminale*, and results are published very shortly afterwards at the end of June or beginning of July.

For those who fail the first time, it is possible to re-take the *bac*. As it is the key to any form of success in France, as well as entry to higher education, it is highly advisable to do so!

EDUCATION IN ENGLISH

The opportunity for a child to be educated at a French school can be excellent for their future prospects, ensuring that they will be bilingual. However, it may also prove frightening and daunting for a child whose command of French is not sufficient. You must also consider the effect upon their education if you will only be living in France short-term, and will be returning to your native country and education system.

The options open to you are:

1. Boarding school in the UK or the US – this may not even be an option, depending upon your financial situation, your company's willingness to pay fees, and yours and your child's attitude to boarding school.

2. Private international schools in France – the same financial criteria may affect your decision, and as well as accessibility to any such schools.

3. French schools with international sections – these are schools within the state system which normally charge a small fee for schooling in English. These schools work towards the *option internationale* of the *Bac*, and teaching is by native English-speakers.

4. French schools that offer high-level English programmes – extra hours of education in English from native English-speakers.

5. French schools with European sections – these will normally offer some extra education in English, but not necessarily given by a native English-speaker.

The American School of Paris (tél. 01 41 12 82 82, fax 01 41 06 23 90, **www.asparis.org**) and British Schools of Paris (tél. 01 34 80 45 90, fax 01 39 76 12 69, **www.britishschool.fr**), private schools in the suburbs, each follow the national curriculums of their 'home' countries. They would therefore allow your children to continue within the same educational system as they may have known before, according to your own nationality.

The international sections of *lycées* probably offer the best option for those who want their children to benefit from an Anglo-French education at a very reasonable cost. Currently there are about eight British sections in France, and about six American sections. The general rule (which varies between sections) is about four hours per week of English language and literature, and two hours a week of geography and history. The International Lycée at St Germain-en-Laye is considered to be the best (tél. 01 34 51 62 64, fax 01 34 51 39 36, **www.lycee-international.com**.

The International option of the *bac* is very highly regarded, and roughly equivalent to S levels within the British education system. It is therefore a good option for those seeking university entry not only in France, but in other countries too.

More information about native English education in France is available from **The English-Language Schools Association France (ELSA-France)**, **www.elsa-france.org**. This website has full information on all schools in France offering English-language education in all categories (state, private, exclusively English-speaking and part-English speaking). ELSA has strong links with the Section Internationale at the Collège & Lycée de Sevres, rue Lecoq, 92310 Sévres (tél. 01 46 23 96 35).

EDUCATIONAL BENEFITS

- *L'aide à la scolarité* – this is available for children at *collège*. It is means-tested, and limited to those who are already receiving another form of family or housing benefit, or benefit for a disabled adult.

- *L'allocation de rentrèe scolaire* – this is available for children between six and 18 years old, under the same conditions as above. Each child will automatically be awarded the benefit. The maximum of joint income permitted to obtain this benefit rises with the number of children that you have.

Both benefits are administered by the *caisse d'allocations familiales*.

HIGHER EDUCATION

Since 1987, France's student population has grown dramatically. However, there has been no similar growth in funding or facilities. Students tend to go to the university nearest to their home, partly to keep down costs by continuing to live at home. Naturally Paris draws a huge student population of not only locals but 'foreigners' in all senses of the word, from other parts of France and from other parts of the world, drawn to the city's academically excellent institutions.

In 2000, 173,000 foreign students were studying in France. The government is currently studying the European standardisation programme of university degrees to work out precisely how to structure French degrees in the future.

The only entrance requirement is normally a pass at *bac*. As a result, there is generally high competition to enrol on the course of your choice at the university of your choice. The university year runs from October until June.

The French degree structure

◆ **Years 1 and 2 –** *DEUG (Diplôme d'Etudes Universitaires Générales)*. This is the core curriculum course which must be passed before continuing with further study. Many students repeat this year, and the DEUG on its own is not highly regarded.

◆ **Year 3 –** *Licence*. This can be passed in most subjects. It is roughly equivalent to a BA or BSc.

◆ **Year 4 –** *Maîtrise*. Roughly equivalent to an MA.

- **Year 5 – *DEA (Diplôme d'Etudes Approfondies)*.** A preparatory year for a doctorate.

- The **Doctorate** is the final stage. There is now a limit of four years for completion of the doctoral thesis.

If there is any doubt over the level of your degree, a *lettre d'équivalence* can be requested from the *Ministère de l'Enseignement et de la Recherche* equating your degree to a French degree level.

In accordance with the European standardisation programme, the French degree structure is being adapted to the '**3-5-8**' or '*LMD*' system, of *bac* + 3 (**Licence**), *bac* + 5 (**Master**), and *bac* + 8 (**Doctorat**). The new system will take into account credits earned at other universities, and notably at foreign universities.

Student resident permits

Some Paris colleges and university departments have agreements with the residence permit authorities of the *Préfecture de Paris* allowing you to submit your application for a *carte de séjour* directly to the college administration. In this case, they will pilot you through the formalities of application and you will only have to go to the *Préfecture* to collect your permit once it is ready. This applies to students of all nationalities.

If you undertake the process yourself, remember to take copies of everything with you, as well as originals. The same rules apply for student *cartes des séjours* as for all other foreign nationals in France.

1. Citizens of one of the original EU member countries do not require a *carte de séjour*.

2. Citizens of one of the countries which joined the EU in 2004 do still require a *carte de séjour*.

3. Non-EU citizens do require a *carte de séjour* (see below).

Students in the second category should consult their own Embassy for up-to-date information on the documents required, which may include some of the items listed below for non-EU students.

Students from other countries

American students require an entry visa before arrival in France. In addition to the basic requirements for Americans applying for a *visa de long séjour* (see Chapter 2), students will also require a letter of admission (*attestation de pré-inscription*) when applying for the first time to a French university, or other similar evidence of enrolment. Academic credentials may be checked by the French Consular services in the USA where you apply for your visa. Nationals of other countries should check with their nearest French Consular office for formalities which they need to complete.

You must apply for your *carte de séjour* within 30 days of entering France. You will need to bring:

1. The original of your valid passport plus copies of the pages indicating the marital status of the applicant, the date limit of the passport and the visa allowing entry into France.

2. Originals plus copies of degree certificates, exam results, etc., to prove the seriousness of your application; and the *certificat*

d'immatriculation, d'inscription, or *pré-inscription* for your course at your college or faculty. For higher education establishments which do not fit into the university category, check with your college administrators for the documentation required.

3. Originals plus copies of proof of residence (see above). If you are staying in a hostel or student residence, you will need a recent signed *attestation* from the director and also a recent bill.

4. Proof of financial resources as above. If you are receiving a grant, you will need a statement on letter-headed paper from the grant-making authority stating the duration of the grant, the amount, and what studies you are undertaking. If you are receiving funds from abroad, you need to take as much evidence as possible with you of monthly payments. If you are being financed by a third party in France, you need to supply a certificate and personal and financial documents relating to your sponsor (enquire for further details).

5. Original plus copies of your proof of social security cover. Either your social security card or an *attestation* stating that you have signed up to the student *régime* of the *Sécu*; or a personal insurance programme either approved by URSSAF, the social security agency, or stating that you have complete cover for illness, accidents and pregnancy.

Student welfare

Students have their own *régime* in the *Sécurité Sociale*, for those between 20 and 28 years old. Students from EU countries will need form EHIC when coming to study in France. Upon arrival they will then need to contact the *direction des régimes spéciaux* of their local university *caisse d'assurance maladie*.

You must join the student social security *régime* if you are over 20 and under 28, and/or you are a foreign student; have no rights deriving from a parent, or from your own paid employment; and you are enrolled in an establishment deemed to fall under the student social security *régime*. Students who receive a French government grant are exempt from the social security fee.

There are also two student *mutuelles* (additional health insurance schemes) available, from which you should choose one to join: either La Mutuelle des Etudiants (137 bd St Michel, 75005 Paris, tél. 0810 600 601, **www.lmde.com**); or La SMEREP (54 bd St Michel, 75005 Paris, tél. 01 56 54 36 34, **www.smerep.fr**). The LMDE site has a well-presented multi-lingual section which explains student healthcare procedures for foreign students.

Housing and other benefits are means-tested on the basis of the income of the student's parents. All students are eligible for limited housing benefit. However, a distinction is made between those who depend solely on their parents for financial support, and those who work their way through their studies. In fact, those who work are worse off in terms of benefits.

Two of the most important places that you will need to find are the *CROUS (Centre Régional des Oeuvres Universitaires et Scolaires)*, and the *CIDJ (Centre d'Information et de Documentation Jeunesse)*, if your university has one. The important Paris *CIDJ* is at 101 quai Branly, 75015 Paris, beside the Eiffel Tower (tél. 01 44 49 12 00).

The *CROUS* will issue your student card, which will allow you a wide variety of discounts (e.g. travel, museum entrance, etc.). The

CROUS acts to some extent as a student union would in a British university, in terms of the welfare and general information services it offers.

The Cité Internationale Universitaire de Paris (www.ciup.fr)

Founded after the First World War, the extensive residential campus on the southern edge of Paris with its own sports grounds and RER station is a popular choice for students in higher education. There 27 nations have their own *college* or *maison*. The main reception centre at 19 boulevard Jourdan, 75014 Paris can be contacted on 01 44 16 65 54, and the admission office on 01 44 16 64 41 (01 44 16 64 68 for the student welcome centre). The College Franco-Britannique (9b, boulevard Jourdan), which can be contacted on 01 44 16 24 00, admits over 200 students of at least third year university level from all over the world, with 50% of the rooms reserved for British students. There are also American and Canadian colleges.

The *grandes écoles*

The *grandes écoles* are the élite higher education institutions (some of which are private), which consistently produce the leaders of French commerce, industry, politics and society in general.

Competition for entry is obviously fierce and very selective. Being a foreigner will probably not help your case, unless you have already attended a top-level university in your own country. However, if you do succeed in graduating from one of these schools, a successful professional life will be almost assured, and you will have a very useful set of future contacts.

English-speaking universities in France

The American University of Paris (www.aup.edu)

◆ **US Admissions Office**, 950 South Cherry Street, Suite 210, Denver, Colorado, 80246. Tel. 303 757 6333, Fax 303 757 6444, e-mail: usoffice@aup.edu.

◆ **Paris Admissions and Summer Programme Office**, 6 rue du Colonel Combes, 75007 Paris. Tél. 01 40 62 07 20, Fax 01 47 05 34 32, email: admissions@aup.edu.

The American University of Paris (AUP) is a private university based in central Paris in the 7th *arrondissement*, near to the American Church community centre. The AUP offers undergraduate courses in a wide variety of subjects, summer programmes and continuing education which will help you develop skills for the French job markets (e.g. web design, screen-writing, accounting). All courses are taught in English. The AUP also offers help with accommodation for its students. Candidates may join the university for either the fall or spring semesters. The AUP also offers distance learning courses.

The British Institute of Paris
The British Institute (**www.ulip.lon.ac.uk**) tél. 01 44 11 73 73, fax 01 45 50 31 55), housed in the same building as the British Council (the cultural affairs department of the British Embassy **www.britishcouncil.fr**), is situated at 11 rue Constantine overlooking Les Invalides. The Institute is an integral part of the University of London, and offers a BA honours degree course in French studies, the only British university department offering the chance to learn French in France. The Institute also offers continuing education courses such as translation. The British

Council regularly organises workshops and seminars with visiting authors and academics.

The Open University

The British distance-learning university, the Open University, has now been operating in France for several years, and has held two degree conferral ceremonies in Paris. All courses are taught in English using proven methods, and cover a wide range of subjects. The obligatory summer schools are also held in France. For further information, write to: Rosemary Pearson, 51 rue de Villiers, 92200 Neuilly-sur-Seine, tél. 01 47 58 53 73, fax 01 47 58 55 25, email: r.pearson@ open.ac.uk, **www.open.ac.uk**.

Other degree courses in Paris

There are an increasing number of **MBA** courses being taught from Paris bases with joint-teaching programmes linked to US universities and business schools. These courses are almost all taught at least partially in English. Details of the courses and schools available will be found in most English-language magazines in Paris. The most renowned French business school is INSEAD (tél. 01 60 72 42 42) near Fontainebleau, now ranked amongst the world's leading schools.

Parsons School of Design in central Paris (tél. 01 45 77 39 66, **www.parsons-paris.pair.com**) offers full-time, part-time and evening classes and bachelor of fine arts degrees in fashion design, illustration, computer graphics, etc.

LEARNING FRENCH

Private language schools and teachers abound in Paris and across France. The quality and value for money that you will receive from these institutions and individuals varies enormously, and you should try to seek local guidance from expatriate groups and colleagues. Sign up early to ensure your place at your preferred school and course. You will normally have a brief test to establish just how much or how little you know. After that you will be 'streamed' into the appropriate class.

Your local *syndicat d'initiative* should be able to provide a list of language schools in your area. Many universities now offer language courses for foreigners. Foreign university students will also normally find that French tuition is included on their timetable.

The best-known Paris language schools for foreigners are the following:

◆ *Alliance Française*, 101 bd Raspail, 75006 Paris, M° Rennes, tél. 01 45 44 38 28, fax 01 45 44 89 42, **www.alliancefrancaise.fr** – the flag-ship of a world-wide network of deservedly renowned French language schools.

◆ *Institut Catholique*, rue d'Assas, 75006 Paris M° Rennes – the renowned private Catholic university in central Paris (open to people of all and no faiths) has a major centre for French language teaching to foreigners.

◆ *La Sorbonne*, Cours de Civilization et de la Langue Française, 47 rue des Ecoles, 75005 Paris, M° St-Michel, tél. 01 40 46 22 11, fax 01 40 46 32 99. Offers courses and diplomas at all levels, including business French.

Cultural learning opportunities

WICE – The Women's Institute of Continuing Education, 20 bd Montparnasse, 75015 Paris, M° Duroc, tél. 01 45 66 75 50, fax 01 40 65 96 53, **www.wice-paris.org**

Based on the Left Bank near Montparnasse, WICE offers everything from art history to creative writing classes and cultural tours of the great Parisian museums and French *châteaux*. WICE also offers English-language teaching qualifications required to make a successful entry to the job market as a TEFL teacher. Despite the name, the clientele is not exclusively female although women account for about 90% of the 1000 members from 25 different countries.

FINDING OUT MORE

♦ **The English-Language Schools Association France (ELSA-France)**, **www.elsa-france.org**. The ELSA website offers easy-to-follow explanations in English of the French school system. For more information in French, you should consult the highly informative and well-presented Education Ministry website at **www.education.gouv.fr**.

♦ **Centre National des Ouevres Universitaires et Scolaires (CNOUS)**, **www.cnous.fr** – each university has a regional centre (**CROUS**). The individual websites linked to this central site are the best place to find out all the practical details of student life, from residence permit centres to housing offers.

♦ **www.edufrance.fr** – multi-language French government website. General information and useful links.

- **www.prefecture-police-paris.fr** – help in English for EU citizens applying for student residence permits, and in French for non-EU students. American students would be better advised to consult the American Embassy website at **www.amb-usa.fr** for current information in English.

- **www.caf.fr** – to find out about means-tested student housing benefits.

- A useful source of information on schools offering education in English across France is the web portal **www.angloinfo.com**, which will allow you to access regional angloinfo websites. Similar help can also be found on the (French only!) site **www.enfantsbilingues.com**.

12

Travelling Around France

Public transport in French cities is generally excellent. Rural regions, however, suffer from a lack of public systems which make cars a necessity. Several major cities, such as Lille, have smaller métro systems based on the extensive Parisian model. Many other cities have chosen to install popular tramways, such as in Strasbourg, Montpellier or Bordeaux.

INTRODUCING PARISIAN PUBLIC TRANSPORT

At some stage during your time in France, you will almost certainly visit or pass through Paris, with its dense public transport system. This is controlled by the *RATP, Régie Autonome des Transports Parisiens* (www.ratp.fr) – also known to Parisians during the regular strikes as '*Rentre Avec Tes Pieds*', (Go home on foot). In spite of the French national hobby of striking, the RATP services offer an excellent public service, with *métro* stations at an average distance of 500m apart in central Paris, the *RER (Réseau Express Régional)* offering fast links from the furthest suburbs into the heart of Paris and between central Paris locations, a dense network of buses and also a small number of night-buses, plus fast links to the Paris airports at Orly and Roissy. In addition to these services, local *SNCF* (French national railways, *Société Nationale de Chemins de Fer*) services also provide commuter trains from the suburbs to all the main Paris stations, where there are inter changes onto the métro or *RER*.

Maps of the bus, *RER* and métro systems are available free in métro stations at the ticket office, and at tourist offices. A recorded 24 hour multli-language (including English) telephone information line on all services operated by the *RATP* can be called on 08 92 68 41 14. In 2001 the *RATP* launched a new campaign to inform and enable passengers with special needs and limited mobility to use the public transport system. Several buses, métros and *RER* stations are now equipped with entries and exits for wheel-chairs. This access plan can be down-loaded from the excellent fully bilingual *RATP* website which is linked to the Paris Tourist Office website and has many excellent links. To access the multi-lingual section, click on *information touristes* and then choose the British flag.

USING THE UNDERGROUND

The métro

♦ In central Paris, stations are close together and trains run 20 hours a day from 05h30 until 01h30. Several lines fork at particular stations. To determine what is the final destination of the train and which stations are therefore served, check both the electronic indicators on the platform and the front of the train as it arrives. The final destination should be highlighted.

♦ One ticket is good for the length of any one trip, providing you have bought the correct ticket. It is cheaper to buy a book of ten tickets (*carnet*) than to buy tickets individually. Tickets can either be bought at the ticket offices (*guichets*) or from automatic vending machines accepting either coins or credit cards. For information on travel passes, see below.

♦ In métro ticket halls and sometimes on the platforms (*quais*), you will find local street-maps with alphabetical street indexes, and major monuments (e.g. schools, churches, government

offices, post offices) will all be indicated. You will also find the
métro exits indicated on these *plans du quartier* so that you can
take the correct exit to arrive as quickly as possible at your
destination.

The *RER*

The *RER* (*Réseau Express Régional)* is a more recent and very
modern system with underground trains running deeper than the
métro. It is an express system with fewer central Paris stops, but
which reaches much further out into the Paris suburbs. Fares vary
according to distance, and the *RER* runs from 05h30 until a little
after midnight. A number of central *métro* stations have
intersections with the *RER*, although the *RER* and *métro* stations
do not always have the same name (e.g. *Opéra métro* = *Auber
RER*).

There are now five *RER* lines (A–E), and each one forks at least
once. As with the London Underground, you will find 'fast' trains
not stopping at all suburban stations. You also need to be sure
that the train you board is going to your correct final destination.
Electronic boards on the platforms indicate both the final
destination and stations where the train will stop. They also
indicate if it is a short or long train, so that you can position
yourself on the platform accordingly, as well as the waiting time
for the train.

To transit from one system to another, you need to pass through
dividing barriers. If you have a travel pass (e.g. *Carte Navigo*) you
will be able to make the transition without any problem. Within
the same zones, métro tickets can also be used on the *RER* also
(e.g. if you stay in zones 1 and 2).

To exit from any *RER* station, you must either use the same ticket you used to get into the system (at which point it becomes obsolete if it is a single ticket), or use a new ticket if you have managed to lose your original ticket. If you have lost your ticket, you may have difficulty leaving the system at main stations, as both full-length barriers and ticket controllers will prevent the only other possible methods – squeezing through with a friend, or crawling under or jumping over the barriers.

Taking local trains in Paris

The French state railway company (*SNCF*) runs local services with frequent stops in the suburbs (*banlieues*) of Paris. These operate at roughly the same times as the *RER* and *métro*. Regular green bus/*métro*/*RER* tickets are not valid on the *SNCF* local lines, and you must purchase yellow tickets the same size as the green tickets, but purchased from the *guichets* or vending machines. These tickets will indicate your final destination on both tickets if you buy a return ticket.

Before boarding the train, you must validate (*composte*) the ticket, as with all *SNCF* tickets. To do this, insert the corner of the ticket into one of the orange machines at the head of the platform, and when the green arrow lights up and you hear a clunk, one corner of the ticket will be automatically removed and date stamped on the reverse side. The ticket is now valid and you can safely board the train. You must repeat this process with your return ticket before joining the train.

Taking the bus

There is an extensive bus network in Paris. One of the most remarkable impacts of the Socialist administration of Paris has been the creation of dedicated bus and cycle lanes across the capital, which are also used by taxis and emergency service vehicles. Cars are banned from these lanes, and there are barriers to prevent lane jumping. These lanes considerably increase the efficiency of bus travel. Passengers line up at the bus stop (*arrêt de bus*) as in the UK. Inside the bus there is a chart of the route and the stops, with information on how many tickets are needed for each distance travelled. Timetables are posted at bus-stops, and most bus-stops also have simple *plans du quartier*. Certain lines run until 0h30 in the morning, but mostly the last bus is about 21h00. Partial services stopping part-way on the bus route are indicated by a line through the final destination. The major stops on a bus route are also indicated on the sides of the buses.

Individual bus and *métro* tickets are identical. However, they are more expensive when purchased from the bus driver. You should punch the ticket in the machine provided to validate it (*composter*) when getting onto the bus, unless you have purchased a travel pass (see below). If you purchase a *passe navigo* (see below) remember that you must validate your pass when you enter the bus using the special card reader.

Once you are on the bus, to request the driver to stop use the red buttons. If you have to fight your way out of the bus because of over-crowding, and the doors close and the driver is preparing to pull away, just shout '*la porte, s'il vous plaît*'.

There are a number of night-buses (*noctambus*) which serve Paris, leaving from the Place du Chatelet every hour on the half-hour until the métro opens once again at 05h30. You can use your *carte navigo* pass on these buses, but you cannot use ordinary bus tickets. *Métros* now also run later on Fridays and Saturday nights, up until 2am.

Choosing your travel pass

All of these services are operated by the *RATP* and regular transport passes and tickets can be used. A single *RATP* ticket (*billet*) currently costs €1.50, and a *carnet* (10 tickets) costs €11.10, or *carnet* child under 10 €5.55. Children under four travel free of charge.

If you intend using public transport on a regular basis, or even for occasional short periods from one day to one week, the most economical and convenient way to use the system is by buying a pass. A free pamphlet in French outlining the passes available and current prices is available at all métro stations.

♦ The c*arte intégrale* is an annual travel pass for *RATP* services, the regional *SNCF* trains, trams and partner services in the zones chosen.

♦ The *carte imagine 'R'* is an annual travel pass for travellers aged under 26 and reserved for school and higher education students.

♦ The *carte orange* is the Paris travelcard covering bus, métro and *RER*. Price varies according to the number of zones you wish to include. Zones 1 and 2 cover the whole of central Paris, up to the end of almost all *métro* lines, but the business district of La Défense is in zone 3. Check at your local station to see which zone you live in. If you go outside your zone, you have to buy a ticket for the whole journey – you cannot simply buy an extra ticket to 'add on' to your *carte orange*. The *carte orange* is now only available on the *Passe Navigo*, a personal card with an electronic chip which you program according to the number of zones which you wish to include on your pass. To obtain your first pass, you must fill out a form which you will obtain either from the ticket office (*caisse*) of your metro, *RER* or local train station, and then send off with several passport-sized photographs. The pass will come back personalised, and with your photo scanned into the card. If you lose the card, it can be replaced at a small cost. Several large train stations, including the Gare du Nord, have *RATP* shops where you can also obtain your *Passe Navigo*. Once you have received your pass, you must go to your local station, and use one of the card machines (*bornes*) to charge the card each month, either for a weekly or a monthly period as required. You can change the number of zones and the time period each month as you wish. These machines have instructions in English. You choose the number of zones you require, the method of payment (*carte bleue* or cash), then you place the card on the reader, pay, and the card is charged. This can also be completed at the ticket office. To enter the metro, *RER* or local *SNCF* service, simply slide the card over the purple card reader. You will hear a beep, and you will see green arrows which light up. You use the same procedure on buses and trams as well, as a way of 'validating' your ticket for the journey.

♦ The *carte hebdomadaire* is valid for a maximum of 12 journeys (2 per day) within a seven-day period, or between two *RER* or SNCF stations, either from one of these stations and central Paris. The price depends on the journey which you choose.

◆ The *carte mobilis* is a one-day travelcard, which should be punched in the machine. The *ticket jeune* for travellers under 26 is a weekend travelcard for Saturday and Sunday, and public holidays.

There are a number of other passes available for tourists which give unlimited travel for a period of days. Ask about these at any métro station, or at your hotel or welcome centre.

The *carte integrale* and *carte orange* above are reimbursed by almost all employers at 50%. Most employers will require you to hand over your monthly tickets at the end of their validity as proof of purchase and use. Families with three or more children are entitled to reduced-rate travel by requesting a *carte famille nombreuse*. Ask at *métro* stations for details.

Taking the tram

Trams have become one of the latest trends in French cities. Some of the major successes are to be found in Lyon, St Etienne, Grenoble, Caen, Montpellier, Nantes, Bordeaux and Nice. Paris caught the tram bug when Socialist Mayor Bertrand Delanoë was elected, and is now an integral part of the drive towards more collective and less individual transport as France grapples with environmental issues which partially dominated the 2007 presidential elections.

In the Paris region, there are currently four tram lines (T1 to T4), mainly serving (for the moment) the suburbs close to Paris. However the first tram line within Paris, on the outer reaches of the city was opened in 2007. This runs from Porte Garigliano close to the Seine in the 15th *arrondissement*, via the Porte d'Orléans and the Cité Universitaire, to Porte d'Ivry on the south-eastern limit in the 13th *arrondissement*. A new extension is planned to take this line on to Porte de la Chapelle in the 18th *arrondissement*. All the tram lines are included in the *Passe Navigo* scheme, and you need to check which *RATP* zones they fall within.

Avoiding problems with public transport

♦ Travel passes, including the *Passe Navigo*, must be shown to inspectors upon request. If you are using individual tickets, do not throw them away until you leave the bus, tram, train or *métro*. Travel passes with accompanying personal identification (coupons with numbers and/or photos) must be produced together. Travel passes are personal and not transferable. Failure to produce a valid ticket or pass can lead to a heavy on-the-spot fine.

♦ A *carte orange* or *Passe Navigo* can be purchased from the 20th day of the month, valid for the following month. Avoid long delays by buying your ticket in advance of the 1st of the month.

♦ Do not put *cartes oranges*, *intégrales*, or *imagine* 'R' into the validating machines on buses. Otherwise they become invalid!

♦ There are alarm buttons on the platforms of all *métros* and *RER*s and in many corridors and within the trains themselves. These have direct links to the ticket offices at stations, and to the train driver.

♦ Most central Paris stations have France Telecom card phones on their platforms and at their exits. These can be operated using ordinary French phone cards, and calls to the emergency services are of course free.

◆ The *RATP* have introduced their own uniformed police force, complete with guard-dogs. You will also see many police and uniformed soldiers with rifles in central Paris stations as part of the *Vigipirate* anti-terrorist campaign.

◆ The *RATP* Lost Property Office (*Bureau des Objets Trouvés*) is to be found at the Police Station at 36 rue des Morillons, 75015, tél. 01 40 30 52 00 (M°Convention), next to the Parc Georges Brassens. The office is open 08h30–17h00 Monday and Wednesday; 08h30–20h00 Tuesday and Thursday (except in July and August when the hours change to 08h00–17h00); 08h30–17h30 on Fridays; and closed at weekends and bank holidays.

'What are they talking about?'
Phrases you will often hear announced over the métro loud-speakers include:

◆ *Les pickpockets sont susceptible d'agir dans cette station. Veuillez veiller à vos affaires personnelles.* 'Pickpockets are at large in this station. Take care of your personal belongings.'

◆ *Suite à un mouvement sociale, le service est très pertubé/ interrompu sur la ligne 1 entre Etoile et Bastille/sur toute la ligne.* 'As a result of strike action, the service is very disrupted/has ceased on Line 1 between Etoile and Bastille/on the whole line.'

◆ *Suite à un incident voyageur à St Germain des Prés, le service est momentanément suspendu entre . . .* 'Following an incident involving a passenger at St Germain des Prés, the service is temporarily suspended.' This phrase is used to cover anything from drunks on the tracks, to brawls, to suicides.

♦ *Suite à une manifestation, les stations Franklin Roosevelt, Champs-Elysées Clemenceau, et Alma-Marceau sont fermées au public. Les correspondances sont assurées.* 'As a result of a public demonstration, Franklin Roosevelt, Champs-Elysées Clemenceau and Alma-Marceau stations are closed to the public' (i.e. no entries or exits). You can still change lines and trains here if you are already in the underground.

Taking taxis

You can normally find a taxi by simply hailing one down on a busy main street, or by going to a *stationnement de taxi* (taxi rank). You will often find taxis waiting for fares outside nightclubs, well-known hotels or theatres.

When the sign on top of the cab is not lit up, the taxi is occupied. When it is lit, the taxi is for hire. If you have ordered the taxi, the meter will be running when the taxi arrives, as you pay for the service from the moment the driver has accepted the call to collect you. Make sure if you catch a taxi in the street that the previous fare has been cleared from the meter. Day and night rates should be displayed.

Finally bear in mind that all taxis will take three passengers, but very few will accept four passengers without prior request by telephone. Extra charges are made for large amounts of luggage, including perhaps the 'excess baggage' of a fourth passenger, if you do manage to squeeze them in . . . !

TRAVELLING BY PLANE IN FRANCE

The national airline, Air France, operates worldwide. The two principal airports are Roissy-Charles-de-Gaulle and Orly, just outside Paris. The airports in Bordeaux, Lyon, Marseille, Nantes, Nice, Strasbourg, and Toulouse all have direct scheduled international flights. The smaller regional airports have become increasingly important in recent years as French airspace has been opened up to low-cost airlines.

Like all other major airlines, Air France now exclusively use electronic or e-ticketing. When you complete your transaction, your will receive an order reference number which you will need to print your ticket at the stations (*bornes*) at the airport, and you will probably be asked for another form of personal identification (e.g. passport number, credit card number or frequent flyer card number).

Travelling to and from Paris airports

If you use public transport to travel to either Orly or Roissy, you must either have the travel pass covering the correct number of zones (1–4 for Orly, 1–5 for Roissy), or buy the necessary ticket(s). *RER* Ligne C goes to Orly, and *RER* Ligne B goes to Roissy-Charles-de-Gaulle-Roissy. The Orlyval train is not included in any travel pass.

Buses to the airports run from the following places:

◆ The *RATP* Roissybus (same rules for travel passes as for the *RER*) from rue Scribe beside the Opéra-Garnier.

◆ Air France buses from Place de l'Etoile (beside the Arc de Triomphe), and Porte Maillot (beside the Palais des Congrés) also serve Roissy. Tickets are purchased on the bus, and prices are comparable to the Roissybus.

♦ The *RATP* Orlybus leaves from Denfert-Rochereau métro in southern Paris. The same rules apply as for the Roissybus.

♦ Air France also operates buses to Orly leaving from Invalides métro in central Paris. The *RER* also leaves from this station for Orly.

TAKING THE TRAIN IN FRANCE

The state-owned railway company, the *Société National des Chemins de Fer* (*SNCF*), operates the most extensive train network in western Europe, with over 21,000 miles of track. The high-speed *TGV* (*Train Grand Vitesse*) trains have been successfully exported to other countries on the basis of their success in France. New high-speed links to southern and eastern France have considerably reduced journey times.

Buying your ticket

If you go to one of the principal railway stations, look to see if one of the counters (*guichets*) has a British flag displayed in the window. If so, the ticket seller should speak some English. A one-way ticket is an *aller-simple*. A return ticket is an *aller-retour*. Tickets are valid for two months from the date of purchase. Once you have validated (*composté*) your ticket by punching it in the orange box at the entrance to the platform, it will be valid for only 24 hours from the date and time punched on the ticket.

> Always remember to validate your ticket <u>before</u> entering the train. A non-validated ticket could lead to a hefty fine. This also applies on local suburban *SNCF* trains.

Making reservations

Tickets can be reserved on most trains, and *must* be reserved on all *TGV* trains. A small reservation fee will be levied, but the exact sum depends on the time and category of the train, and of your ticket. Reservations include the choice of first or second class and window or aisle seats.

You can either make your reservation in person, or over the telephone by calling the appropriate station. The website **www.voyages-sncf.com** is one of the most popular and successful on-line services in France. Tickets reserved over the phone or on-line and paid for by credit card must be collected within 48 hours from an *SNCF* station. Tickets reserved on-line can be sent to your home. You can also use the automatic ticket machines in the major stations to make reservations, at the same time as buying your ticket. If you make an on-line reservation, you can also choose an electronic or e-ticket which you print out at the station at the automatic ticket machines (normally using your *carte bleue* and a reservation number), and then validate (*composté*) as a normal ticket. All reservations will include a carriage number and seat number.

Choosing when to travel

The *SNCF* recently introduced a new ticket pricing system. Basically, reserving in advance as much as possible before your trip will allow you to access the most advantageous prices. Tickets for travel in peak holiday periods are now generally more expensive, even in less sought-after time brackets. You should check the *SNCF* website (**www.voyages-sncf.com**) and information leaflets for current promotional details. A notable recent innovation are the *Prem*'s tickets, starting at €20 for certain TGV journeys. Check the promotions pages of the SNCF website for details, and book your ticket as far in advance as possible.

In peak holiday periods – *Toussaint* at the beginning of November, Christmas, the spring school holidays, the May bank holidays, and in July and August – you should definitely make reservations on all main-line journeys to avoid the discomfort of three hours standing in a corridor.

Reduced price tickets

The *SNCF* offers a number of interesting reductions available to young and old individuals and families. Leaflets concerning these offers, partly printed in English, are available in all main-line *SNCF* stations. The '*Guide du Voyageur*' (in French), is available free in all main stations. This is an indispensable guide to all the current ticket reductions and services offered by the *SNCF*.

♦ For regular and frequent travellers, check out the variety of annual cards and reductions available.

♦ The *Carte Escapade* is aimed at people aged 26–59. It currently costs €85 for an annual subscription. With this card, reductions vary from 25% to 40%, for all return journeys of more than 200km, including a Saturday night stop-over, or a day trip on a Saturday or Sunday. For more details see **www.escapade-sncf.com**.

♦ If you have at least three children under the age of 18, you qualify for the *carte famille nombreuse*. This offers very significant savings, up to 75% of the price of standard tickets.

♦ The *carte enfant* + offers cheap travel for children under 12, and for those accompanying them. Up to four adults and other children are included in the deal, and do not need to be related to the holder of the card. The *Jeune Voyager Service* arranges the appropriate care of children travelling alone. For more details see **www.enfant.plus-sncf.com**.

◆ The *carte 12–25 ans* offers reduced travel rates within that age group. Reductions vary from 25 to 50%, depending on your travel dates and when you reserve. For more details see **www.12-15ans-sncf.com**.

◆ The annual holiday ticket (*billet de congé annuel*) is available to those in and out of work, including the self-employed, and also to retired people. There are certain conditions attached to availability for the unemployed. The reduction offered is 25%.

◆ Group travel (ten people and over) has a tariff structure linked to the size of your group.

◆ For **les seniors** (over 60), the *carte seniors* operate in a very similar way to the *cartes 12–2 ans* with reductions from 25 to 50%. For more details see **www.senior-sncf.com**.

◆ A guide is available for those with mobility difficulties. At your local station ask for the free *Guide du voyageur handicapé*, or download the PDF from the website **www.voyages-sncf.com**. Details of stations with facilities for handicapped travellers and those in wheel-chairs (*fauteuil roulant*) can be found on the dedicated pages on this website. You can also reserve the appropriate places on TGV trains. Certain *guichets* are also equipped for travellers with impaired hearing. A ticket is required for domestic animals transported by train, but guide-dogs travel free with their master or mistress and are not required to wear a muzzle. To access the dedicated service for handicapped travellers on the SNCF pay telephone reservation service, within France dial 3635 and say '*Accès Plus*', or dial 41 after the introductory message. There is also a dedicated website, **www.accesplus.sncf.fr**.

♦ If your train is more than 30 minutes late arriving, and it is a *grande ligne* train, you will be entitled to a reimbursement of up to one third of your ticket price. You will be given a form to fill in and send to the SNCF with your claim, and you will receive a voucher in return. This service does not apply to all promotional tickets.

Travelling at night

Three options exist for those travelling overnight.

1. Reclining seats (*sièges à dossiers inclinables*) are available in certain trains in second class carriages. You should reserve these seats in advance.

2. The famous bunk-beds (*couchettes*) are available in first class (four to a cabin) and second class (six to a cabin). The current cost is €17, and reservations should be made. If you use one of the reduction cards or options mentioned above, you can save up to 25% on the price of *couchettes*.

3. Sleeping compartments (*les voitures-lits*) are also available on certain trains: individually in first class, and for two to three people in second class. Enquire at main stations for further details.

No matter which option you choose, take great care over money and personal belongings on night trains.

Transporting animals

Larger domestic pets are charged at about 50% of the price of a second class ticket. Small dogs, less than 6kg, transported in a bag or basket, cost a maximum of €5 to transport. One thing to remember is that if another traveller objects to your pet, you may have to change seats or even carriages. If you take your animal on a night train, you must reserve a private cabin for the journey.

Transporting vehicles

Motorail is a European network of over 100 services within France and Europe which allows you to transport your car or motorbike by train. In the UK and Ireland, you should contact Rail Europe UK to make advance bookings, which are strongly recommended. If you book in France, you will be given a *guide du voyage* containing practical information at the same time as you receive your travel documents.

Vehicles are generally loaded about one hour before departure, and are normally available for collection about half an hour after arrival. Loading and collection times will be marked on your tickets. Both services are performed by the relevant staff. Motorbikes are always loaded and unloaded by the driver.

Generally, loading and collection take place in the station where the passenger boards the train. If it does not, a free shuttle bus (**navette**) will transport you between the loading or collection point, and your place of departure or arrival. A free guide is available from main SNCF stations. For information on Eurotunnel services, contact a travel agent or the company itself. For bicycles, see below.

For more details in English see **www.raileurope.co.uk**. On the SNCF website, you can also find full details in French of the country-wide *Autotrain* service.

DRIVING IN FRANCE

One of the priorities set by President Chirac in 2002 was to reduce incivility on the roads, and the number of accidents and deaths due to traffic accidents. A firm campaign was launched to tackle one of the world's best known bad habits – French driving. This includes hundreds of radar speed traps across the country in accident black spots, heavy fines, and point deductions for holders of French driving licences. If you contest a fine or point reduction, the rule is that you pay first and contest later. If you delay paying a speeding fine, or any other fine such as parking or using a mobile phone whilst driving, it will quickly be automatically increased, and may eventually lead to your bank account being blocked. Foreign drivers in France are not immune from punishment even if they driving with a foreign or international licence.

Parking, especially in Paris, is *spécial* in the French sense of the word. Many people would say that the best advice would be to bring along a can-opener to manoeuvre yourself in and out of the available slots, or to escape from the mess somebody else has made of your neat parking.

A resident's parking permit (*vignette de stationnement résidentiel*) can be obtained from your local town hall, which gives you the right to preferential parking rates and access. If you receive a parking fine, you need to buy the appropriate stamp (*timbre fiscal*) at a tobacconists, affix the stamp and send the payment. Failure to do so in the specified time limit will lead to an increased fine. If your car is towed away, you will need to make enquiries at the nearest *commissariat* to find out which car pound is holding your car, and you may well face a costs contribution plus fine combination.

A French Government leaflet in English, *Welcome on France's roads* clearly explains the basic road rules, safety limits and regulations. You can find this on **www.securiteroutiere.equipement. gouv.fr/IMG/pdf/Depliant_welcome_2007-08.pdf**, and on the British Embassy website, **www.britishembassy.gov.uk/france**.

Driving papers
You must always carry your driving licence with you when driving, as well as the original registration document and the car insurance documents. You must be at least 18 years old to drive in France. Although the annual car tax (*vignette*) has been abolished for individuals, it is still required for a company car.

British drivers in France
Officially, it is no longer necessary to exchange a UK driving licence (*permis de conduire*) for a French licence if you are resident in France.

Applications for international driving licences, which are valid for three years, should be made at your local *préfecture*. You should note however that international licences are not valid in the bearer's country of residence.

American drivers in France
US visitors who stay in France less than 90 days can drive in France with a valid US licence although it is advisable to carry a translation. French residents (who have either a *carte de séjour* or *carte de résident*) can drive in France for up to one year from the start date of their residence permit. In this case either a 'sworn' translation or an international driver's licence is also obligatory. American students may drive with an American licence throughout the duration of their studies.

Fourteen American states have official agreements with France which allow holders of state licences to exchange their licences for French licences. These states are: Arkansas, Colorado, Connecticut, Delaware, Florida, Illinois, Kansas, Kentucky, Michigan, New Hampshire, Ohio, Pennsylvania, South Carolina, and Virginia. This agreement allows you up to one year to exchange your American license for a French *permis de conduire*, after which time the exchange is no longer possible. In practice, you should allow up to three months for the successful exchange of licences. The whole process takes place at the *prefecture de police* and must be completed before the end of the first year of residence.

To exchange your licence you need to obtain and complete the necessary form from the prefecture; to provide your US driver's licence with a notarised translation into French; a proof of your current address (rental agreement or EDF or France Telecom bill, a photocopy of both sides of your *carte de séjour*); and two passport size photographs. As with any French administrative application, make sure you have originals and copies available of all of these documents.

If you hold a US licence from another state, you must take the two-part French driving test (part written, part practical) after a series of lessons from a recognised French driving school which will allow you to fulfil the obligation to take the test in a dual-control car. Some concessions are made for the fact that your knowledge of French may be limited when you take the practical test, and a translator may be allowed to accompany you. For up-to-date information on regulations concerning American drivers in

France, you should check the specific information given on the American Embassy website, **www.amb-usa.fr**.

Replacing a lost licence

If you lose your licence or it is stolen, you must report it at the nearest police station to where the incident happened. They will give you a receipt valid for two months, which acts as a temporary licence. During that period go to your local *préfecture* and request a new licence. Take with you:

- the receipt of your declaration of loss or theft
- a piece of official identity
- the completed form requesting a duplicate licence
- a proof of residency (e.g. tenancy agreement, electricity bill, etc.)
- three passport size photos.

It can take three to six weeks to obtain your new licence. You will also have to pay the appropriate fee.

Lost or stolen US driving licences can only be replaced by the Department of Motor Vehicles in the driver's home state.

IMPORTING A CAR

You can import a car for up to six months in one year without completing customs formalities. A new or used car on which VAT (*TVA* in France) has already been paid in another EU country can be imported into France by a French resident free of French VAT.

Otherwise, VAT is payable *immediately* upon entry into France. You can pay at the point of importation or at your local tax office. You will then be issued with a customs certificate (*Certificat de Douane 846A*) permitting you to register the vehicle in France. The same form will also be required even if VAT has already been paid, to prove that this obligation has been met.

Tourists (anyone staying no more than 90 days) can bring a car or motorbike into France duty-free and retain their foreign number plates, but must display a national sticker beside the licence plates. Cars brought in for more than three months need French licence plates, which requires registering the car.

US temporary residents who hold a *carte de séjour temporaire* are exempted from customs duties if they can show:

a) that they will stay in France less than one year
b) they that have a permanent residence outside France
c) that they have lived outside of France for at least one year
d) that they have owned the vehicle for at least six months.

Long-term residents are not entitled to exemption from customs duties on imported vehicles, and the car must carry French licence plates and be registered in France. You must also have paid all duties on the vehicle in the country of export.

REGISTERING A CAR IN FRANCE
Registering an imported car
Imported vehicles must be registered in France within three months of entry. To do this, you must contact the local *direction régionale de l'industrie, de la recherche et de l'environnement (DRIRE)*. After the local vehicle inspection centre (*inspection des mines*) has checked that your car meets French construction and

use regulations, you will receive a certificate from *DRIRE* which will allow you to apply for the registration certificate (*certificat d'immatriculation*, more normally known as a *carte grise*). This happens at the *préfecture*, or the *préfecture de police*, or local *mairie* in Paris. They will provide a checklist of documents required, which are:

1. Proof of origin of the vehicle or copy of the certificate of sale.

2. The foreign registration document.

3. The customs certificate 846A (see above).

4. A manufacturer's certificate of construction. This is available from a local car dealer, the French importer, or the manufacturer. *Officially* it is no longer required, but it may be asked for. It can also be very expensive. The point of the document is to prove that the vehicle meets European safety standards.

5. A completed request for a registration card (*demande de certificat d'immatriculation d'un véhicule*), available from the *préfecture*, or the *préfecture de police*, or the local *mairie* in Paris. This document should be accompanied by your passport and proof of residence.

6. A technical test certificate if your vehicle is more than four years old. All vintage vehicles and vehicles over four years old are subject to regular testing every two years.

Once you finally receive your car registration, new number plates must be installed within 48 hours. They can be made up and fitted at local garages for a small fee.

Registering a new car

Before using a new car, you must obtain the *carte grise*. In theory this can be issued immediately if you go to the appropriate office, but in practice, applications are generally made by post and take about 15 days to process. You will need a new form to apply for a new *carte grise*, the certificate of sale, the technical certificate from the *inspections des mines*, a piece of official identity (e.g. *carte de séjour*) and a proof of residency less than three months old (e.g. electricity or telephone bill in your name).

Registering a second-hand car

Once again you have 15 days in which to register. Vehicles less than ten years old cost the same to register as new vehicles; those which are more than 10 years old cost half as much to register. You will need ID and proof of residence (as above), and the *carte grise barrée* (old registration document of the car) supplied by the former owner.

Cars more than four years old must have the necessary technical certificate dating from less than six months before the purchase. You also need a *certificat de situation administrative* from the seller.

Moving home

Even if you stay in the same *département*, you must change the address on your *carte grise*. This is free, and can be done immediately at the local *mairie* or *préfecture*, by presenting a new proof of residence and your *carte grise*. If you fail to do this, you could face a fine of €90.

Replacing your *carte grise*

If you lose your *carte grise* or it is stolen, you must report it to the police. You will be issued with a temporary document which will allow you to use your car. It will also allow you to apply for a new *carte*. You will need an official piece of ID, a proof of residency, the receipt of your police statement of loss, the form requesting a duplicate *carte*, and the necessary technical certificate for vehicles more than four years old.

Selling your car

If you decide to sell your car once you have moved to France, you must supply the following documents to the buyer before the sale is complete and legal:

1. The *certificat de vente* – it is your responsibility to obtain this from the *préfecture* or *sous-préfecture*.

2. The '*carte grise barrée*', i.e. 'crossed-out'. You must write across the carte in indelible ink, '*vendue le* _____ ' (sold on _____) and fill in the date. You must then sign the amended *carte*.

3. If the car is more than four years old, a technical certificate dated less than six months before the date of the sale proving that the car is roadworthy (see above).

4. A *certificat de situation administrative* – to obtain this, go to your local *préfecture* with your *carte grise*. You will need to submit the registration number of the vehicle, the model, and the power of the engine. The *certificat* will certify that there are no outstanding fines relating to the vehicle.

Within 15 days of the sale of the car, you must hand in the second copy of the *certificat de vente* at the *préfecture* at which it was previously registered. Restrictions apply on the sale of cars imported duty-free which are regulated by the French Customs Office.

INSURING YOUR CAR

Fully comprehensive insurance is advisable to cover the costs of breakdown or accidents. Third-party motor insurance for unlimited liability is compulsory in France. You will need to shop around to find the best policies and prices. Third-party insurance is required for the import of cars whether they are occupied or not, and if you opt to take out a policy before arrival you must have proof ready for French Customs at the point of entry (land or sea). The Customs Offices themselves offer temporary insurance for up to 30 days at these same points of entry.

RE-FUELLING YOUR CAR

Garages are placed at intervals of 24km along all motorways, and are to be found across Paris. Many of the Parisian and suburban garages are self-service. '*Faites le plein, s'il vous plaît*' means 'Fill her up, please', if you do find yourself being served. A favourite tactic in any French industrial dispute in order to bring pressure on the government is to try to block access to petrol refineries and Paris. The result is panic buying, and long queues at the pumps.

Leaded petrol is now sold only in one grade (*essence super*). Unleaded is sold in two grades: *essence sans plomb*, and *super sans plomb*. The minimum quantity that you can buy is five litres. Diesel (*gazole*) is cheaper and readily available.

ROAD RULES

The most important thing you need to remember is that in France you drive on the right! Equally important is the fact that in built-up areas, you must give way to traffic coming from the right – the famous *priorité à droit* rule. In less built-up areas, traffic on main roads has priority over traffic from side roads. The exception to the rule of priority is at roundabouts. Traffic entering the roundabout has priority, EXCEPT when signs such as '*Cédez le passage*' (Give way) or '*Vous n'avez pas la priorité*' are displayed.

Health and safety precautions

◆ Seat belts are obligatory in France, including in the rear of the car if they are installed. You can face an on-the-spot fine if you disobey this rule.

◆ Random tests are made for drink-driving in France, which is a major killer on the roads. The legal limit is now 80mg alcohol per 100ml of blood – not much more than one glass of wine. You may face an on-the-spot fine, a court appearance or a driving ban if you are found guilty. The best solution is not to drink alcohol at all when driving.

◆ Speed limits are reduced in bad weather. Generally on toll motorways (*autoroutes à péage*) the maximum speed is 130kph, and 110kph in bad weather. The minimum speed in the outside (overtaking) lane is 80kph during daylight on flat roads with good visibility. For dual carriageways and toll-free motorways, the speed limit is 110kph; for other 'departmental' roads the limit is 90kph; and for roads in built-up areas the limit is 50kph. The limit on ring-roads is 80kph.

◆ Cars made in the UK and Ireland must adjust their headlights in order not to dazzle on-coming traffic. Headlight converters made from pre-cut black masking tape must be fitted over the headlights. If another driver flashes his headlights at you it is to indicate that he has priority and that you should give way.

◆ If you break down, try to move the car to the side of the road and flash your hazard warning lights. The red warning triangle should be placed 30m behind your car (100m on motorways). Emergency phones (*postes d'appel d'urgence*) are at 4km intervals on main roads, and every 2km on motorways.

◆ If you have an accident, you should call the police immediately by dialling 17. The ambulance service will also be alerted if necessary. You and the other parties must complete and exchange an accident statement form (*constat à l'amiable*) and exchange insurance details. If possible, persuade witnesses (*témoins*) to stay and make statements.

POLLUTION CONTROLS

Environmental issues linked to road and public transport are one of the major preoccupations in French Government policy. Generally, France remains car-friendly. However local municipal authorities, notably in Paris, have made firm efforts to reduce the number of motorists by dissuasive methods such as the prioritising of bus lanes, and a marked decline in street parking facilities. Amongst the measures which you should be aware of are the following.

◆ Pollution controls in Paris. To combat pollution in Paris, notably during the summer months, regulations may be announced and enforced whereby you can only drive on alternate days. This depends on the last two numbers before the letters in a number plate. On one day only even numbers (*pairs*) will be allowed to drive, and on the next day it will be the turn of uneven numbers (*impairs*). Listen for warnings on the TV and radio.

◆ Eco-friendly car incentives. In 2006, the Government introduced an eco-tax on environmentally-unfriendly cars, based on gas emissions and/or the power of the engine. This tax is applied only to new vehicles at the moment of registration. In 2007, the Government also introduced a '*bonus-malus*' scheme, allowing car constructors to reduce the price of more eco-friendly cars. The cars which do not fall into this category include jeeps, and people carrier (*Espaces*) cars popular with families.

TWO-WHEELED TRANSPORT

Non-motorised forms of transport – bikes, roller-blades and 'scooters' – have experienced a huge rise in popularity ever since the near-general strike of 1995. In Paris cycle lanes now run the length and breadth of the city with protective barriers to stop encroachments from motorised vehicles. On Sundays, the *quais* of the Seine and the canal banks are reserved for bladers and cyclists. The Bois de Boulogne and the Bois de Vincennes are also popular cycling venues.

It is possible to hire bikes at over 200 *SNCF* stations in much the same way that cars are hired (i.e. collect at one station and deposit at another). A leaflet available at *SNCF* stations gives the list of stations and prices for the bike hire service. For short journeys, you can put your cycle in the luggage van for free. For longer journeys, it needs to be registered, and you should really send it a few days in advance. The *SNCF* also offers a door-to-door collection and delivery service for bikes.

One of the new 'must haves' for French cities, along with trams, is the 24-hour self-service bike hire system. This began in the provincial cities such as Lyon and Rennes, and in Paris the *Vélib* bikes have been an instant success. Basically you apply for a card, take out a subscription lasting from a week to a month, go to one of the bike stands (*bornes*), identify yourself, take a bike and away you go. The instructions on how to use the service are available in eight different languages at the stands. When you reach your destination, you return the bike to the nearest stand; and when you want to move on again you repeat the process as many times as you like or need within the same day. To find out more about the Paris system, which operates in just the same way as all the provincial cities, go to the multi-lingual website **www.Velib.paris.fr**. One point to bear in mind about cycling in France is that French cyclists are only French drivers on bikes! Take care when cycling in the major cities, and always take the necessary security precautions.

SAILING IN FRANCE

At sea
Neither sailing boats nor motor boats with motors less than 6CV require permits. However, for coastal navigation, three types of permit exist:

- *La carte mer* – required if you intend to sail a boat with a motor between 6 and 50CV. This permits you to undertake daytime sailing, within a limit of about 9km.

- *Le permis mer côtier* – for boats with motors over 50CV. This permit also covers night-time sailing, but within the same geographical limit.

- *Le permis mer hauturier* – this allows all forms of sailing. To take the test for this permit, you must enrol in a boat school.

Further details are available on all of these permits from the Bureau de la Navigation de Plaisance, 3, place Fontenoy, 75007 Paris, tél. 01 44 49 80 00.

On rivers

Permits are also required if you intend to sail on French rivers, if the boat is more than 5m long or travels at more than 20kph. To enrol for these permits, contact a boat school.

- *Permis C* – also known as the *coches de plaisance*, this allows you to sail a boat less than 15m long at less than 20kph.

- *Permis S* – also known as the *bateaux de sport*, this allows you to sail a boat less than 15m long but which travels at more than 20kph.

- *Permis PP* – also known as *péniches de plaisance*, this permits you to sail a boat more than 15m long.

A permit is not required on certain water-ways if you decide to take a barge holiday in France. Unless you possess the *Permis PP*, you must hire a boat of less than 15m at a speed of less than 20kph. The hirer will give you a *carte de plaisance* for your stay on the boat, which will be your sailing permit.

FINDING OUT MORE

- **The French Travel Centre**, 178 Piccadilly, London W1V OAL, tel: 09068 244 123, fax: 020 7493 6594, **www.franceinlondon.com**. Open Monday–Friday 09h00–17h00, Saturday 10h00–17h00. French Railways Ltd, The Rail Europe Travel Centre, 179 Piccadilly. Tube: Green Park or Piccadilly Circus.

◆ **www.equipement.gouv.fr** – the transport ministry website. For information in English on road rules in France, see the on-line Government pamphlet *Welcome to France's Roads* available at available at **www.securiteroutiere.equipement.gouv.fr/IMG/pdf/ Depliant_welcome_2007-08.pdf**.

◆ **www.voyages-sncf.com** – the popular website for checking train times and ordering tickets. These can either be sent to your home or collected at the station.

◆ **www.ratp.fr** – the excellent multi-lingual website for the Paris transport authority, with suggestions for day-trips, amusing the children, etc., plus all the usual travel information you would expect.

◆ **www.eurostar.com** (within Europe) or **www.eurostartickets.com** (USA and Canada only) – both sites offer times and tickets, but the North American site offers discounted tickets for these travellers.

◆ **www.eurotunnel.com** – bilingual site for the underground-overground option.

◆ To find out more about the ***Motorail*** and ***Autotrain*** options for transporting your car by rail, you can call 08448 484 550 and place a call-back request within the UK.

◆ **www.bison-fute.equipement.gouv.fr** – the transport ministry's excellent French-only site with travel updates, road works and closures, and school holidays dates (i.e. when not to travel).

◆ **www.eurolines.com** and **www.hoverspeed.com** – coach travel to France. The Hoverspeed site offers both ferry and coach information. Eurolines has an extensive network covering France.

◆ **www.brittany-ferries.co.uk, www.poferries.com** – cross-channel ferries to the UK and Ireland.

◆ **www.airfrance.com**; **www.britishairways.com**; **www.flybmi.com** (British Midland) – for regular flights to Paris and major French cities.

◆ **www.britair.com**; **www.ryanair.com** – airlines offering domestic flights in France, and to provincial French airports.

◆ For more information on rollerblading in France, including the famous 'Friday Night Fever' mass rollerblade in Paris, check out the multi-lingual website **www.paris.roller.com.ft**. On this website you can find out about how to join the Paris roller association. Another useful website covering roller meetings across France is **www.rollerenligne.com**.

◆ For more information on self-service bike hire in Paris, go to the multi-lingual website **www.velib.paris.fr**.

13

Enjoying Your Leisure Time

France is the land of the *bon viveur*, literally the 'good-liver'. A great deal of importance is placed upon the pursuit of leisure. Relaxing, building bonds with family and friends, and exploring new activities are all ingrained elements of the French way of life. A great deal of stress is laid upon encouraging *solidarité* between ages and social classes.

PUBLIC HOLIDAYS AND FÊTES

No introduction to France would be complete without mentioning the public holidays and *fêtes*. It is important to know when these holidays occur, since many public services will shut down or run reduced services, whilst private commerce comes to a stand-still. Transport is often heavily booked in advance at holiday periods.

Although the provision of public holidays is generous, they are rigidly linked to the precise date. If a holiday falls on a Saturday or Sunday, then it is observed on that day, and no working day is given in lieu. However, if a holiday falls on either a Thursday or a Tuesday, then many people will take the link day to make a long week-end. This is known as *faire le pont* – literally to make a bridge.

The *Fête Nationale* (Bastille day) on the 14 July is always accompanied by huge public street parties in Paris and throughout France. Popular balls are organised at local fire-stations (*bals des sapeurs pompiers*) on the night of the 13 July. There are usually other free open-air parties not only in Paris but also in major cities. On the 14 July, France parades her military glory along the Champs-Elysées under the President's scrutiny, before the traditional garden party at the Elysée Palace, and a magnificent *son et lumière* firework display near to the Eiffel Tower.

On 21 June each year (once again strictly observed on that date) is the newer *Fête de la Musique*. Although not a public holiday, it is an extremely popular occasion when free concerts are given in almost every church and café and seemingly on every street corner. The fête was created to encourage music-making (*faites de la musique* – a French play on words), and has been a tremendous success with vast open-air concerts in the major cities.

At the beginning of September each year are the traditional *Journées du Patrimoine* (National Heritage weekend), commonly known as *les Portes-Ouvertes* (the 'Open Doors'). Another recently invented festival, this is the annual occasion when the public can view the great state residences and buildings normally closed to the public, including the Elysée Palace in Paris, the Assemblée Nationale, and many embassies usually on restricted access. Local *mairies* (town halls) will be able to tell you where to find lists of buildings open to the public. The concept of this festival has recently been imported to the United Kingdom.

The main Christmas meal in France takes place on Christmas Eve, when the family and perhaps close friends gather for *le réveillon* (the vigil) meal. Traditionally the meal will include rich elements such as oysters (*huîtres*) and French specialities such as Champagne, *foie gras* and truffles (*truffes*). The traditional

Date	Occasion
1 January	New Year's Day – **Jour de l'An**
March/April	Easter Day and Easter Monday – **Pâcques** NB: *Good Friday is not a holiday in France.*
1 May	Labour Day – **Fête du Travail**
8 May	Liberation Day – **Fête de la Libération**
May	Ascension Day – **l'Ascension** NB: *Date depends on the date of Easter.*
May/June	Whit Monday – **lundi de Pentecôte** NB: *Date depends on the date of Easter.*
14 July	National/Bastille Day – **Fête Nationale**
15 August	Assumption day – **l'Assomption**
1 November	All Saints Day – **Toussaint**
8 November	Remembrance Day – **Fête de la Victoire 1918**
25 December	Christmas Day – **Noël** NB: *26 December is not a holiday in France*

Fig. 12. Public holidays in France.

French Christmas dessert is a *bûche de noël*, a sweet 'Christmas log' cake which may contain alcohol. Many families then go to the packed churches for Midnight Mass. You then have a week to recover from the meal (even though only Christmas Day is a holiday in France), before the second *reveillon* (sometimes known as *St Sylvestre*), on New Year's Eve. This meal is often five or six courses long, including similar elements to the Christmas meal. You should note that in France greetings cards are traditionally sent to celebrate the New Year, not Christmas itself. You can send cards right up until the end of January. You should reply to each card that you receive with a card of your own. The French are also great fans of telephoning to present their best wishes for the new year. Christmas celebrations continue on 6 January with the feast of the Epiphany (*Fête des Rois*), when almond pastry tarts (*galettes*) are eaten in homes and offices. By tradition the portions are distributed by the youngest person, calling out from underneath a table! The cake contains a small prize (*feve*), and the person who finds the prize is 'crowned' king or queen with the paper crown supplied with the cake. Christmas finally finishes on 2 February with the feast of Candlemas (*Chandeleurs*), which is the real French pancake day, despite the world famous *Mardi Gras* (greasy Tuesday) before Lent.

FRENCH DINNER PARTIES

Dinner parties in France normally begin at about 20h00–21h00. Try to be reasonably on time so as not to spoil a carefully prepared meal by leaving it to simmer longer than intended. Written invitations should be acknowledged by written replies. Normally, a French dinner consists of the following elements:

◆ Starter (*entrée*) normally accompanied by white wine.

◆ Main course (*plat*) accompanied by red wine, unless white wine is appropriate.

◆ Cheese *before* dessert, served either by itself or with a light salad.

◆ Dessert perhaps accompanied by a special dessert wine.

◆ Coffee, served at the table. This may or may not be followed by liqueurs.

Very grand dinners will have a sorbet between each course, to clear the taste buds. It is not advisable to take wine as a gift for your hostess. French people are generally knowledgeable about wine, and will normally have carefully selected what they wish to serve with a particular meal.

A bottle of Champagne is a good present, which need not be expensive. Flowers are cumbersome for a hostess when she is about to serve dinner. For foreigners, bringing a product or gift from your country is an original idea, and provides a talking point at the table. A small box of good chocolates is another popular gift, which can be purchased from specialist shops, or even at the *boulangerie*.

If you do not wish to drink alcohol, mineral water is almost always available at French tables and in all restaurants. Smoking is very prevalent in France, and etiquette regarding smoking at the table – and even between courses – will vary according to the hosts and the company you keep. As with many table manners, it is very much a game of 'follow my leader'. If you object to somebody smoking beside you, a discreet request rather than a loud haughty lecture will achieve the effect you require.

You may well find a rack or block beside your plate, which is a knife or fork rest. In France, it is quite common to keep the same cutlery throughout several courses. Bread is normally in plentiful supply on French tables, and should be broken with your hands, not cut with a knife. Butter is not normally served with bread.

Whilst business associates may well be invited to dinner, there is rarely 'shop talk' at the table. If you do not know the rest of the party well, remember that the French are generally conservative and dress accordingly. The fading custom of sending thank-you notes is nonetheless greatly appreciated, and will probably ensure your popularity with your new friends.

Formality and etiquette are part of the French fascination with rules and regulations. If you are worried about making gaffs (*faux pas*), then invest in one of the many etiquette guides available.

EATING OUT IN RESTAURANTS

Finding good restaurants which offer value for money can be difficult. The best Paris restaurant guide in English is the annual *Time Out* guide, but all major newspapers and entertainment guides have regular weekly updates, depending on the style of meal you are looking for. Whilst guides can be very useful, recommendations from locals, friends or colleagues are often more reliable.

Generally, restaurants offer a choice between meals at a fixed price chosen from a menu or *formule*, or choosing from the whole menu, which is known as eating *à la carte*. The formule is normally more economical, and generally involves a selection of the dishes offered in the menu. It may be a starter (*entrée*) and main course (*plat*), or a main course and dessert, or all three. A small jug of wine (*pichet*) is also sometimes included. Alternatively, you can ask for a jug of tap water (*une carafe d'eau*), which is free. Mineral water must be paid for. Some restaurants will only offer a lunchtime set menu (*formule du midi*). Be careful to check this before you set out for the restaurant in the evenings, especially if you are on a limited budget.

The menu should always indicate if service is included (*service compris*). This may affect your decision as to whether to leave a tip, especially in expensive restaurants. If you order a meat dish, depending on the meat, you will be asked how you liked it cooked – *Quelle cuisson?*

- *saignant* = rare
- *à point* = medium rare
- *bien cuit* = well-done.

The French like their meat cooked very rare compared to the British, so you should perhaps over-compensate if you do not like rare meat.

Foreign and regional food

The choice of restaurants available will depend on your location. Non-French food is widely available, and as in the UK the choice reflects France's colonial past. Vietnamese and North African food (*couscous*) are popular, and Chinese and Italian food is widely available. Indian food is rarer. British cooking is still eyed with suspicion and/or mirth in France, and there are no truly British restaurants.

What you will find in France is a great choice of restaurants offering regional specialities. It can be great fun when visiting a new area to try not only the local cheese and wine, but also the local dish. Some are now universal, and you will find *boeuf bourguignonne* (Burgundy beef stew), for instance, available everywhere.

Fast food and take-aways

Fast food is widely available now in France, and major international chains have outlets in most principal towns and cities. Chinese and Indian take-aways are still not common, but home-delivery services are widespread. Some restaurants do offer *plats à emporter*, but this will mean ordering your food at the restaurant and squeezing up to the counter while you wait. Alternatively go to a *traiteur* who offers Italian or Chinese/

Vietnamese/Thai (the three tend to be mixed together) dishes sold by the portion.

VISITING CAFÉS AND PUBS

Cafés are one of the great traditions of French society, ranging from the high-brow literary *salons* of St Germain des Prés in Paris to scruffy street-corners, and encompassing every style in between.

Drinking at the counter (*comptoir*) is cheaper than at a table (*en salle*) or on a terrace (*en terrasse*). The same rules apply in cafés to ordering alcohol as to ordering coffee or tea. Exploring the local cafés and finding one that suits you, where you can while away half an hour with the newspaper, a book or friends for the price of a coffee, is another of the joys of France.

Those cafés which display a red *tabac* sign also double as tobacconists, offering a wide range of products at the cigarette counter (e.g. phone cards or fiscal stamps). Many also offer a *service restauration* at least at lunchtime, with sandwiches and hot meals available. Some of the terms for these meals you will need to know include:

♦ *Croque-monsieur* = ham and cheese toasted sandwich.

♦ *Croque-madame* = as above, but with a fried egg served on top.

♦ *chèvre-chaud* = hot goat's cheese normally served on toast, with a small mixed salad. Either a starter or a main course.

♦ *Francfort-frites* = Frankfurter sausage and chips. Sausages such as *saucisse de Toulouse* are more like a Cumberland sausage and will be served with other vegetables and a sauce.

◆ *Garnis avec...* = served with: chips (*frites*), mashed potato (*pommes vapeur*), fried/roast potatoes (*pommes sautés*), pasta (*pâtes*).

◆ *Salade* – Be careful here. In French this means both lettuce, which may be all you receive, or for instance, a *salade de tomates* (a plate of sliced tomatoes). A *salade mixte* will be a side-salad of lettuce plus perhaps chicory (*endives*) and tomatoes. Salads which are served as main courses will normally have a list of their ingredients.

Some cafés also become centres of nightlife. There are over 60 Irish pubs across France in the principal cities, most notably Paris. However, you should note that whilst they appear to be like English and Irish pubs, the prices are very much higher. Do *not* walk in and offer a round of drinks to your friends unless you are prepared, or feeling very generous!

A pint normally costs about €5 in a pub, and spirits are also about €7–8 per glass. The cost of a glass of wine will depend on its size and quality. The standard French person will drink a half-pint (*demie*) of whatever is on tap (*pression*). This is one local custom you should take up quickly!

GOING TO CABARETS AND CLUBS

The French have been famous for generations for their cabarets and nightclubs. Nightclubs, almost by definition, fall in and out of fashion very rapidly and regularly. You should check the style of a club by using a guide, or by asking somebody whom you know already goes to the club. Styles vary widely, even at the same club, depending on the day of the week. The trendiest Paris nightclubs have a very exclusive door-policy, so swot up in advance on what to wear and how to act.

French nightlife gets going much later than in the UK. Bars generally close at 02h00, and nightclubs will generally start to fill up from about 01h00, and then stay open until dawn. The entry price may include one drink (*une consommation*), but after that be prepared for high prices.

ATTENDING PARTIES

Cocktail parties usually begin about 19h00, and will last for a couple of hours. Informality over the time of arrival may not be matched by informality over dress, and you should try to find out roughly what is expected of you.

If you decide to organise a more traditional British-style party, do not expect your French guests to bring a bottle with them. In France, the host traditionally provides all the requirements for an evening's entertainment. One way to get around this is to call a party a *soirée à l'anglaise*, literally an English evening, and gently explain the bring-a-bottle concept to your French guests. You should warn both neighbours and the *concierge* that you will be organising a party, and post polite notes in French in the entrance hall of your building, apologising in advance for any inconvenience caused.

Encourage your guests to leave quietly, and be careful of the level of noise. The police may be asked to intervene at rowdy parties after 22h00. Your neighbours will normally be forgiving if you make an excuse such as 'It's my birthday'. However, remember you only have one birthday a year!

MARKING BIRTHS, MARRIAGES AND DEATHS

Although these are not leisure activities, it is appropriate to know a few of the social customs of the 'hatched, matched and despatched' business which still thrives in Republican France, so that you do not make any blunders. Obviously there is no Court Circular page in French newspapers, but both *Le Figaro* and *Le Monde* carry social announcements, as well as *Libération* to a lesser extent. The choice of paper depends entirely on the class pretensions and politics of those concerned.

Births

Births (*naissances*) are often announced not only by cards as in the UK but also by a small advertisement in one of the papers named above. Typically, a birth announcement will be roughly translated as, 'Marie and Pierre are pleased to announce the arrival of their new sister Jeanne', followed by the name and address of the parents.

Infant baptisms are heavily on the decline in France. For Catholic families, they normally take place during the Parish Mass on Sunday mornings and will be followed by a family lunch. Coloured sugared almonds (*dragees*) are often distributed, pink for girls and blue for boys.

Marriages

No religious wedding ceremony may take place in France until a civil marriage has first been performed by the mayor at the town hall. This applies to all religions and denominations. If a large religious ceremony is to follow, then normally only close family and friends will attend the wedding at the *mairie*. However, many people choose to stick to civil marriage. Being invited to be a *témoin* (witness) is an honour equivalent to being a bridesmaid or usher.

Wedding lists are very popular in France, and are an easy way of dealing with the problem of presents. The style of the wedding is of course entirely personal to the couple and may range from the unusual to the strictly traditional. A traditional Catholic wedding will take place in the course of a Nuptial Mass in the bride's home parish.

As with British weddings, French weddings can be the occasion for a great show of finery. As ever in France, be careful to find out as much about the dress code as possible. The wedding invitation may well read like a genealogy of the couple, with grandparents and parents of both sides listed.

The French tradition in wedding receptions is the opposite of the British. Everybody is invited after the wedding to the *vin d'honneur*, to toast the couple's health and happiness. But after that the reception is limited, ranging from a seated dinner (*dîner placée*), to a *soirée dansante* (dance). At a French aristocratic wedding, this will normally take place at the family *château*.

Finally, one tradition which is widely observed is to form a wedding convoy after the ceremony at the *mairie* or church, with drivers all sounding their horns at the same time as they drive along.

Deaths

Generally you will receive a *faire-part* (card announcing a death), including the same genealogical list as you would find on a wedding invitation – only longer. For instance, a *faire-part* announcing the death of a grandmother would begin with her spouse, include any surviving brothers and sisters and their spouses, and then move on to mention each child and their children, sometimes each by name.

The French are very attached to the tradition of writing to express condolence. The *faire-part* will announce when and where the funeral is to take place, if donations should be made in place of flowers, and whether it is a 'family only' affair (*dans la plus stricte intimité*).

At a French Requiem Mass, each mourner will be invited to take part in the ritual of absolution, the *absolut* (sprinkling of holy water) as a final farewell. This is not obligatory if it contradicts your own faith. If you do wish to participate, move at the instruction of the undertaker, and then 'follow the leader'. Burial is still much the most common end for French men and women, and cremations are rare. It should be noted that French crematoria are to say the least much less 'user-friendly' than British ones.

ENJOYING THE PERFORMING ARTS

France is traditionally very generous in state patronage of the arts. The result is a rich variety in the performing arts, which is by no means concentrated only in the major cities. Tourist information centres will be able to tell you what forthcoming productions and events are planned in your own area.

Music

Regional festivals and the system of *conservatoires* (music academies) ensure a broad availability of music in the more populated areas. Paris naturally has a high concentration of fine concert halls, but there is a very important musical life outside of the capital also. Each summer, for instance, Radio France organises a classical music festival in Montpellier.

Popular music concerts take place all over France, with world-renowned singers touring. The *Printemps de Bourges* festival is a major jamboree and recruitment session in central France for rock fans and recording artistes. *L'Interceltique* at L'Orient in Brittany is a vast international Celtic gathering with participants from Wales, Scotland, Ireland, Spain and beyond.

Opera

Opera flourishes in Paris, not only in the new Bastille Opera House, but also at the Opéra-Comique, and sometimes also at the old Paris Opéra (the Palais Garnier), and in other theatres such as the Théâtre Chatelet. There are also important opera houses in Bordeaux, Lille, Lyon, Nancy, Nice and Montpellier (where there are in fact two opera houses). Both traditional and modern operas are included in their repertoires. The Paris Ballet is now housed at the grand old Opéra-Garnier, and provides a full programme each season. Visiting ballets also regularly appear in Paris.

Theatre

The theatre thrives in France, with many small theatres offering the chance for new actors and productions to appear before the public. The most famous French theatre is the Comedie-Française in Paris, which now has three theatres. Several Paris venues regularly offer productions in English, from small repertory companies to the *Bouffes du Nord* directed by former British National Theatre director Peter Brooke. Outside of Paris, the annual Avignon Theatre Festival is world-renowned.

Carnivals and fiestas

Although the Catholic tradition of carnival is much less present in France than elsewhere in the Catholic world, it is still observed with a certain exuberance in northern France, notably in Dunkerque, and in Nice in the south. In the summer months, in the areas bordering Spain which have been heavily influenced by Spanish immigrants from the 1930s onwards, Spanish-style fiestas take place, including regular bull-fights. The most notable centres for these fiestas are Nîmes and Beziers.

VISITING GALLERIES AND HISTORIC MONUMENTS

France is home to arguably the world's greatest museum, the Louvre, which is the centre-piece of the cultural jewel which is Paris. A good guide-book to Paris (there are hundreds to choose from) will be a worth-while investment. However, you should remember that there is a hidden wealth of art galleries, museums and historical monuments across France.

From the gothic cathedrals of Amiens, Rheims and Rouen in the north to the painter Chagall's hideaway at St Paul-de-Vence in the south, via the Baroque splendours of Versailles, the *châteaux* of the Loire valley and the restored medieval ramparts of Carcassone, France is packed with fascinating and well-preserved historical monuments. The municipal art galleries (*musées des beaux-arts*) of Lille and Rouen are particularly fine. Driving through the valleys of the Dordogne region, you will come across ruined castles, and across France you will find many ancient shrines around which grew up often well-preserved medieval towns. Each time you intend to visit a new city or region, buy yourself a regional guide-book if you can. This will allow you to get the best out of even a short stay. The best series of guide books for France remains the **green Michelin guides**, which are also available in English.

GOING TO THE CINEMA

Cinema is one of the great passions of the French, which they consider to be the 'seventh art'. Paris has two film festivals of its own sponsored by the city, and other festivals take place throughout the year linked to particular themes. In addition to the famous Cannes film festival, there is also an American film festival at Deauville and a British film festival at Dinard each year.

Films in English with French sub-titles are widely shown and are marked *v.o. (version originale)*; *v.f. (version française)* means that films have been dubbed. *Premiers* (first nights) are great occasions, but there are plenty of *avants-premiers* now which are advertised in the press. Wednesday is the day that new films come out in France, and is worth avoiding at cinemas if you want a quiet night out.

The French are very attached to experimental art cinemas, and these in particular have been threatened by the arrival of cinema passes from the large chains.

WATCHING AND PLAYING SPORT

As with so many other activities, the French are nothing if not passionate about sport. A French player or team who wins a competition in no matter what discipline can be certain of a hero's welcome on the Champs-Elysées when they return to France, as well as endless hours of television coverage – until or unless they are knocked out of a competition, when TV interest noticeably evaporates.

Details of local facilities – which are widespread and generally high-standard – can be obtained from the local *mairie* or *syndicat d'initiative*. Sport is very well-regarded in France as a means of social interaction, and some of the poorest and most troubled areas have the highest sporting take-up rates.

Soccer is one of the national obsessions, especially since the World Cup hosted by France in 1998. To celebrate this occasion, the French built themselves a magnificent new stadium just north of Paris. The leading clubs are Paris-St Germain (**PSG**) and Olympic Marseilles (**OM**) in the south, Lens and Lille in the north, Nantes in the west and Auxerre in Burgundy, although there are regional clubs all over France who participate in national and international league.

Rugby is another national obsession, especially beating the British whenever possible. This is most notably during the Six Nations tournament each year. Rugby is particularly strong in the south-west around Toulouse, and in central France near Brive-le Gaillard (literally 'Brive the strong'). Tennis is also a favourite pastime, encouraged by the French climate. The Roland Garros competition just outside Paris and the Paris Open Tennis championships rival Wimbledon in drawing the great names to play. Basketball is another popular sport, and France's geography also favours water-sports, from swimming to surfing to water-skiing. If you enjoy sailing, be sure to read Chapter 9 before setting sail from the coasts of France.

Winter sports have always been a French speciality due to the mountainous Italian, Spanish and Swiss borders. The ski resorts are very well-developed, and often full at peak holiday periods. In the summer months, mountaineering and hiking are also popular pastimes. Cycling dominates news coverage for at least several weeks each year when the Tour de France weaves its way across the country and into Paris. Cross-country cycling is increasingly popular.

Horse racing enthusiasts will find plenty to please them in France. Deauville and Paris are both well-known centres for horse-racing. The great races each year are the *Prix de l'Arc de Triomphe* at Longchamps on the first weekend in October (the occasion of a British mini-invasion for the French equivalent of the Derby), and the *Prix de Diane* at Chantilly in June (which is really the equivalent of the Ascot Gold Cup, with lots of silly hats included). In August, the action moves to Deauville for the holiday season.

ENJOYING HOBBIES

Joining a club or society can be a good way of meeting people and making friends in your own neighbourhood. It can also be a good opportunity to practise or improve your French. The Regional Directory at the end of this book will give you information on how to contact clubs and societies in your area which are specifically for foreign residents. Otherwise the local *mairie* will also be able to point you in the right direction for finding groups such as ramblers (*randonneurs*) or wine-tasters, or indeed whatever your own particular interest might be.

If you enjoy fishing, you should note that you will need a licence (*carte de pêche*). There is no examination for this, but you do have to pay. For further details contact the Union Nationale de Pêche,

17 rue Bergère, 75009, Paris tél. 01 48 24 96 00. A junior card exists for children under 16. There are also cards valid for 15 days for holiday-makers. You should also take a look at **www.unpf.fr** the French language website of the national federation of French fishers.

VOLUNTEERING

Another way of meeting people is to join a charitable association. Giving a little of your time as a *bénévole* (volunteer) can make a lot of difference to the well-being of both the charity and the people it seeks to help. The largest charities in France are those helping people affected by AIDS (*SIDA* in French), cancer research, the Red Cross (*Croix-Rouge*) and charities such as Abbé Pierre's '*Emmaus*' Project for housing assistance for poor families. One of the most well-known charities is the *Restos du Couer*, which are mobile soup-kitchens helping the homeless.

To find out more about volunteering with English-language associations, take a look at **www.britishinfrance.com**. This website covers English-language associations in the Il de France, but also provides links to other groups outside of Paris. The associations are not exclusively for British citizens, and all welcome native English-speakers of other nationalities.

GOING ON HOLIDAY

France is consistently the most popular tourist destination in the world. As a foreigner in France, you will probably want to take advantage of the wonderful opportunities all around you to explore your new home. This need not be expensive, and can be easily done using public transport as well as private vehicles. As a first step, you should try contacting the tourist office (*office de tourisme* or *syndicat d'initiative*) for the town you are thinking of visiting. The French have a sometimes curious 'herd-instinct' and tend to leave the cities in droves to escape each other, only to find that the resorts are full of their compatriots doing likewise.

If you can take a break out of high season, you will enjoy it more, it will probably be cheaper, and you will certainly have more choice over accommodation. Chapter 12 includes details of some offers available from the *SNCF* train service. The *gîtes* system (small country properties) offer the opportunity for self-catering in pleasant surroundings. Hotels range from the cheap and cheerful *Formule 1* outside major towns, to the luxurious *Relais Châteaux,* with a wide range in between.

HOLIDAY CHECKLIST

◆ Check your dates – do they coincide with the school holidays?

◆ Check the weather and any travel offers.

◆ Reserve your accommodation and tickets as far in advance as you can. If you are going to a small town, the hotels may close out of season, or may you find that a local event means all the hotels are full when you arrive.

◆ If you are taking your car, or you wish to hire one, take the appropriate documents with you.

◆ Buy yourself a good local guidebook so that you can get the most out of your trip. The green Michelin guides cover the whole of France.

◆ Don't forget to switch out the lights when you leave – and *bon voyage!*

FINDING OUT MORE

Weekly entertainment guides coincide with new films every
Wednesday. Magazines come out on Thursdays. The newspapers
publish their critiques on different days.

◆ Amongst the best Paris guides are, **in English**: *The Free Voice*;
  FUSAC (listings only); *Where* (monthly subscription magazine,
  tél. 01 43 12 56 56). **In French**: *Pariscope*; *Zurban*; *A nous
  Paris*; and *Officiels & Spectacles*.

◆ Nationwide coverage can be found in the magazine *Nova*; *Aden*;
  the weekly supplement of *Le Monde*; *Libération* and *Le Figaro*
  (every day); and the supplement to *L'Express*.

◆ Each summer the main French newspapers publish free
  supplements listing the hundreds of festivals across France, in
  major cities and small towns. It is well worth checking these
  supplements to find out what is going in your home town or
  your planned holiday destination.

See also Chapter 12 on Travelling in France for further useful
holiday links. Each of the French regions has a tourist office in
central Paris, known as *La maison de Savoie* (for example). Check
the *Pages Jaunes* for current addresses and telephone numbers.

14

Discovering the Regions of France

This chapter provides a brief introduction to some of the regions of France which are most popular with the English-speaking communities. If you do not find the region you are looking for, you should not worry about being 'lost' in the French hinterland. Four points of contact in particular can provide help in most parts of France in finding local contacts and information:

◆ *Association France-GrandeBretagne* – the Franco-British cultural and friendship society with branches all over France. To find out about local branches, contact the Paris office at 183 avenue Daumesnil, 75012 Paris, tél. 01 55 78 71 71 (see also **www.britishinfrance.com**).

◆ **www.avf.asso.fr** – *accueils des villes françaises*. This partially bilingual welcome website can help you find out about local amenities in your new town or city, and put you in touch with useful organisations, as well as the local EDF, etc.

◆ **www.cnous.fr** – use this website to find the contact details of your local student centre. Many of the linked local sites are bilingual, at least in part.

◆ **www.europe.anglican.org** – the Church of England has chaplaincies covering almost all of France. In some places there are permanent churches, whilst in others congregations share local churches. Current contact numbers and times of services can be found on this website. Remember that English-speaking churches are a focus for expatriate communities who can offer valuable local advice.

REGIONAL TRANSPORT

One of the major changes in France in recent years has been the increase in high-speed links between provincial cities and regions, and Paris, London and beyond. This is due to two factors. Firstly, the number of low-cost airlines serving regional French airports, and allowing regular links notably to British airports. Secondly, the French rail system and its high-speed TGV system has been extended to Strasbourg. It used to take more than four hours to reach Strasbourg by train: the travelling time has now been reduced by two hours. Regional commuters to the capital are now a common phenomenon, and this may be an option which you wish to consider in order to access different lifestyle opportunities. You should always check the current services offered when deciding on where to live or buy property, as commercial arrangements change frequently according to economic factors.

THE SOUTH-WEST OF FRANCE – MIDI-PYRÉNÉES

This is the largest administrative region in France, covering 50,000 square kilometres and home to three million people. Bordered on both sides by mountains (the Pyrenees and the Massif Central) the region is larger than Switzerland, Belgium or the Netherlands. In 2001 it was the region with the highest number of job creations, and the fourth highest number of foreign investors in France. The three most important employers locally are the aircraft construction and space industries; agriculture and food (accounting for about 10% of the working population); and information technology and communications, for which this is the second most important region in France.

Tourism is also a major employer in the region. The number of British tourists on the Atlantic coast rose by between 5–10% in 2000, and the impact of the low-cost airline links to **Bergerac** and **Poitiers** is bound to ensure that this number continues to rise. The south-west is particularly well-endowed with excellent wines, from the cheaper Bergeracs to the richer Bordeaux such as Médoc. It is also home to the most famous of French specialities *foie gras.*

Despite being grouped together in a large administrative unit, the area is a mixture of ancient rival cities and cultures who are still jealous of their ancient rights. There is no point in asking inhabitants of the two principal cities, **Toulouse** and **Bordeaux**, what is good about the rival city; they will simply tell you, 'Nothing at all'! Whilst Bordeaux and the coast of **Acquitaine** (the name of the medieval dukedom covering this area) is solidly right-wing, the hill country beyond Toulouse gave the Socialists some of their highest scores in 2002.

The ancient city of **Toulouse**, *'la ville rose'* as it is known because of the pink brick buildings, is centred on the Capitole and the Place Wilson. It is home to some 100,000 students at its university, renowned for health, food safety and environmental studies; about 30% of the city's population is under 25. The city suffered a major blow in September 2001 when the chemical factory AZF exploded, killing 30 people, wounding 2,000, and leaving thousands more homeless. The future of the site remains very unclear. New developments in the Airbus industry (the A380) were set to create thousands of new jobs, but current economic uncertainty concerning Airbus has created unexpected economic tension in the region.

One local writer described **Bordeaux** as the town where, *'it is as rainy as Nantes and as hot as Seville'*. Home to some 220,000 people, with 700,000 living in the total urban area (two-thirds of the *Bordelais* live in the city suburbs), and with some 70,000 students, the city was renowned as somewhat closed and sleepy until recently. The ancient heart of Bordeaux reflects the commercial strength of this once-major port. Fine 18th century mansions line the narrow medieval streets and the banks of the **Garonne** river, newly restored to create an impression of St Petersburg. The port remains the symbolic heart of the city, but the real economic heart is not only the wine trade, but also the aeronautical industry once again. The opening of the first tramway in 2006 allowed the rejuvenation of the poorer Right Bank of the city, but the city's long-standing traffic problems are still unresolved. One of the major problems is the lack of bridges, and rush-hour travelling times can be very extensive. Finally, with 20% of the city budget spent on the arts each year (opera, ballet, museums, theatres and galleries), the city is an important cultural centre, even if it is renowned for the enigmatic 'discreet charm of the bourgeoisie'.

Below the Pyrenees lies the former independent kingdom of **Béarn**, centred on the Anglophile city of **Pau**, with its English church, 19th century English villas, and a French hunt that could have trotted out of the Cotswolds, founded by the first English visitors. For centuries this region was criss-crossed by pilgrims on their way to the great Spanish shrine at Compostella (giving rise to many magnificent abbeys), or to the local French shrine of **Rocamdour** in the Dordogne valley. Now pilgrims flock to this region to visit the shrine of **Lourdes.**

The Midi-Pyrénées region has 400km of beaches on the Atlantic coast, which are the centre of the surf industry in France, which employs about 4,000 people locally from Bordeaux to **St Jean de Luz**. The surf capital is the jewel of the Atlantic coast, **Biarritz**, which forms the flamboyant part of an urban conglomeration of **Biarritz-Bayonne-Anglet**. Locally the saying goes that, '*You work in Bayonne, you enjoy yourself in Biarritz and you sleep in Anglet*'. Whilst Biarritz is full throughout the tourist season, Bayonne is slowly recovering from a period of decline.

This furthermost corner of France is the **Basque** country, and cultural sympathy for the nearby Spanish Basques runs very strong, and there is a train link from Bayonne in France to San Sebastian in Spain, further reinforcing economic and cultural links. There is a strong Basque nationalist movement in the area, with constant demands to allow the teaching of the Basque language in schools and the creation of a separate Basque *département*.

The strong British communities in the south-west are traditionally to be found in the **Dordogne** valley, and a newer community in the **Tarn-et-Garonne** region between **Cahors** and Toulouse. Whilst the former is mainly a retired community, the latter has proved to be entrepreneurial. Local reaction to these communities tends to be a mixture of jealousy of their property purchasing power, and grateful thanks for helping to revive dying villages. The rural **Lot-et-Garonne**, centred on **Agen**, is still cheaper than the other two regions, despite a growing number of foreign households.

There are two major international airports in the south-west. Bordeaux is planning to expand its airport with a low-cost terminal, and there are already regular links to Luton, Birmingham, Bristol, Manchester and Southampton. Toulouse airport had more than six million passengers in 2007, with low-cost carriers ranking as the second most important airline. Other regional airports with international links include Lourdes and Bergerac, and efforts are being made to re-establish the low-cost link to Poitiers. Carcassone has also seen significant increases in low-cost flights to the UK and northern Europe. Currently it takes three hours for the TGV to link Paris and Bordeaux. The TGV link from Paris to Toulouse takes five hours. A high-speed Paris–Madrid train link via Bordeaux and Angoulême is planned for 2010–2016, and this will reduce the train journey from Paris to Bordeaux by one hour.

Useful contacts

- **Conseil régional de Midi-Pyrenées**, 22 boulevard du Maréchal Juin, 31406 Toulouse, cedex 4, tél. 05 61 33 50, fax 05 61 33 32 66, **www.midipyrenees**. The main local newspaper is *La Dépêche du Midi*.

- **www.aquitaine.angloinfo.com** is a comprehensive website with current information on community associations, schooling and business groups across the south-west region. This is a very useful link for anybody moving to the region. On the international schools and universities page, you will find a list of English-language education opportunities in the region.

- **American Presence Post** (commercial matters only), 25 allée Jean-Jaurés, 31000 Toulouse, tél. 05 34 41 36 50, fax 05 34 41 16 19, Monday–Friday 09h00–12h00, 14h00–17h00.

- **The British Consulate**, 353 boulevard Wilson, 33073 Bordeaux, tél. 05 57 22 21 10, fax 05 56 08 33 12. Go to

www.britishembassy.gov.uk/france, then choose the Bordeaux consulate for local advice and associations contacts, including churches and sports clubs. Church services are held across the region and there are churches in Bordeaux, Toulouse, Biarritz and Pau.

- **Bordeaux-Bristol Association** (library) 13, quai de la Monnaie, 33800 Bordeaux, tél. 05 56 92 26 21.

- **Bordeaux British Community**, **www.bordeauxbritish.com** (no employment or housing advice).

- **Americans in Toulouse**, email: americansintoulouse@yahoo. com, **www.americansintoulouse.com** – an association for English-speakers of all nationalities.

- **Dordogne Study Centre**, tél. 05 53 81 79 62, fax 05 53 80 54 47. **www.johnairs.tripod.com**. GCSE, A level and adult education.

- **Bordeaux International School**, **www.bordeauxschool.com**, tél. 05 57 87 02 11, fax 05 56 79 00 47 – bilingual education from juniors to high school.

- **Toulouse – Lycée Polyvalent International** (section Britannique), tél. 05 61 15 94 94.

- There are Anglican chaplaincies which operate across the region. For current contact details, and times and places of services, consult **www.europe.anglican.org.**

THE NORTH-WEST OF FRANCE

Brittany

With its rugged coastline and English weather ranging from glorious sunshine to pouring rain, its Arthurian legends and

Druidic standing stones (*menhirs*), and a strong cultural identity including a language that looks suspiciously like Welsh, there is a strong natural attraction between the *Bretons* of **Bretagne** and their neighbours in **Grande-Bretagne** and Ireland. The region around Quimper, **Cornuaille**, even has the same name as the French for Cornwall. This ancient former independent duchy is happy, loud and proud of its difference from the rest of Latin France, even if remains one of the bedrocks of French Catholicism. Every year, the *Festival Interceltique* at **Lorient** draws a crowd of up to 500,000 people from across the former Celtic kingdoms of northern and western Europe for a frenzy of Celtic music, bagpipes, parades and the great Breton celebrations known as the *fest-noz* (which probably loses a little something in translation, but is the Breton for a good party!).

With the notable exceptions of **Rennes**, **Vannes**, and the former capital of the Dukes of Brittany at **Nantes** (currently 'in exile' as the capital of another region), Brittany is a region that lives from the land and the sea. Both the local economy and politics reflect this, and in the 2002 elections the highest scores for the Ecology Party, *les Verts*, were recorded in Brittany. 'Local boy' Jean-Marie Le Pen received a resounding rejection from the fair-minded Catholic-influenced Bretons, along with their neighbours across western France. (Le Pen's name is typical of Breton names, many of which are preceded by 'Le'.)

Some 80% of the Breton economy is composed of small and medium-sized companies, including many service industries linked to agriculture, the food industry and tourism, which plays an important rôle in local economic life. The region is dominated by **Rennes** with its 206,000 people, including 55,000 students (of whom 3,000 are foreign students), who generate a healthy cultural life. The city has undertaken a number of important infrastructural developments in recent years, including transport links, housing developments and high-speed Internet access. The Atlante business park is the principal site of the other Breton speciality of recent years, the development of information technology services.

Leaving aside historical arguments about whether it is or is not in Brittany, **Nantes** is now one of France's leading cities. It has a flourishing university, and is a major economic centre for the west of France. The city has benefited from renovation, including an extensive tram service across the city, and the redevelopment of the former port areas around Beaulieu. The city also has an excellent cultural programme, including the annual non-stop classical music festival.

Brittany has seen a major British influx in recent years, and community associations, and churches and some school facilities are now available to assist your integration. A few international school facilities do exist, but generally you will be reliant on the local education system for schooling. However, one major advantage that local education does offer is that it is ranked as the best in France, from kindergarten through to the highest success rate at the *bac* since 1998. This has much to do with the Breton belief in the value of education as a way of achieving success. Education is another way of reinforcing the Breton identity, with 35 *écoles Diwans* (and 2,000 students) learning the Breton language, and some 300 students enrolled for courses in Breton at Rennes University. This is not to everybody's taste, least of all the guardians of the national constitution, the *Conseil d'Etat*. Conscious of the calls from the small number of extremist Breton nationalists for a degree of autonomy to which Paris does not agree, and of the dangers of the Basque and Corsican examples, French remains the official language of these schools, despite the subject matter.

Calls for the 'reunification' of Brittany with a return of **Nantes**, the university city and cultural capital of western France, to the Breton fold, and disputes over the teaching of Breton, both highlight the difficulties France faces as it moves towards greater measure of decentralisation. But nobody denies (at least in Brittany) the positive economic effect of a strong local identity, including the first regional private TV channel, TV Breizh, founded by the Breton director of France's leading TV company.

Normandy

Ever since the Norman invasion of 1066, the British have been busy trying to turn the tide by launching regular invasions of the area nicknamed 'lower Kent'. Normandy offers all the advantages of proximity to both Britain and Paris that many people seek, but this also has proved to be something of a hindrance in its current economic development. The coastal areas suffered considerably during the D-Day landings of the Second World War, with much of **Caen** and even more of **Le Havre** destroyed in bombing. But inland you will still find ancient villages and *châteaux*, half-timbered houses and medieval abbeys. Normandy is also France's 'cider country', although other local specialities include the *Calvados* liqueur and the great French cheese, *Camembert*.

The ancient capital of Normandy is **Rouen**, home to about 106,000 people including just over 30,000 students. This cultural masterpiece on the banks of the Seine, with its magnificent medieval cathedral at the centre, is 120km from the sea. Nonetheless its port receives some 4000 boats a year, as the last major port before Paris. In recent years, the city has begun the restoration of the quaysides, and sought to exploit its maritime links. But the city suffers from its proximity to the capital. It is only one hour by train from Paris, and some 1,500 people commute to the capital each day. Rouen has also suffered from the AZF explosion in Toulouse (see above). A number of high-risk sites surround the city, and their eventual closure would lead to severe difficulties. However, in the Rouen region there are new information technology and communications companies being established.

Le Havre (with a population of 191,000 people) has always been a major port, but suffered doubly from the ugly post- D-Day bombardment concrete reconstruction, and from heavy job losses and social conflict in the 1980s and 1990s. In recent years, central government has come to the aid of the town, and the port remains the fifth largest in Europe and the second largest in France. The Port 2000 project is intended to redevelop the port to rival Hamburg or Rotterdam. The continued presence of the oil refinery industries and the Renault car works still provides the mainstay of employment in this area, along with the newer industry of waste recycling, but the current mayor is seeking to restore the pre-war leisure industries which made Le Havre a rival for **Deauville** across the bay. A small university was founded in Le Havre in 1984, which now has about 8,000 students.

In a survey in Rouen in 2002 (*Libération*, 25 January 2002), 24% of Rouen inhabitants said that if they had to leave Rouen to live somewhere else, they would choose **Caen**. In 2006, a major survey of the best cities in France (in *Le Nouvel Observateur*), listed Caen as the sixth best city in France. Although the city suffered from the D-Day bombardments, the British bombs appeared to have spared the Abbaye aux Hommes et aux Dames, including the tomb of William the Conqueror. Caen today is a busy university town, just over two hours from Paris by train and with regular ferry links to the UK. To the east lie the sandy beaches of **Houlgate, Cabourg** (home to Marcel Proust), chic **Deauville** and picture-postcard **Honfleur**. From May to September, there are direct trains to the Norman coastal resorts from Paris. To the west lies **Bayeux** (and its tapestry), and the rural Norman peninsular region centred on **Coutances**.

On the southern edge of Normandy the smaller city of **Evreux** is another Norman town which suffers from the same commuter effect as Rouen. However in this lower part of Normandy near **Chartres** (with its world-famous cathedral), the proximity to Paris has worked in the local favour. Small and medium-sized businesses have grown up around the pharmaceutical and aeronautic industries in the area.

To the west of Chartres lies **Le Mans**, the capital of the **Sarthe** *département*, renowned for its annual motor-race. The area remains economically healthy, with 28% of the population working in industry (as opposed to 19% nationally), and the food and car industries still the major employers along with the insurance industry. A new business district has been developed, and the town is home now to some 20 call centres.

The Loire valley

Below Normandy and stretching out to Nantes lies the famous valley of the châteaux. The towns and cities which line the valley are now within easy striking distance of Paris, but are also considered to offer a better quality of life. In November 2006, in a league table of the best cities in which to live in France, the magazine *Le Nouvel Observateur* ranked Angers the second best city in France, whilst Nantes was ranked eighth, and Orléans was ranked fifteenth. Currently the university town of Angers appears to be the most 'Anglo friendly' of the Loire cities, with an English Library and several schools with international sections.

Nantes has a major international airport, with almost three million passengers each year, and low-cost links to London and Barcelona. La Rochelle airport has also seen a significant increase in low-cost flights to the UK, but only the link to Stansted is currently open all the year round. Low-cost flights also operate to Dinard on the Breton coast, and there are also small airports at Brest and Caen. By train, Chartres, Evreux, Le Mans and Rouen, all in Normandy, are one hour from Paris. In the Loire valley bordering Normandy and Brittany, Orléans is an hour from Paris, Angers is ninety minutes from Paris, and Tours-Paris Montparnasse takes just over one hour. The ferry companies all continue to operate services from the major ports the length of the Breton and Norman coastlines. The principal local newspaper for this region is *Ouest-France*.

Useful contacts

◆ Brittany and Normandy are both within the Paris consular districts of foreign embassies. There is an **American Presence Post** (commercial matters only) in Rennes at 30 quai Dugouy-Trouin, 35000 Rennes, tél. 02 23 44 09 60, fax 02 99 35 00 92.

- With the growing British presence in western France, a small number of associations creating a more formal community structure are now developing. For details of English-language services, including schooling in English, and community associations, consult the following sites: **www. brittany. angloinfo.com**; **www. normandy.angloinfo.com**; or **www. loire.angloinfo.com**.

- There is an **Anglican church** in Rouen and regular services in Caen and Coutrances. Services are held throughout the summer at the English church in Dinard, and a multi-point chaplaincy covers the wider Brittany region (see **www.europe.anglican.org**).

- **www.britline.com** – on-line banking facility in English from the Crédit Agricole bank, with over 10,000 British clients who have purchased property principally in Normandy.

GOING TO LIVE IN PARIS

Faced with the necessity to convert to Catholicism in order to attain the throne of France during the bitter Wars of Religion in the 16th century, the Protestant King Henri of Navarre (Henri IV) came out with one of his best one-liners: '*Paris vaut bien une messe*', 'Paris is well worth a Mass'. The same sentiment remains true today. For more information, see *Living & Working in Paris* (How To Books), where I provide a detailed description of the city and its suburbs, and all the practical information needed to make a success of life in the capital.

The Ile de France is composed of eight *départements* including Paris itself, and is home to some 12 million people representing about 19% of the French population and 21% of the working population, and receiving 36 million visitors a year. The best universities and most prestigious companies are to be found in the city and its nearby suburbs, and it still represents your main opportunity for entering French society.

Whilst there is obviously a very high urban concentration, you are not forced to live entirely surrounded by cars and concrete. The region includes 2,400 square kilometres of forests, and almost 10,000 square kilometres of farmland and natural parks. The outer suburbs, which have good transport links to the city centre and business districts, combine country living with city amenities.

Useful contacts

◆ The contact details of the principal English-speaking Consulates are given at the end of Chapter 2.

◆ Conseil régional d'Ile de France, 33 rue Barbet-de-Jouy, 75007 Paris, **www.iledefrance.fr**.

◆ **www.paris.france.org** – Paris city council (*Mairie de Paris*) website.

◆ **www.britishinfrance.com** – website of the 60 British and Franco-British clubs and associations in and around Paris, many of which are international in nature and welcome members of other nationalities.

◆ **Principal churches and community centres**: The American Church, 65 quai d'Orsay, 75007 Paris M° Invalides; The American Cathedral, 23 avenue George V, 75008 Paris, M° George V; St George's Anglican Church, 7 rue Auguste-Vacquerie, 75116 Paris, M° Etoile, Kléber; St Joseph's RC Church, 50 avenue Hoche, 75008 Paris M° Etoile; St Michael's

Anglican Church, 5 rue d'Aguesseau, 75008 Paris, M°
Concorde.

◆ Paris has a number of English-language schools, all of which
  are private. The best known are The British School of Paris in
  Croissy sur Seine (**www.britishschool.fr**), the American School
  of Paris in St Cloud (**www.asparis.org**), and the International
  School of Paris (**www.isparis.edu**), and Ecole Active Bilingue
  (**www.eab.fr**) in central Paris. There are also several
  international sections at state-run *lycées* and *collèges*. The
  Lycée International at St Germain en Laye is a very highly-
  regarded school (**www.lycee-international.com**), with partnership
  arrangements with several more junior schools in the western
  suburbs. For a full selection of bilingual opportunities, see the
  (French only!) site **www.enfantsbilingues.com**, and go to the
  Plan du site and choose *Trouver une école bilingue*.

◆ **Bookshops**: Brentanos, 37 avenue de l'Opéra, 75002 Paris,
  www.brentanos.fr, M° Opéra; WH Smiths, 248 rue de Rivoli,
  75001 Paris, **www.whsmith.fr**, M° Concorde.

◆ **Free community publications**: France-USA Contacts,
  www.fusac.fr (jobs, accommodation, entertainment); The Paris
  Voice, **www.parisvoice.com** (more lifestyle articles but also
  accommodation and jobs). Both available at churches,
  Consulates, bookshops and in Anglophone bars.

◆ *Time Out*, **www.timeout.com/paris** – quarterly listings in English
  available at the same distribution points as FUSAC.

THE NORTH OF FRANCE – NORD-PAS-DE-CALAIS

From Calais to the forests of Chantilly, through **Picardy** and the
ruddy fields of Flanders, this area of France has been invaded,

conquered and reclaimed more times than most French people would probably care to remember. The mixture of faded splendour, ruin and revival in this area are a testament to economic riches past and present. Dominated for centuries by the textile and cloth industries which are still vital to the region, then by mining and the steel industry, and now by the car and transport industries, this part of France is a melting pot of French, British and Belgian influences.

Whilst the Channel ports today are simply ferry ports to many people, **Dunkerque** has strong associations for many British people with the Second World War. The damage inflicted on this part of France can be seen in towns such as **Abbeville**, where scattered relics of the former glory of the region stand forlorn amongst drab post-war reconstructions.

Although the town of **Calais** commemorates medieval English occupation with its famous Rodin sculpture of the hostage Burghers of Calais handed over to Edward III of England, 19th century English visitors were made much more welcome on the region's **Côte Opale**. From **Le Touquet** where the local 'gentry' still retire in the summer months to what was known as 'Paris-Plage', to picturesque **Boulogne-sur-Mer** or popular **Berck-sur-Mer**, the northern coast is a popular local holiday destination.

The regional capital of **Lille** only became part of France in the 17th century when Louis XIV conquered the region. The city is an architectural gem which strongly reflects its Flemish origins, with the main square more reminiscent of the Grand Place in Brussels than of other French cities. Only one hour from Paris by train, and the second stop of the Eurostar trains from London, Lille has developed a strong international identity through its quick links to nearby Belgium and Germany. It is no surprise that Lille and the north is renowned for its selection of beers!

Excellent shops are complemented by a fine cultural life and a large university. But whilst Rouen suffers from its proximity to Paris, Lille suffers in part from its proximity to Belgium. When it comes to nightlife, the night-owls think nothing of flitting across the border to Belgium to round their night off. The great annual event is the **Grande Braderie de Lille**, when, for an entire weekend, the city is transformed into one vast open-air market.

If Lille reflects Belgian culture, a strange English influence can be felt in former mining towns such as **Lens**. When the mines were founded, the French mine-owners turned to their British counterparts for ideas as to how to house the miners. The result is row upon row of terraced red-brick houses which could have been imported from County Durham. Add to this the religion-like role of football in local life, especially in Lens and Lille, plus the local taste for beer and chips, and you could be forgiven for wondering precisely where you are.

It was in this region that Henry VIII of England met François 1 of France at the Field of the Cloth of Gold. Although the textile industry has now diminished in size and importance in the local economy, it still employs about 36,000 people locally. The closure of the pits and steel works has started to be compensated for by large car factories near **Douai, Maubeuge** and **Valenciennes**, employing around 20,000 people. The transport industry has increased in importance, most notably as a result of the Channel

Tunnel. Finally, information technology and communications account for about 29,000 jobs in this region. But despite all of these factors, unemployment remains consistently above the French average at about 14%.

To the south of the region, **Amiens** is the capital of the *département* of the Somme. The cathedral is one of the finest Gothic cathedrals in the world, and attests to the former wealth and power of the cities in this part of France. This area is much more concerned with agriculture than industry, and has suffered from heavy flooding in recent years. You should make careful enquiries about flood zones (*zones inonndables*) when considering purchasing property near here.

Closest to the capital lies the forest and town of **Compiègne**, with its former royal palace beloved of both Napolèons, and the valley of the **Oise** leading down to **Chantilly** with its *château* and racecourse, which has always had strong British links.

Useful contacts

◆ The region is amply served by **transport links**, with ferries to the UK, high-speed trains to Paris, Belgium, the Netherlands, Germany and the UK, and two international airports at Lille and Beauvais, along with France's main international airport, Roissy, on the regional border. The principal local newspaper is *La Voix du Nord*.

◆ **The British Consulate**, 11 square Dutilleul, 59800 Lille, tél. 03 20 12 82 72, **www.britishembassy.gov.uk/france**, (choose the Lille Consulate for local advice and associations).

- **The British Community Association www.bca-lille.com** social activities for British residents and their families and friends.

- **The British Cultural Centre**, 4 place du Temple, 59000 Lille, tél. 03 20 54 22 79 – includes a library, language cassettes, newspapers and periodicals. Open afternoons in the school year.

- **Anglican church services** are held in Lille, Arras, Boulogne-sur-Mer, Calais and Chantilly.

- **English Language Montessori School**, 34a rue Victor Hugo, 60500 Chantilly, tél. 03 44 57 83 72, for teaching entirely in English for children aged two to six.

- **Association des Parents Anglophones de la région de Chantilly**, BP302, 60634 Chantilly, www.aparc.com, email: info@aparc.com – English classes for English-speaking children from kindergarten to high school. Qualified teachers and preparation for the international GCSE and American SAT.

- **Ecole Active Bilingue Jeannine Manuel**, Ecole Internationale de Lille Métropole, 418bis rue Albert Bailly, 59700 Marcq-en-Barouel, tél. 03 20 65 90 50, fax 03 20 98 06 41. International boarding school for pupils aged 11–18.

EASTERN FRANCE – ALSACE AND CHAMPAGNE

Surrounding the Place de la Concorde in Paris stand statues representing the great cities of France. For decades, the statue representing **Strasbourg** was covered up as France struggled with her shame at losing the long-disputed lands of Alsace and neighbouring **Lorraine** on what is now France's eastern border. The constant exchanging of these disputed territories has resulted in Alsace in a land of neat half-timbered houses decked with geraniums in villages with Germanic names; a predilection for beer (this is the home of Kronenbourg) and fruity white wines more akin to German vintages; and a local dialect, **elsaesserditsch**, which appears to basically be a Frenchified version of German.

As a region Alsace has many particularities, including different local laws based on German law. You should consult a lawyer well-versed in local law before considering any legal transactions in Alsace. Nonetheless, it remains an integral part of the French republic.

Although the region has suffered from a spate of company closures recently, there is still a fairly resistant economy, even if the region finds itself caught between two economic cycles. 70,000 *Alsaciens* work in neighbouring Germany and economic worries in the region's principal trade partner weigh heavy on the local population. As one local said, 'If Germany coughs, then Alsace catches the flu'.

The other strong local presence is American companies who have chosen to base their European operations in what feels like the heart of Europe. The regional capital, **Strasbourg**, is 700km from the North Sea, one hour by train from Basle, and as close to Paris as to Prague or Munich, and equidistant from Barcelona and Warsaw. In the new enlarged European Union, which takes in almost all of these destinations, the city could well become the permanent capital of the Council of Europe (which is currently shared with Brussels and neighbouring Luxembourg). The European Court of Human Rights and Europol are both already housed in the city, which has 71 diplomatic representations.

The city itself (264,000 people, with 453,000 people in the total urban area) has a strongly developed cultural identity. This is partly due to the 49,000 students at the university, of whom almost 16% are foreign. The local **Riesling** and **Sylvaner** wines are matched in importance by the local beers, and fine food is a local priority, with over 150 varieties of local **charcuterie**. However, in the German tradition, it is not possible to buy fresh bread on Sundays when the bakers are all closed.

Some 25% of Strasbourg's budget is devoted to the arts and the Opéra du Rhin is a combined project of the main Alsacien cities. The city was home to Gutenberg, and there is an antique book market every week by the rose-coloured cathedral, which is the centre-piece and pride of the city. The ancient city centre groans under the winter invasion for the great *Foire de Noël*, or *Christkensmänk*, when half of Europe descends to buy their Christmas baubles in the self-proclaimed 'capital of Christmas'.

Strasbourg has one of the youngest populations in France, with 40% aged under 25. One of the greatest problems that the city faces is obvious tensions between the quiet, conservative older generation and the younger generations, in particular in the difficult *cités* surrounding the city. This has flared up into remarkable violence in recent years.

The Champagne region
The baptism of the Carolingian King Clovis in 496AD by St Rémy is hailed as one of the great moments in French history. The cathedral built on the traditional site of the baptism, **Reims**, subsequently became the coronation church of the French kings

and represents one of the greatest achievements of the French Gothic cathedral builders.

The region that Reims came to dominate has in itself become synonymous not simply with luxury, but with the French *joie de vivre*. The real capital of the Champagne industry is in Epernay. This industry is now largely controlled by the multinational luxury goods companies. Overall, the Champagne region is suffering economically. In neighbouring Lorraine, a similar situation prevails as in Alsace, with more than 50,000 *Lorrains* now working in Luxembourg.

In 2007, the *TGV-Est* line was opened, and this is rapidly changing the prospects of the eastern region of France. Travelling times from Paris to Strasbourg have been reduced from four and a half hours to two hours and twenty minutes, and for Paris to Nancy from three hours to one and a half hours. Reims is now only 45 minutes from Paris, as opposed to one and a half hours before, and is expected to develop rapidly. The main airports for eastern France are Strasbourg, and Mulhouse close to the Swiss border.

Useful contacts

♦ The principal airport for the region is Strasbourg. The main local newspaper is *Les Dernières Nouvelles de l'Alsace*.

♦ **US Consulate-General**, 15 avenue d'Alsace, 67082 Strasbourg, tél. 03 88 35 31 04, fax 03 88 24 06 95, Monday–Friday 09h00–13h00, 14h00–17h00, **www.amb-usa.fr**. For British citizens Strasbourg falls within the Paris Consulate.

◆ There are English-speaking community associations in Strasbourg (**www.esc-alsace.org**) and Mulhouse. Americans in Alsace (**www.americansinalsace.org**) offers helps and assistance when settling in the region. There is an Anglican church in Strasbourg, and you can find more details of other community associations and services on **www.alsace.angloinfo.com**.

◆ Details of current bilingual schooling opportunities can be found by consulting the angloinfo website, or by consulting **www.enfantsbilingues.com**. Go to the *Plan du site* and choose *Trouver une école bilingue*, and then scroll through the list which is classified by *département* number.

THE RHÔNE-ALPES REGION

There is a line running across France which originally marked the ancient frontier between the kingdom of France and the Holy Roman Empire, and which today passes through the three most important French cities in descending order. It begins in Paris and ends in Marseilles on the south coast, and the mid-point lies at France's second city, **Lyon**, the capital of the Rhône-Alpes region.

Lyon occupies a unique position at the junction between Marseilles and Mediterranean Europe, and Paris and northern Europe, which has been the basis of both its fortune and its disappointments. Separated from Paris by the plain of the **Burgundy** wine region, the city is naturally turned to the south by the plunging vineyard valley of the **Rhône** which leads to Marseilles and the Mediterranean Sea. The ancient capital of the Gauls at the junction of the **Rhône** and **Saône** rivers is now a city of 1.3 million people, with a student population of about 83,000 and a strong international community.

Lyon follows the Parisian model of dividing the city into *arrondissements*, and has also followed the Parisian example by electing a Socialist mayor. The former mayor and ex-prime minister Raymond Barre described the city when he arrived as 'a rich city, happy to be rich and careful not to show it'.

The city has always been considered 'the French Manchester', and the wealth, ingenuity and success of Lyon business is historically well-known, beginning with the silk and textile industries, and spreading in the 19th century to banking (Crédit Lyonnais) and other industries. In recent years Lyon has shrugged off its 'closed' image and opened up to international contact, with its eyes set on southern Europe. The St-Exupéry airport is the second most important airport in France, served by both the TGV and a web of major *autoroutes*, as well as 80 international airlines. Lyon has also looked to a strategic development with Geneva, to align the three 'alpine' cities; but a Mediterranean link to Genoa, Barcelona and Marseille has also been toyed with. The Euro Institute, Euronews and Interpol have all chosen to set up their headquarters in Lyon.

In an effort to secure a new regional status, Lyon has aligned itself with the eight other major cities in the region. But the most important move has been a concerted effort by both industrial Lyon and commercial Marseille to develop the entire southern region by working together to ensure that companies choose the south and not Paris or elsewhere as their French or European headquarters. The strongest local presences in Lyon are the pharmaceutical industry, information technology and logistics based near the airport. Some 40% of companies in the Lyon region are local subsidiaries of American companies.

As befits the second city of France, the cultural life and city transport are both of excellent quality, with music and theatre playing an important role. Lyon is also much appreciated for its parks, which account for 15% of the total surface area of the Rhône-Alpes region. This in turn has had a positive effect. Certain villages saw their population rise by as much as 50% between 1990–99, and in the city one in four *Lyonnais* arrived between 1990–1999, with half of those in the 20–29 year-old category arriving in the same period.

The opening of the *TGV Méditerranée* fast-link has transformed not just the Lyon-Marseilles axis, but also the local economies of towns and cities the length of the line in both the Rhône valley and neighbouring Provence. Part of Lyon's problem has been the same as that experienced by so many other towns in the region; that it has always been merely a stopping point on the great north-south trek from Paris to Marseilles, which in the past led from the capital to the empire. Lyon is now seeking to exploit once again its unique point of junction to place itself at the heart of economic Europe.

The second city of the region remains **Grenoble** in the **Isère** *département,* close to the mountains of the **Savoie** on France's Swiss and Italian border. Grenoble is an ancient and popular university city which has developed important high-tech and electronics industries. But it is the TGV towns on the way south which are due to see the greatest changes in coming years. One such town which is seeking to break out of its 'staging post' role on the *autoroute* and railways is **Valence**. A city of some 200,000 people, it has a new TGV station and link, 6,000 students who have relocated from Grenoble, a growing number of businesses, and a rising property market, with the chance for commuters to appreciate a small-town life and fast-track links to Marseille, Lyon or beyond.

The mountainous region of **Savoie** beyond the Isère is centred on **Annecy** and **Chambéry**, and is home to nearly a million people. The main economic activities of the area remain tourism and traditional agriculture. This ancient independent kingdom (the palace of the Dukes of Savoie is to be found in Annecy) has a number of its own local dialects and strong regional folklore, as well as a culinary tradition which includes both wine and the well-known **Comté**, **Tome de Savoie** and **Reblochon** cheeses. As in many other frontier zones, in the **Haute-Savoie** (beyond Annecy) the natural tendency is to look to nearby Geneva across the Swiss border.

Useful contacts

- **The British Consulate**, 24 rue Childebert, 69002 Lyon, tél. 04 72 77 81 70, M° Bellecour or Cordeliers, **www.britishembassy.gov. uk/france**.

- **The American Presence Post** (commercial matters only), 16 avenue de la République, 69002 Lyon, tél. 04 78 83 36 88, fax 04 78 38 33 03, Monday–Friday 10h00–12h00, 14h00–17h00.

- Details of community associations can be found on two websites covering this region, **www.lyonexpat.com**, and **www. frenchalps.angloinfo.com**.

- There are **Anglican churches** in Lyon, Grenoble, Annecy and Evian.

♦ Details of current bilingual schooling opportunities can be found by consulting the angloinfo website, or by consulting **www.enfantsbilingues.com**. Go to the *Plan du site* and choose *Trouver une école bilingue*, and then scroll through the list which is classified by *département* number. In Grenoble, the *cite scolaire internationale* (**www.ac-grenoble.fr/ cite.scolaire.internationale**) also has an English section.

THE PROVENCE-ALPES-CÔTE D'AZUR REGION (PACA)

More than any other region in France, except for Paris, this is where many foreigners and French people want to be. You only have to say the word **Provence**, and an image of sunshine (on average 300 days a year) and bountiful vegetation, beaches and mountains, olives and wines, all spring to mind. If the British are thought to have over-run the area in recent years (almost two million British tourists visited the **Côte d'Azur** in 2001 out of a total of 40 million tourists), they are in fact only following in the footsteps of their ancestors who first made the southern coast fashionable in the 1860s.

But Provence is much more than a string of over-developed fishing villages with beaches. It includes the ancient seat of learning at **Aix-en-Provence** and the former Papal city of **Avignon**, now a cultural capital. It also contains the Roman arena at **Arles**, the Alpine regions and an open door on to the world and its cultures at **Marseille**.

On the borders of the Isére and of Italy, the **Haute-Alpes** *département* centred on **Gap** draws not only on the economic dynamism of the region to the south, but also looks to Grenoble and Turin to develop economically. Like the adjoining Savoie region, the area depends heavily on both winter and summer tourism in the Alps, and 80% of the working population are employed by the tertiary sector. Information technology and biotechnology is also beginning to play an important rôle locally.

The **Alpes-Maritimes** *département* has for almost 150 years been the centre of attraction in Provence. Originally part of the Italian kingdom of Piedmont-Savoie, **Nice** and the surrounding areas retain a heavy Italian accent and strong links to their neighbour. Nice is a cosmopolitan city, with its Promenade des Anglais, its Russian cathedral, and its Franco-Italian ambiance. **Cannes**, however, remains definitively French, even if there is a strong American presence each year for the international film festival. The former village of **St Tropez** needs no introduction, and represents the first transformation of this formerly quiet area into a media circus.

The second transformation is to be found just beyond Cannes in the ten communes which form the French 'Silicon Valley' of **Sophia Antipolis**, founded in 1969, uniting 23,000 jobs in information technology, 1,300 companies and some 60 nationalities. The atmosphere is predominantly young, with a mixture of students finishing their masters' degrees and young twenty- and thirty-somethings lured by the sun, the scenery and the chance of a dip in the pool at lunchtime.

Provence has become France's economic success story, turning a tide of high unemployment by successfully reinventing itself after dependence on agriculture (which is still highly important locally) and the post-colonial crash of Marseille. The chemical industry, including the perfume industry around Grasse; the pharmaceutical industry; the aeronautic and the micro-electronic industries, are all heavily represented in Provence. Together with the information technology industries, these varying strands have so far allowed the region to resist the worst impacts of the global economic slow-down.

Perhaps the greatest symbol of this regional renaissance is the local capital itself. **Marseille** was founded in c.600 BC. Today it is a thriving multicultural city of 807,000 people, the third city of France, but determined to become a pivotal city in the southern European Mediterranean sphere. It was the great port of the French empire, a city of spices and dates, coffee and sugar, of Africans, Algerians, Armenians, Greeks and Italians, who all came to make their fortune beside the French. The Suez Crisis and the gradual ending of the empire, including the war with Algeria, brought ruin, and the city of colours became faded, shabby and sad.

Suddenly in the 1990s the city started to fight back, partly helped by the British author Peter Mayle and his *A Year in Provence* and a subsequent return to lifestyle values which the city and region now represent. But to complement this 'back to lifestyle basics' campaign, industries such as telecoms, television production and IT-related industries have all been heavily encouraged. The Euroméditerranée development in the heart of Marseilles is the largest economic and urban redevelopment project in France, bringing new life back to the derelict docks and warehouses with a combined arts, audiovisual and multimedia development. The arrival of the TGV Méditerranée and its three-hour link to Paris in 2001 has added to Marseille's chances of success, as the city enjoys its return to grace, favour, and creative activity, from fashion to fine art to music.

Despite its 2,600 years of age, Marseilles remains a young city, with 70,000 students shared between the split university sites of Marseille and **Aix-en-Provence**, the ancient university and noble city which was home to Cézanne, only half an hour to the north of Marseille. Aix was voted the best place to live in France in January 2002 in a nationwide survey (*Le Point*, 11 January 2002).

Slightly further north again in the Vaucluse département lies **Avignon**. Dominated by the ancient Papal Palace which dates from the Great Schism, the city is one of the cultural capitals of France each summer with its theatre festival. Whilst Avignon and Aix cultivate sophistication, sleepy **Arles** with its Roman ruins feels like the poor country cousin. Arles lies at the entrance to the **Camargue**, the great natural reserve separating Provence from the **Languedoc** on the western coast, and draws its local colour from the **Gîtanes**, the traditional French gypsies who congregate in the Camargue, whose colourful clothing has inspired local folklore and also local designer Christian Lacroix. Conscious of its role as a regional capital, one of the projects of Marseille is to develop an economic link up the Rhône valley to Aix and Avignon, both of which also benefit from the new TGV link.

Despite the success and the beauty of the PACA région, it cannot mask a number of profound problems. One major problem is that it is a victim of its own success, especially in terms of property prices.

Many people simply cannot afford to accept a new position in the region because of the high property prices. The huge influx of both foreigners and French retirement-age purchasers has pushed house prices through the roof. A second problem manifested itself again in 2002 with severe flooding especially in the Vaucluse *département*, leading to massive damage and over 20 deaths.

Other problems which the area faces are both demographic and social. The area has experienced both high immigration, high unemployment amongst the immigrant communities, and high crime rates. Not all the local woes can be pinned on **Maghrebin** immigrants, but most are attributed to them. The result is that PACA is the region which most solidly supports Jean-Marie Le Pen and his **Front National** party.

Useful contacts

♦ The main international airports are Nice and Marseille. The main local newspaper is *La Provence*. Both airports are well served by low-cost airlines.

♦ There are **American Consulates** at Place Varian Fry, 13006 Marseille, tél. 04 91 54 92 00, fax 04 91 55 55 09 47; and 7 avenue Gustave V, 06000 Nice, tél. 04 93 88 89 55.

♦ **The British Consulate**, 24 avenue de Prado, 13006 Marseille, tél. 04 91 15 72 10, **www.britishembassy.gov.uk/france**.

♦ There are **Anglican churches** in Marseille, Nice, Cannes, Menton, Monaco, Beaulieu, St Raphaël and Vence.

♦ Details of community associations can be found on **www. riviera.angloinfo.com**. The Anglo-American Group of Provence (**www.aagp-provence.com**) has its own library, and the British

Association of the Alpes-Maritime (**www.angloinfo.com/online/ ba**) has branches across the region. There is also an Australian community association.

◆ **British Association of the Alpes-Maritimes and the Var** – branches in Nice, Cannes, Menton and the Var, c/o Holy Trinity Church, 11, rue de la Buffa, 06000 Nice. Local current contact details on the British Consulate webpage.

◆ **The British Chamber of Commerce Riviera** (**www.bcc.jr-sr.com**) and the Nice branch of the **Franco-British Chamber of Commerce** (**www.francobritishchamber.com**, tél. 04 93 62 94 95) provide two good points of entry to the local business community. Further business association links can be found on the Angloinfo site.

◆ Local English language media: *The Riviera Reporter*, 56 chemin de Provence, 06250 Mougins, tél. 04 93 45 77 19; *The Rivera Times*, 8 avenue Jean Moulin, F-06340 Drap (Nice), tél. 04 93 27 60 00, **www.mediterra.com**; *Var Village Voice*, **www.varvillagevoice.com**, tél. 04 94 04 49 60; Riviera Radio, 10-12 quai Antoine I, MC98000 Monaco, tél. + 377 97 97 94 94.

◆ **School near Aix en Provence**: International Bilingual School of Provence, **www.ibssoprovence.com**, tél. 04 42 23 03 40, fax 04 42 24 09 81, email: ibs.of.provence@wanadoo.fr – co-educational day or boarding international school, primary and secondary level education, American, British and French examinations offered.

◆ **Schools near Cannes**: **Mougins School**, **www.mougins-school.com** – curriculum based on British national curriculum for pupils aged 3–18 from 25 different countries; **International School of**

Sophia Antipolis, Centre International de Valbonne (CIV) Anglophone section, BP097, 06902 Sophia Antipolis, tél. 04 92 96 52 00, fax 04 92 96 52 99 – 570 pupils aged 9–18, who study for the international *bac*. Boarding facilities available.

◆ **School in Monaco**: **Lycée Albert 1er**, International section, Place de la Visitation, 98015 Monaco, tél. +377 93 15 80 54, fax +377 93 15 80 59 – co-educational day school for ages 16–18. Six hours per week of English tuition, with the international *bac* on offer.

◆ **School in Nice**: **International School of Nice**, www.isn-nice.org, tél. 04 93 21 04 00, fax 04 93 21 69 11, email: 101644.1546@ compuserve.com – non-profit private co-educational day school for pupils aged 4–19. General American curriculum but the international GCSE and *bac* are both offered.

◆ **Bookshops** – Ad Hoc Books, 8 rue Pisancon, 13001 Marseille, tél. 04 91 33 51 92, email: adhocbooks@libertysurf.fr; Book in Bar (coffee bar and bookshop), 1bis, rue Joseph Cabassol, 13100 Aix en Provence, tél/fax 04 42 26 60 07. **www.bookinbar.com**.

THE LANGUEDOC-ROUSSILLON

Basking warmly in the sun between the mountains of the **Massif Centrale** and the Mediterranean coast, and between the gentle wilderness of the **Camargue** and the Pyrenees, lies the **Languedoc**, literally the 'the language of the d'Oc' or more correctly **Occitane**, which was the language of the medieval troubadours. From **Nîmes** to **Perpignan**, and from **Béziers** to **Carcassone**, the region is rich in history and drama which the quiet countryside conserves amongst its hills and vineyards.

Whilst Nice and the Côte d'Azur have a distinctly Italian feel, the
Languedoc is under the charm of Spain, or more precisely
Catalonia. The city of **Perpignan** was one of the capitals of the
kings of Catalonia in the Middle Ages, and the ancient summer
palace of the kings dominates the picturesque artists' village of
Collioure. When the Spanish Civil War broke out in the 1930s,
hundreds of thousands of Spanish refugees fled to France and
settled in the Languedoc. The cities close to Spain echo to the
sound of the **flamenco**, which seems to suit the region – soft and
slow at times, and exuberant and loud at others. Nîmes and
Béziers in particular have adopted the traditional Spanish fiesta,
with thousands descending on the cities for fiestas in mid-August,
complete with bullfights. With the end of the French empire in the
1950s and 1960s, thousands more refugees – the ex-colonists
Pieds-Noirs, Moroccans and Algerians – also flocked to the
region. This has replicated the same tensions as in neighbouring
Provence.

Nîmes has taken on an increasingly important rôle in the region.
Frequently amongst the hottest cities in France, it has become
one of the points of entry for the massive influx of north
European visitors to the region. At the centre of this Roman city
stands the great amphitheatre, which is a centre of bullfighting,
whilst nearby stands the stately Pont du Gard.

The regional capital **Montpellier** shares many similarities with Aix-
en-Provence. An ancient university city of some 225,000 people
(491,000 in the total urban area), it is currently one of the most
popular cities in France. It is expected to grow to 825,000 people
by 2030, with approximately 1,000 new arrivals each month. There

are about 61,000 students in Montpellier, including many at the famous school of medicine. The lively city, 'an old "young" city', as it was recently described, has a packed cultural life centred around numerous festivals, opera, theatre and the beach. Only 12km separates the city from the sea, and the mayor is determined to envelop those kilometres to extend his city to the seashore.

Whilst the city has become a magnet for young twenty- and thirty-somethings seeking fun in the sun, a job and more space to live in, the economic life of the region has not really kept pace. A number of important IT companies (e.g. IBM, Dell, Cap Gemini) have all opened significant sites in the city, but not enough to meet the demand for jobs. Montpellier, like the whole region, suffers from higher than average unemployment, currently running at over 14%. Small companies come and go, but they account for the largest number of local employers.

Attempts to develop a new TGV link to Spain to spur the local economy, running from Nîmes via Montpellier and across the border, have started and stopped and started again several times since 1989. At the moment the planned completion date is 2015-2020.

One city in particular which has a great interest in the project is **Perpignan**, almost at the Spanish frontier, which should be linked to Barcelona airport by a *TGV* route of less than one hour in 2006. The symbol of the ancient Catalan capital of 133,000 people, the *Castillet* fortified gatehouse sums up neatly the components of this region: a red brick gatehouse with an oriental turret. The city has constantly acted as an entry point for new arrivals to France, notably a large *Maghrebin* immigrant population in addition to the Catalan settlers. The red brick echoes the city of Toulouse in the north-west of the region.

Like Montpellier, Perpignan lies only a few miles from the sea. It lies close to the popular beach resorts of **Canet** and **Argèles**, and in the summer the *Festivales de Perpignan* liven up the evenings. It also has a very high unemployment rate at 17%.

A result of the heavy Spanish influence on the region is the strong Catholic tradition seen not only in the Spanish-style Holy Week processions in Perpignan, but also in the confraternities of penitents in medieval costumes which can still be found in other places such as **Aigues-Mortes,** or the **Gîtane** festival of St Sarah at **Les Sts Maries de la Mer**, both in the Langedoc Camargue.

The anti-Cathar Albignesian crusade of the 13th century is named after the city of **Albi**, with its fortified cathedral built to repel attack. The Cathars were hugely popular in the region, and included many noble supporters who gave refuge to the Cathars in the last stages of the crusade in the now-ruined *châteaux* of the Cathar hills and mountains, a popular tourist route in the region.

Béziers is a busy port surrounded by vineyards, typical of this region which is home to José Bové and his agricultural supporters. Situated 60km from Montpellier, the town has little economic development but that may change when a new motorway is opened.

The population of the Languedoc coastline swells in summer, with numbers reaching as high as 200,000 for the towns around **Agde**,

and **La Grande Motte** reaching almost ten times its resident
population. In addition, the region's permanent population is
growing fast. In addition to the 'neo-rurals' as the younger
'idealists' are known, the largest influx is from the 'papy-boom'
generation reaching retirement in France.

If you want to follow the path of the region's other persecuted
minority, the Protestants, you need to climb into the hill country
of the **Cévennes** where the 18th century rebels against Louis XIV
are commemorated each year at *L'Assemblée du Désert,* France's
great open-air Protestant festival. This area was immortalised by
Robert Louis Stevenson in his epic donkey trek and travelogue in
1879.

Alternatively you may wish to head for the fortified city of
Carcassone, restored in the 19th century to its medieval splendour.
Passengers at Carcassone airport have risen to 215,000 a year since
the arrival of daily flights to London and Charleroi, making this
the most important international airport in the region.

Up to 75% of local property transactions are British purchases
and although the 20-50% increases in house prices they have
provoked is less welcome, foreign contributions to the local
economy and village life is more than welcome. One village of less
than 600 souls now boasts a Belgian baker, a Danish hotel owner
and a British church organist!

Useful contacts

♦ The principal international airports in the region are
  Carcassone, Montpellier and Nîmes. There is also an airport at
  Perpignan. The main local newspapers are *La Dépêche du Midi*,

and *Midi-Libre*. In Montpellier, there is also *La Gazette de Montpellier*, with an important entertainment guide.

◆ The Marseille consulates for both the UK and the USA are responsible for this region.

◆ Details of local English-language community associations, schools and services for the English-speaking community can be found on **www.languedoc.angloinfo.com**. The British Community Association website can be found at **www.bca-montplellier.com**. There is also an American Library in Montpellier (**www.bibliotheque-americaine.com**).

◆ The Bookshop, 6 rue de l'Université, 34000 Montpellier, tél. 04 67 66 09 08. **www.bookshop-montpellier.com**.

Further Reading

GUIDES

There are a wide variety of guides to France for all tastes and budgets. The classic series remains the Michelin guides, for general information, restaurants and hotels. The annual *Time Out* guides for France and Paris are amongst the best guides available.

HISTORY

France & Britain 1900–1940; Entente & Estrangement, Philip Bell (Longman, 1996).

France & Britain 1940–94; The Long Separation, Philip Bell (Longman, 1997).

Index